BIRMINGHAM IRISH
MAKING OUR MARK

BIRMINGHAM IRISH
MAKING OUR MARK

By Carl Chinn

I dedicate this book to my Dublin wife Kay and to our children, Richard Michael, Tara Chantelle, Catríona Marianne and Rochelle Louvaine. The blood of the Irish and the English runs in their veins. Their names reflect this and we have brought them up to be proud of both traditions. As for Kay, Kathleen Mary Ann Doyle, my debt is simple. My love of and for an Irishwoman defines my life.

Birmingham Irish: Making Our Mark
Copyright © 2003 Carl Chinn.

The rights of Carl Chinn to be identified as authors of this work have been asserted by them in accordance with the
Copyright, Design and Patents Act 1988.

CIP catalogue record for this book is available from the British Library.

ISBN: 070930241X

Published by Birmingham Library Services.

Designed and produced by Birmingham City Council.

Front and back cover photographs: Front, Birmingham St. Patrick's Day Parade 2002 © West Midlands Fire Service.
Back, Carl at Birmingham's Irish Club presenting his BBC WM Sunday Show after the city's St. Patrick's Day Parade 2002.
With him are Phil Castlton (left) of the West Midlands Fire Service, Mark Jarmek of the Fire Department, New York, Paul
Smith of the WMFS, a second generation Irish Brummie, and Andy Horan of the FDNY. © Pat McCool of *The Harp*.

CONTENTS

ACKNOWLEDGEMENTS

This book has been many years in the making. In 1988, Maureen Messent interviewed me for the *Birmingham Evening Mail* about my first book, *They Worked All Their Lives. Women of the Urban Poor in England*, (1880-1939). She asked me what other books I had in mind. I stated a history of the Irish in Birmingham. Since then, and in between many other projects, I have been collecting evidence, shaping my thoughts and visiting those parts of Ireland from which originate so many of the Birmingham Irish. Despite this work over a long period, this book has come at me in a rush. For the last three years, I have been promising my wife Kay, my Irish pals and Martin Flynn of Birmingham Library Services that I would write it. Finally, I committed myself to a publication date and launch at Birmingham's Irish Club and that was it. However, I had only a few weeks in which I could actually do the writing.

That I was able to write *Birmingham Irish* so quickly is the result of three factors. First, because of the years of putting together my thoughts in my mind. Second, because of the urging of Roger Swift, an esteemed historian of the Irish in Britain, to write '"Sturdy Catholic Emigrants": the Irish in early Victorian Birmingham' for the work he edited with Sheridan Gilley and called *The Irish in Victorian Britain. The Local Dimension* (1995). And third, because of the photocopying and supplying to me at home of evidence from Birmingham Central Library.

I thank Peter Drake and Caroline Forman for this vital service. *Birmingham Irish* could not have been written if they had not laboured to send me the copies of newspaper cuttings, books and other material that I needed. In previous years, a number of other librarians also sent me various pieces of evidence that I had identified and I would like to acknowledge Richard Albutt; Patrick Baird, head of service; and Doreen Hopwood, genealogist. Birmingham Libraries possesses one of the best, if not the best, collections of local history material in the world and the librarians who work in this field are dedicated and knowledgeable. Joseph McKenna is another esteemed librarian in Local Studies and History. During his time there, he has written The Birmingham Irish, a pioneering and invaluable work, and he has been involved with the Irish Studies Group. And, as Central Library Manager, Martin Flynn has played a key role in this book. He prompted and prodded me to write it and has read various drafts and commented on them. I thank him and his dad, Enda Flynn, for checking historical details. My gratitude goes also to Andy Willis for the scanning of the photographs; Jim Warren for handling the book design and liaison with printers; and Pam Gaffney for the proofreading.

Additionally I wish to show my appreciation to Gail Hill, my part-time secretary at South Birmingham College, who typed up all the many memories sent to me and made the job of

including them easier and manageable. Thanks are also due to Sarah Edwards, archivist of the BirminghamLives Archive at South Birmingham College, and Rachel Hopkins, librarian at South Birmingham College's Digbeth Campus, who added up numbers for me relating to various matters from my gathering of evidence from the 1881 Census.

A number of other people must be recognised. They are Rev. T. A. Farrel, formerly Diocesan Treasurer, Archdiocese of Birmingham, who gave me books on Birmingham's Catholic churches; Gearóid Mac an Mhaoir, who was always on the end of a telephone line for me to check Gaelic spellings – and any mistakes are mine and not his; and Michael Foley of Small Heath, a mine of information about all things Irish in Birmingham. I also wish to pay tribute to the work of John Fitzgerald of Minstrel Music and Brendan Farrell of the *Irish Post*. John has been involved in so many positive activities and for many years was the man who energised the Irish music scene in Birmingham. He continues to be a major figure locally. So is Brendan. He has become a good friend and on the many occasions I have met him over the last decade he has never let me forget that I planned to write this book. The Irish community in Birmingham owes much to Brendan, as it does to John. Not only has Brendan photographed and written about the Birmingham Irish, but also he is responsible for many important cultural events and initiatives. In particular, he pressed BBC WM to bring in the award-winning Irish Show of Bob Brolly MBE.

I would also like to show my gratitude to Bank of Ireland Shirley Branch and Stena Line. Bank of Ireland Shirley Branch twice provided me with funds to travel around the west of Ireland so that I could visit the places from which so many of the Irish of Birmingham have come. This was a vital exercise that allowed me to understand the west of Ireland better, to find out about the de Berminghams, to feel the tragedy of the famine and hear the anger of the Land War. In particular, I thank Andy Smith, Area Manager Midlands, Kevin Monahan, Brendan Murphy, Tom Queenan and Margaret Gales for their backing and encouragement. Those two visits to Ireland were also made possible by the generosity of Stena Line. I am grateful to Maggie Roche, National Account Manager, and her colleagues for helping me achieve my ambition of writing a book on the Irish of Birmingham that differed from those on the Irish of other places. It was important to me to appreciate the circumstances of rural Ireland and not to write only of the Irish when they reached England. Stena Line have also played a major role in making the Birmingham Saint Patrick's Day Parade one of the biggest in the world through their support in bringing Irish marching bands to Birmingham.

There are a large number of evocative and moving photos in Birmingham Irish. I thank all of those who have allowed me to use them and they are acknowledged with regard to a particular photograph. However, I wish to make a special mention of the West Midlands Fire Service and the *Birmingham Evening Mail*. The photograph on the front cover of this book and other photos elsewhere are by courtesy of the West Midlands Fire Service. In particular, I thank Chief Officer Ken Knight and photographer Edward Ockenden. I also thank Roger Borrell, the editor of the *Birmingham Evening Mail* for allowing me the use of some of the *Mail's* photographs.

I want to show my appreciation for those people and organisations that made the launch of this book so successful. They are Birmingham Library Services; The Irish Club, Birmingham; Little

Jimmy and friends; Tommy Dempsey and Dempsey's Lot; Joe Murphy, Paul and Aidan O'Brien and Karl Brazil of Juno; South Birmingham Comhaltas; the Birmingham Irish Pipes and Drums; and Michael Collins, that renowned monologue man. The launch was also supported by South Birmingham College and I want to record my gratitude for the college's wholehearted backing of all that I do. In particular, I thank Alan Birks, Principal; John James, chair; Barry Coleman, Assistant Principal; and Peter McNally, Health and Safety Director. A second generation Irish Brummie born and bred in Digbeth, Peter has a special responsibility for relationships with the Irish community and was a key figure in saving the Irish Club in 2001.

This is a book of two parts. In the first four chapters, through a painstaking search of the 1851 and 1881 Censuses and a host of reports, I have striven to reach out for the voices and lives of the Birmingham Irish of the nineteenth century. In doing so, I have felt it vital to understand the economic, political and social conditions that prevailed in Ireland and which were the cause of mass emigration. In an age of mass emigration from central and Eastern Europe, Italy and even England, Wales and Scotland, the movement of the Irish was on a scale that was unprecedented. The second part of the book looks at the Irish in Birmingham from the inter-war decades until the late 1970s. There is some reference to later years, but this is not a history of the Birmingham Irish in the 1980s and 1990s. In this second part of the book, I did not have to reach out for the voices and lives of the Birmingham Irish. For many of them have written to me and shared with me their experiences and their family photographs. I decided that it would not be right for me to integrate such precious words into chapters of my writing. Instead I believe that these voices and photos should stand on their own, although wherever possible I have tried to provide a context for these memories. I thank all those who gave me the honour of letting me know about themselves and their feelings.

FOREWORD

I grew up in Springfield on the edge of Sparkhill. When we were young, me and Our Kid spent hours playing football over Sarehole Rec. Most of the other lads were Irish Brummies from Sparkhill and whenever a newcomer joined in the question would soon be asked 'Are you Brummie Brummie or Brummie Irish?' But never was that query intimidating, it was just something that was put almost as a matter of course - and once the answer was given then that was the end of it. Me and Our Darryl were amongst the few Brummie Brummies as most of the others were second generation Irish. Two especial mates were Paul and Séan McGonigle. I see Paul still down the Villa and we have met up at a lot of dos over the years. Then there was Michael Tighe, who I seem to recall was a bit older than us and almost took on the role of a leader; and Brian Higgins, who was a fine player and who I see occasionally at Vaughans in Hall Green and there were many others.

As we became teenagers, Sarehole Mill on a Sunday was like one huge football match. There would be fifteen, twenty-a-side or more and Our Old Man would be playing in the midst of it making sure everything was done fair. Often, an Irish Brummie I played football with comes up to me and asks to be remembered to Mr Chinn. It was on those Sunday afternoons in the autumns, winters and springs of our teenage years that we came to know one of the finest footballers ever to come from Birmingham. His name was Noel Fagan. He and his brother, Paddy, joined us regularly. Noel was light of foot, fast, skilful and tough – and he was on the Villa's books. But never was he cocky, he still came along to the rec and joined in and didn't expect any special treatment. Things didn't work out for Noel but I was privileged to have played football with someone of a rare talent. Then there was Micky Doyle. Micky was slight of build and small of height, but he was one of the hardest blokes I ever met. Uncompromising but fair, Micky always respected Our Dad. He was the kind of kid who would drop everything for you if you needed him and he would no more have thought of turning his back on a pal than of denying who he was. And there was also Gerry Delaney. What a magic player Gerry was and what an even better player of Irish football. It was Gerry's dream to make it in Ireland, but without any qualifications in the Irish language, he was unable to break through.

As we hit our late teens, we all drank in the 'Horse Shoes' on the Stratford Road, Irish and English together, and then me and Our Kid and Big Dave Evans moved on to make our local the 'Royal Oak' on the corner of Alfred Street and Stoney Lane, Sparkbrook. This came about because of my family's bookmaking business down The Brook. On Saturdays and in the school holidays and then in the university breaks, me and Our Darryl worked in Our Dad's betting shops. One was on The Lane, the Ladypool Road, and the other was on the opposite corner to the 'Oak'. We'd been working in the shops since we were thirteen and got to know well many of Our Dad's punters who were Irish lads. Generous, witty and clever, they taught us much.

One of them was called Jack. In those days of the late 1960s and early 1970s, a lot of the Irish lads were earning good money on the lump on the building sites. Jack and his pals would come in to the shop on a Saturday morning in new suits, put their bets on, have a drink and come back for another flutter in the afternoon. The next week they would work in that suit and the following Saturday they would buy another new one. There was many a man's shop in Brum that depended upon the trade of Irish building workers. Whenever they had a good win there was always a big tip, say a ten bob note or even a quid. And that was a lot then. Sometimes in the winter when the dark nights meant racing ended earlier, I went off to the match. I always remember Jack warning me not to get into any trouble. I saw him a while ago. Like so many of his pals he had not married and he had lived for the day. Now he wasn't doing so well. But he was still that intelligent, concerned bloke he had ever been and told me how he watched out for me on the TV and that I was sound. That meant a lot.

There were so many characters amongst the Irish we knew. There was Jimmy the Talking Horse. Did you want to know the sire, the dam, the grandsire, the granddame of a horse? Ask Jimmy. And there was Bunty. Quiet, reserved and polite, Bunty was a bloke who no one could push around – nor can they still. Another soft-spoken chap was Pat Duffy, a fine Irish footballer at Glebe Farm in his day. Pat lived locally and had done well as a subcontractor. It is his nephew, Anthony Duffy, who is chairperson of the Birmingham Saint Patrick's Day Parade committee. Oh and there was Pedro. A raylly one, a real Dub, Pedro and his mates were sharp, quick of tongue and walked with the distinctive walk of the inner-city Dub. Paddy Cahill was another Dubliner. When I stood for Parliament as an independent in Sparkbrook in 1983, Paddy backed me all the way and traipsed the streets with me and my other mates; and when I went to Finglas, he always asked me to pop into the 'Bottom of the Hill' and leave a pint in for a childhood mate.

It was the crowd from the 'Royal Oak' who helped me out in that election, even though we had no absolutely no hope of winning. English, Italian and Irish Brummies, we all mucked in together. The gaffer of the pub was John McGrath, God Rest His Soul. We were notoriously slow at leaving the 'Oak', especially on a Sunday, and his cry was always, 'Come on now, time to go, it's family allowance day tomorrow!' The 'Oak' played a big part in our life, me and Our Kid. I started drinking there because of one of our punters, Harry Gillan. Harry was from Belfast and had been great pals with my Uncle Ron Chinn and my Uncle Bernard Chinn, and now he is like an uncle himself to our kids. Throughout the football season Harry comes to the match with us and gives us a powerful link to our past. It was because of Harry that we got to know Billy and Mag Hughes, or Mag Byrne as she is known still. They were both from big families that had come over before and during the war and they lived in Durham Road and elsewhere in Sparkhill.

It was that way that Our Kid met, fell in love with and married Sandra Hughes. So my niece, Natalie, and nephews, Séan and Daniel, are of good Brummie Irish and Brummie English stock like our own kids. Billy is one of the most intelligent and thoughtful men it is my honour to have met and he is an essential part of our match-day gathering. He came to Brum as a youngster, having being born in the Coombe and grown up in and around Capel Street. Mag was just eight when her mother fetched her and her brothers and sisters over here to be with her dad. Hailing from Dominic Street, Mag's accent is still that of a proud inner-city Dub. Billy's sister, Angela, is married to Joe Travers, another Dubliner, and through them, I came to know and become good pals with Brian Travers of UB40. Brian is proud of his Irish heritage and is as proud of Birmingham and all its peoples. Unlike so many others who have made it big, Brian has not cut and run. He and his wife Lesley, also a second generation Irish Brummie, live locally and they maintain a wholehearted commitment towards the city we love and to its wellbeing. When we were fighting to save Longbridge from closure a few years back, I rang Brian and he and the other members of UB40 came and spoke at the great rally in Cannon Hill Park and also were interviewed on numerous radio stations. Their support was strong and welcome.

There were so many Irish folk who we knocked about with. There was Big Patsy McGlinn, a Roscommon man, who would cram us into the back of his transit and take us to any Villa away match. On a Sunday night, if we couldn't get the stopback off John McGrath, we would go to the 'Bridge House Hotel' in Acocks Green. It was owned by Big Patsy's sister. We had some cracking nights there, singing and eating sandwiches. Patsy's sister made us especially welcome. Me, Patsy and Billy Hughes ran the 'Royal Oak' social club for many years, along with a couple of other pals, Joe O'Connor and Peter Goodman. Peter and Joe knew Kay's cousins, the Kehoes, in Dundalk. Then there was Little Jimmy, so well known now for his musicianship, Peter and Mary, and second generation Irish Brummies like Roger Cardall. Roger lived across the way in the maisonettes in Alfred Road, close to Billy and Mag Hughes, and was the groomsman at our wedding. And I can't forget Bob Emmett. What a bostin pint of mild he served at the 'Gate' in Studley Street and what a crack he was. Many's the bet I have taken there, and at the stopback in the 'Oak' - or else at John Hegarty's 'Railway', or yet again at the 'Clifton'. That's where I met Big Danny, the biggest punter we ever had. Each Saturday I would buy him fresh salmon and ducks' eggs from Westwood's on the Stratford Road.

I held up my 21st birthday party down the 'Oak' and we often took Our Winnie down there. Aunt Win was Our Nan's sister. She had a beautiful voice and knew all the Irish songs. It was from her that we learned 'County Down', 'There's One Fair County in Ireland', 'Carlow Mussletoff' and many more. Our Winnie had them from her mom, Great-Granny Wood, who was born on The Curragh. Granny Wood was the daughter of a British soldier, Granddad Kendal, and an Irish girl. They married and had Granny and her younger brother in Ireland. Coming back to Worcester when Granny was small, the marriage broke down. All we know of Granny's mom is that she was called Clancy and that, as Our Nan recalled, 'she coughed her heart of its cusp in the Workhouse'. It was Our Nan's dearest wish to see The Curragh before she died and to pay her respects to her mom and the gran she had known only through a few stories. Years later, when we visited friends of Our Mom and Dad's in Dublin, they took us to Kildare. The Irish soldiers were good to us. They let us in to The Curragh and told us where the oldest barracks were. Our Nan and Our Mom broke their hearts for that poor Irish wench who left home for love only to die abandoned and friendless in the hated workhouse.

It was to the 'Oak' that I took Kay on our first date. We'd met twice in Benidorm and then wrote to each other for months. One Sunday in January 1978 she came to Brum and we got engaged there and then. It was the third time we had met. We were married on 6 September that year at the Church of the Annunciation in Finglas West. Since then, Ireland has become a major

part of my life and I have learned much about Dublin from Kay's mom and dad, Mick and Aggo, her dad's sister auntie Maureen, her three brothers Liam, Michael and Joseph and her sister, Brenda.

Over the last few years, I have learnt more about other parts of Ireland through many friends such as Gareth Savage of Carrickfergus who was in my class at Fircroft College of Adult Education when I first began teaching and who has been a true mate from that time. Then there are our very good friends Peggy and Eddie Falahee from Roscommon and Limerick, who have brought me into a knowing of the west of Ireland; and Brendan and Josie Mulvey of Leitrim and Sligo, who welcomed me into their home and allowed me to share the wonders of their counties. Amongst our other pals are Laura Grigg whose family hails from Monaghan and whose husband Bill is English; Maurice Long of Kerry; Gearóid Mac an Mhaoir of Achill; and Paul O'Brien, a talented Irish musician who plays with the exciting Celtic rock band, Juno. Phil and Chris Creean and Marion and John Harkin, are also big friends of ours. Our kids went to school with theirs at Saint Bernard's and we often have a jar with them and Pat and Ray Vaughan at Vaughans up the road. That connection with Saint Bernard's continues with Our Rochelle, whose best friend is Róisín McGrath. Her mom and dad, Margaret and Kevin, are second generation Irish Brummies and live across the road. I am continuing to learn through my editorship of *The Harp* and my friend and partner, Pat McCool and his Brummie wife, Sue. Originally from the north of Ireland, Pat is everywhere, taking photos, delivering papers and pulling in advertising. The photo on the back cover is one of his. I have many more friends amongst the Birmingham Irish. They are too numerous to mention individually, but I value the pals I have in the county associations of Roscommon, Mayo, Wexford, Carlow, Tyrone, Limerick, Kerry, Monaghan, Donegal, Wicklow, Galway, Armagh, Longford and others.

I am also honoured to have become close friends with a number of second-generation Brummie Irish firefighters. They are Paul Smith, a founder of the Midland Republic of Ireland Soccer Supporters Club and a staunch Dubs supporter in Irish football; Sean McMenamin, who freely gives so much of his time to go to Romania to work in orphanages and make a better life for the orphans in Siret; and Paul 'Ned' Kelly, who was one of the younger ones who used to play football with us over the rec and who is now retired from the force. At the invitation of New York firefighter Andy Horan and his brothers, we and others went to New York to pay our respects at the first anniversary of the horror of 11 September 2001 when terrorists destroyed the Twin Towers and murdered so many people.

I am a proud English Brummie and I am proud to live in a city where English and Irish are so bonded and in which Irish Brummies have made their mark so strongly and so successfully. The Birmingham Irish have given much to the city we love and to which we belong. I hope I have done justice to you in this book.

My Granny and Granddad Wood with some of their children in the 1940s. On the back row are Gladys, Nancy, Bobby, May, and my Nan Lil. On the front row are Rosie, Granddad and Granny and my auntie Win. Sitting on the floor is Doreen. The three other lads, Billy, Georgie and Alfie were in the forces. Another sister, Junie, had died young.

CHAPTER ONE
FROM BIRMINGHAM TO ATHENRY AND BACK

No one will ever know if the Irishman William Bermegham wondered at the connection between his name and that of the city in which he and his Scottish-born wife, Mary, lived. An annealer of iron, he must have worked in blistering, grimy and perhaps dangerous conditions, toughening metal by heating it up and then allowing it to cool slowly. Where he collared and whether or not he was in regular work is not given in the 1881 Census, that vital source that allows us to grab a hasty look at the couple, but he couldn't have been drawing a lot. If he had been he would have been able to afford something better than a tiny back-to-back house up a yard in Pickford Street, in the midst of working-class Birmingham. Running between Bordesley Street and Fazeley Street, halfway between Moor Street Station and the 'Old Crown' in Deritend, the town-side of Pickford Street was dominated by a canal wharf. Here were gathered coal merchants and a timber and slate merchant, and opposite was the skin and hide market in New Canal Street. Noxious smells from this place melded with the pungent whiffs wafting from the tin smelting company and metal rolling works just up the way in Fazeley Street.

Twenty years later, J. Cuming Walters went 'exploring' into the poorer parts of Birmingham, mostly in the eastern and southeastern quarters, and wrote a series of articles for the *Birmingham Daily Gazette*. He was indignant that the poor of the supposedly best-governed city in the world had to crowd 'near the ill-smelling canal; or in the vicinage of factories which pour out their fumes in billowing masses from the throats of giant stacks'. As an outsider in an industrial city, William Bermegham would have been affected keenly by the reek of the overcrowded urban landscape, the more so if he had come from the clear air of the west of Ireland as did so many of his fellow Irish in Brum. Mind you, Pickford

Street was by no means one of the poorest or most unsanitary spots in the city – nearby New Canal Street, Park Street and Bartholomew Street all vied for that unwelcome title as a 1904 report by Birmingham's Medical Officer of Health revealed. Focusing upon the Floodgate Street area, it made plain that even in a poor neighbourhood some people were worse off than others. The most appalling loss of life through poverty hereabouts was in Park Street, where there were many lodging houses and in which the death rate was 63.5 per thousand people. Poverty also killed disproportionately in Allison Street, which had a mortality rate of 49.6.

Numbers 2-6, number 23 court, Park Street, 1904.

By comparison, in Pickford Street the figure was 23.4 people. This was low for the district, but it was still almost 50% more than in the prosperous working-class ward of All Saints – and that again was higher than in wealthy Edgbaston, on the south-west of Birmingham and upwind of the malodour of city life. (J. Cuming Walters, 'A Second Glance Around', *Scenes in Slumland. Pen Pictures of the Black Spots in Birmingham*, articles reprinted from the *Birmingham Daily Gazette*, March 1901; and City of Birmingham Medical Officer of Health, *Annual Report*, 1904).

William Bermegham was 29 in 1881 and his wife was four years younger. Living with them was James C. Mapp, a four-month-old baby born in Birmingham and given as 'Nurse Child' under the Census column of relationship to the head of household. Nothing more reaches out to us about this family, except perhaps as to the pronunciation of William's surname. It may well be that William's information was written down by the enumerator, as often it was in poorer neighbourhoods, and thus it was recorded as it was said with the 'n' missing from Bermingham. As for the 'e' of Birmingham, in the Middle Ages and into the Early Modern period, there was no standardised spelling and so Birmingham could be spelled as 'Bir', 'Ber' or 'Bur'. Interestingly, Brummies pronounce the 'g' strongly and the 'n' weakly so that Birmingham is spoken locally as Birmigum or Bermigum– as with William's name. In fact Bermigham and Birmygham are listed amongst the 140 and more ways of spelling Birmingham by J. A. Langford in 1868.

William was not the first Irish man of his name to live in the city. In 1851 a William Brimagem aged 34 resided in number 3 house 14 court in Digbeth, right in the shadow of Saint Martin's. His surname is very close to Brummagem, the West Midlands dialect name for Birmingham. This pronunciation emerged in the later Middle Ages when the 'ing' of Birmingham became softened to 'idg' and when the 'i' and the 'r' in Birmingham were shifted in local speech. Because spelling was not standardized, Birmingham could also be given as Bermingham or Burmingham. In the latter case this became Brumingham and then Brummagem, although Birmingham could also become Brimagem as in William's surname.

A farm labourer from Galway, William lodged with two other agricultural workers from his county, eighteen-year-old Martha Burke and Philip Chapman, in the home of John and Mary Kelly. Both were also from Galway, where two of their three children had been born. Crammed

into this tiny back house with them were seven more lodgers: two women and one other man from Galway; two chaps from Kerry; and one man from County Cavan. Conditions in this house must have been stifling, with so many packed into so little space and with all of them having to share a vile cess pit outside and overflowing miskins, a space for rubbish. Water would have been drawn from a polluted well or would have been bought stale and brackish from water carts. Having to arise early to troop out of the city centre to whatever farm, William would have returned tired and probably dispirited late at night. Perhaps his only entertainment was to go to the Bull Ring late on a Saturday afternoon to hark at the pitchers of goods and watch the entertainers.

There can be little doubt that both William Bermegham and William Brimagem had a deep bond with the city. Were there any tales in their families that helped explain that link, or were they unaware that in the Middle Ages, when Birmingham was a small market town, the lords of the manor carried their name? Did they know that the land upon which Pickford Street was laid had been part of the demesne, the estate held by the de Berminghams themselves and not rented out to tenants, and that the de Berminghams had lived prosperously just opposite Digbeth in a manor house surrounded by a moat – hence Moat Row? And did they ever go into the parish church of Saint Martin's, just a short distance up the hill in the Bull Ring and look at the effigies of three members of the de Bermingham family, one of which is in the style of the late thirteenth or fourteenth century and is ascribed to a Sir William? It is believed that this is the oldest piece of surviving art in Birmingham, but which William it represents is uncertain for there were four lords of this name in that period. Whatever the case, the tomb indicates a family of some standing and influence, as do the other two monuments. The one in stone is that of Sir Fulk, one of the most powerful members of his family.

A fierce warrior, he was prominent in the wars against the French and fought at the Battle of Crécy, when the English bowmen destroyed their more numerous opponents. It is also likely that ten years later he was present at the victory at Poitiers. The third tomb is in alabaster and is that of Fulk's son, Sir John.

Pickford Street had a population of 282 in 1904, and it is unlikely that it was much higher in 1881 when William lived there. A few streets away from the marked Irish presence in the locality of Park Street and Allison Street, William was one of only eleven Irish folk in the street – although that number could be increased significantly by seventeen if English-born members of households with Irish mothers, fathers or relatives were included. That would mean that about 10% of the street's people could be seen as first or second generation Irish. By contrast Digbeth had 82 Irish people and was close to large numbers of Irish not only in Park Street and Allison Street but also in Edgbaston Street. Slaney Street was also populated markedly with Irish folk and was, in fact, one of the most Irish streets in Birmingham with 77 Irish-born inhabitants, many of whom were from Mayo and Galway and some of whom were from Tipperary. If the close relatives of these Irish folk were taken into account then another 120 could be added to the figure of the Irish in the street. The population of Slaney Street was 311, making folk from Irish households almost three quarters of the total.

Located in the Gun Quarter close to the present Post and Mail building and the West Midlands Police headquarters of Lloyd House, Slaney Street was swept away by the redevelopments of the 1960s, but it had been associated with the Irish from the beginnings of large-scale migration to Birmingham in the mid-1820s. In 1881 one of its residents was William Crawford, a gun finisher. He and his wife Ellen, a boot tip maker, lodged with William Loftus, who was also Irish. Aged 55 and 40 respectively, the couple had three

Slaney Street in the 1950s.

sons: Robert, Martin and James were born in Birmingham, all worked as errand boys and they ranged in age from fourteen to seventeen. Their father worked in a skilled and highly sub-divided trade. Different craftsmen made the various parts of a gun so that there were many processes involved in manufacturing the final product. It was the finisher who fetched in the pieces, distributed them for the last stages of work and then put the gun together and adjusted the several parts. For all the skills involved, the gun trade was precarious, dependent as it was on the export market and the uncertain demand from the wealthy for sporting guns. Gun workers often experienced lean times, explaining why so many of them lived in poor quality housing such as that in Slaney Street, which had been declared as decaying back in the 1840s.

Like William Bermegham, William Crawford probably did not suspect that there was something about him that marked him out from his fellow Irishmen and women in Birmingham and which held him faster to the city than did the fact of residence alone. For whilst Ellen, his wife, originated from Mayo, William himself hailed from Athenry in Galway. The finest medieval walled town in Ireland, it is a setting in which history reaches out powerfully into the present not only through its old buildings but also through a pervasive feeling that awakens the past.

Sacked in 1597 by Red Hugh O'Donnell, the town was so badly damaged that it never really recovered. But the subsequent decline of Athenry meant that the layout of the Middle Ages did not disappear, so that today it boasts still its medieval castle and walls, parish church, Dominican priory, market cross and street plan within its town walls. This old look is enhanced by the base of a bargaining cross in the fair green, two medieval bridges across the River Clarin and remnants of a Pre-Reformation church dedicated to St. Bridget outside its town walls. It is Athenry, this most historic of towns, that ties together William Bermegham, William Crawford, the de Berminghams and Birmingham itself.

Athenry, with the de Bermingham castle in the background.

Like so much of England, following the Norman Conquest of 1066 the minor manor of Birmingham became the property of a foreigner who had served William the Conqueror well. William FitzAnsculf was the commanding lord of Dudley, and Birmingham was one of the many manors locally of which he took possession. Few Anglo-Saxons retained any land or power and everywhere the Normans and their allies were in the ascendancy. One hundred years after the most decisive and traumatic change in English history, Birmingham's Lord was a man called Peter. Whether or not he was a Norman cannot be ascertained but it is likely that he was, given that he had been the steward of the great lord of Dudley. Peter's father, William, had also held Birmingham but it was the son who was to have

the greater impact. For in 1166 it was Peter who gained from Henry II the right to hold a market in his manor. It was this development that led to the transformation of Birmingham from a small agricultural spot into a new town focused upon Saint Martin's and the Bull Ring. Without the market charter Birmingham would not have grown, it could never have become the greatest manufacturing city in the world and it would not have become a magnet to migrants from across England and Ireland who were looking for work, hope, expectations and a future.

Peter de Bermingham had three sons, of whom two are noteworthy. The eldest, William, succeeded his father as Lord of Birmingham and went on crusade in 1191, whilst Robert was a key figure in the Norman invasion of Ireland. A warlike people who craved land above all else, the Normans were swift to attack others and violently take hold of their estates. They had already rampaged through England, much of Wales, parts of the Lowlands of Scotland and Sicily before a force of Norman-Welsh knights and Flemish landed at Bannow Bay, Wexford in May 1169, under the direction of Strongbow, Richard de Clare, Earl of Pembroke. He had decided to help Dermot Mac Murrough, the king of Leinster, against his enemies. A short time later Strongbow himself arrived with reinforcements and within the year he had captured Dublin, married Mac Murrough's daughter, Aoife, and, upon the death of his Irish father-in-law, become king of Leinster. Concerned at the waxing strength of one of his subjects, Henry II came to Waterford with a large force. He took the submission of many Irish princes and asserted his overlordship of Strongbow and thus Ireland. Importantly, Rory O'Connor was acknowledged as ard-rí, high king, of that large part of Ireland that had not been conquered by the Normans, and in turn Rory recognized Henry as his overlord and agreed to collect an annual tribute for him from across Ireland.

In the succeeding years, Henry showed no respect for the agreement. Ignoring the rights of Irish lords, he granted their lands to his followers, whilst other Normans took it upon themselves to attack Irish lands and carved out semi-independent fiefdoms. Amongst them were the de Berminghams. It may be that Robert de Bermingham was one of the 200 knights who came to Ireland with Strongbow, for it was the Earl himself who gave Robert 'Offaly west of Offalen'. As a younger son there were few prospects for him in England and, like others of his ilk, he would have seen Ireland as a land that could be taken from its ancient rulers. As with their invasion of England, the Normans justified their depredations by dubious claims of legality but there can be no doubting that the overarching reason for their offensive on Ireland was to wrest land from the Irish. Robert's father, Peter, must have visited his son for in 1173 the Lord of Birmingham witnessed a document in the country; whilst three years later, Robert and his brother William both witnessed a grant there.

Little more is known of Robert, but for the fact that he established the de Berminghams in Ireland. The family comes to notice again in 1234 with Peter de Bermingham, who may have been the son of Robert. The Lord of Tethmoy in Offaly, he was known as Piers Primaster and was involved in bloody disputes with the local Irish. The next year, Peter joined Richard de Burgo (also known as Burgh, from which name is derived Burke) in the invasion of Connacht. This was as great an act of treachery as any by the Normans. The O'Connors, who dominated Connacht, had kept their part of the agreement and remained faithful to Henry, but the niceties of diplomacy were overridden by a large and fearsome Norman force. Made up of 500 mounted knights and hundreds of archers and other footmen, it crossed the Shannon by storming Athlone and then went on to burn and plunder Connacht. So devastating was the pillaging that large numbers of Irish leaders were

forced to submit to the aggressor and rapidly most Irish lords were stripped of their estates in all but Leitrim and Roscommon.

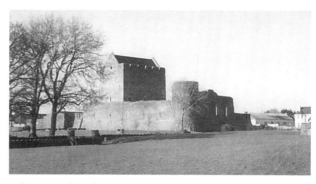

Athenry Castle and outer walls.

It would seem that Peter Primaster was a leading figure in the depredations, for he witnessed grants and received Dunmore in Galway. So strong was his presence that by 1249 the whole area between the River May and Ballysader Bay had become known as 'Mac Feorais's country'. Mac Feorais is the Gaelic for Fitz Piers (FitzPeters), and from which derives the modern Irish surname Corish. Peter was not the only de Bermingham to gain through taking lands from the Irish of Connacht by might. His son Meiler (Myler) became the Lord of Athenry and began what was regarded as the premier barony of Ireland. Certainly, Meiler was in possession of Athenry by 1244 when he was granted the right to hold a market in the town, although probably he had dispossessed the Irish before, as it is believed that he founded the local Dominican priory three years earlier.

Athenry commanded a strategic ford over the River Clarin halfway between Galway City and Loughrea, where de Burgo had built his major castle. Meiler controlled the locality from a strongly built keep. Just two storeys high, it was entered at the second floor by a ladder that was drawn up nightly. The second floor was reached by wooden stairs, whilst the main floor must have been dark, smelly and cold. It had a garde-robe or latrine at its north-western corner, consisting of a projecting 'room', only part of which still remains. There are no windows on the second floor and no fireplaces, suggesting that the fireplace was in the middle of the first floor room – and with no chimney the atmosphere must have been heavy and smoky. The keep was built close enough to the north-western part of the surrounding curtain wall to allow it to overlook the wall, whilst there are wall towers at the north-eastern and south-eastern corners of this outer wall. The south-western corner of the curtain wall was fortified by the gate. This was a place of defence and not beauty, providing protection from a people who strove to regain their rightful lands.

Athenry Castle.

Similarly, the de Berminghams of Tethmoy had to fight hard to maintain their gains and often used stealth and treachery to do so. Owning lands that straddled the border of Kildare and Offaly in the Irish Midlands, their main castle was at Carbury in Kildare. Located on the eastern side of the Bog of Allen and to the west of the Wicklow Mountains, Castle Carbury is now a castellated manor house that incorporates much of the original de Bermingham castle. Built on a hill, there is a fine view of four other de Bermingham castles: Mylerstown, Kinnafad, Carrick Castle and Grange. According to a Scottish source, in 1305 'Piers Brunychemham the baron, a notorious traitor and perjuror' invited Murtagh O'Connor, king of Offally, his brother Calvagh and others to a feast of the Festival of Holy Trinity. On 'that very day, when the meal was over, the moment they (the Irish) rose from the table, he himself, with twenty-four men of his following, cruelly slaughtered them, and sold their heads to their enemies.' Most callously and horrifyingly, it is stated that Peter himself took a young son of the O'Connor and to whom he was godfather and flung him to his death over the battlements. Married to Ela Odyngsells of Maxstoke in Warwickshire, Piers was killed in 1308. According to the Annals of the Four Masters, 'Rory O'Connor and O'Flynn afterwards led a troop of cavalry to the plain of Connacht, the level part of Roscommon, and slew Mac Feorais'.

Both branches of the de Bermingham family were prominent in the even more turbulent and violent years that followed the invasion in 1315 of Edward Bruce, the brother of Robert the Bruce of Scotland. Accompanied by 6,000 warriors, he stormed across Ireland, making and breaking alliances and attacking all who were a threat to his ambition to becoming undisputed king. Felim O'Connor, the king of Connacht whose strength was focused upon Roscommon, was drawn into the skein of Bruce's ambition. Felim was only twenty years old and his claim to overlordship was challenged by his cousin, Rory. Richard de Burgo, the dominant lord in the west, put his weight behind Felim and the two marched to do battle with Edward Bruce in Ulster. Craftily, Edward turned Felim, by promising the Irish leader backing for his claims in Connacht. Of course, Felim was unaware that the Scot had made the same promise to his hated rival, Rory. Felim's forces withdrew and de Burgo was defeated. But when Felim and his men arrived back in Connacht, they were overwhelmed by Rory's forces.

Desperate, Felim approached de Burgo, who had escaped to his stronghold in Galway. The Norman agreed to support Felim and scratched together an army that included Richard de Bermingham. The second son of Meiler, Richard was sheriff of Connacht in 1299, 1310 and 1316.

Because of his ferocity in war he became known as Risteard na gCat, Richard of the Battles, and the Bermingham Tower in Dublin Castle is named after him. The allies clashed with Rory in Mayo, killing him and scattering his men. But swift to move where the power lay and determined to try and wrest back from the Normans his family's lands and power, Felim once more took the side of Edward. He pulled together Irishmen, gallowglass mercenaries from the Western Isles of Scotland and whoever else would take his side and marched on Athenry. On the feast day of Saint Laurence 1316, and led by William de Burgo and Richard de Bermingham, the Normans rode from without the town and crossed its moat. In 'a fierce and spirited engagement' that was believed to have been 'the bloodiest battle fought in Ireland for many a long day', the Irish were shattered. Felim was killed as was O'Kelly, King of Maneach, and most of the Irish princes and chiefs of Connacht and Munster. Irish writers mourned not only the deaths of the 'many kings' who 'were slain in the great defeat, around the great plain', but also the loss of hope that the Normans might be thrust back east of the Shannon. In a brutal reminder of the victory, the town seal of Athenry was made to show the heads of Irishmen impaled on pikes.

The Birmingham Tower, Dublin Castle.

Richard de Bermingham's cousin, John, Lord of Tethmoy was as fierce. A year after the decisive battle of Athenry, which is regarded by some as a turning point in Irish history, Edward Bruce

attacked County Louth. John quickly pulled together a force that mastered Edward and killed him at Faugher. The Scot's head was cut from his body and John de Bermingham, as had his father with the head of Murtagh O'Connor, presented it to the king. Rewarded with the Earldom of Louth and the Barony of Aberdee, John rose further to become justiciar of Ireland in 1321. In common with other Norman lords, it seems that John was haughty and disdainful of the authority of the king and he was involved in private wars with other magnates. Such conflicts may have been small-scale but they were as brutal as bigger battles and they had dire effects on the common people and lesser lords. Obviously believing himself to be above the law and acting as a semi-independent ruler, John allowed his illegitimate brother, Robert, and his gang of 'evildoers' to wreak havoc and commit 'homicides, arsons and other crimes upon the inhabitants' of Louth.

Stirred into action and led by the sheriff and coroners, the Gernons, Cusacks, Hadsors, Clintons and other families came together in a posse and chased the Earl and his band of bullies to Balbriggan. The wrongdoers were charged 'to surrender themselves; but the said Earl, maintaining the said persons in their evil courses, with armed force and standard displayed as in war, assaulted the sheriff and coroners and slew several of their following'. Roused to a terrible anger, the posse slaughtered John de Bermingham and his followers. John's probable brother, William, also met a terrible end, hanged upon the king's orders in 1332. However, the de Berminghams of Carbury continued as a line until the death of Sir William Bermingham, Baron of Carbury in 1562. His heir died without issue, and thus William's title and lands reverted to the Crown. Still, many Berminghams remained locally and unlike the Baron of Carbury, they fought the English as an Irish Catholic family. In the rebellion of 1641 against the English and Scottish settlers, and again in the Jacobite wars from 1689, Berminghams were prominent. Their loyalty to Ireland and their faith led them to lose their lands.

The de Berminghams of Athenry also went on exercising control in their fiefdom. As with their cousins in Kildare, increasingly that power was wielded not as Norman outsiders and conquerors but as an Irish family. That remarkable change was wrought by Irishwomen. As Seumas MacManus expressively explains:

On the day when the victorious Richard, Earl of Pembroke, surnamed Strongbow, married Eva, daughter of Dermot MacMurrough, King of Leinster on the blood-soaked battlefield of Waterford (1170), the Irish conquest of the Norman conquerors was begun . . . As generation succeeded generation all the Irish clans, in the five-fifths of Eirinn, were united in ties of blood with, and helped to conquer to Gaeldom, all the Norman families.
(Seumas MacManus, The Story of the Irish Race, 1990 edition).

These Sean Ghalls, old foreigners, became almost more Irish than the Irish, despite the strenuous efforts of English kings to stop this process of assimilation. The de Berminghams were amongst those who were 'gaelicised'. The wife of Richard of the Battles was called Fionualla, and her name suggests strongly that she was Irish; whilst his son, Thomas, was married to Edina, daughter of MacEgan – and again, presumably she was an Irishwoman. In the fifteenth century the Irishness of the de Berminghams was emphasised by their association with the O'Connors, the same ancient Irish family with which they had fought in the past and which they had wronged, and in 1478 the parliament held at Drogheda took protective steps 'for the chastisement of the Berminghams'.

As Catholics, the Berminghams suffered badly in the terrible wars of the seventeenth century in which the Catholic gentry and nobility of Ireland had their land stolen from them and given to Protestant settlers from England and Scotland. Some of the Berminghams made their way to Spain and France, along with many other 'wild geese' of the Irish who fled oppression and sought refuge with England's enemies. It is ironic, then, that a family that bloodily set itself up in Ireland became profoundly Irish and that in the late nineteenth century two men who held its name came to work in the city of Birmingham, the ancestral home of the Berminghams. Even more ironically, the presence of William Bermegham, William Brimagem and William Crawford of Athenry arose precisely because of the dire economic conditions in Ireland, economic conditions that were themselves largely the woeful result of the Protestant Ascendancy on both rural and urban Ireland.

Further Reading

Justin Pinkess, *The Lords of Birmingham and Their Manor 1066-1554*, unpublished manuscript, 1988 (I thank Sheila Fowler for this source. Sheila herself was deeply involved in this meticulously researched work).

James Charles Roy, *The Fields of Athenry. A Journey through Irish History*, 2001.

Etienne Rynne, 'Athenry', in Anngret Sims and J. H. Andrews, *More Irish Country Towns*, 1995.

CHAPTER TWO
THE TRUE DUTIES OF CITIZENSHIP

The Birmingham Saint Patrick's Day Parade 2002. Photo West Midlands Fire Service.

No one can ignore the Irish in Birmingham today. That was made clear on 17 March 2002 when at least 100,000 people flocked to the city centre to take part in or watch the annual Saint Patrick's Day Parade. Revived six years before, each year the parade had drawn in greater numbers and this time it was joined by four firefighters from the Fire Department New York. They had been invited to Birmingham as a show of solidarity following the atrocity of 11 September 2001 when terrorists attacked the Twin Towers in Manhattan and murdered so many innocent people. That day was one of the most stirring in my life. Standing at the parade's start at Camp Hill, my eyes rushed hither and thither - pulled as they were by the beauty of the Irish dancers' costumes and by the inspired themes on a variety of floats. As much as my eyes were helter-skeltering about, so too were my ears seeking to hark at a medley of pipes, drums, singers and records. It was as if the whole of Birmingham had turned out – English and Irish, black and white, Asian and European – and was trying keenly to catch hold of the enchantment of the day.

Moving down from Camp Hill, the parade was led by the New York firefighters and the Birmingham Irish Pipes and Drums band, marching proudly in their own tartan. Behind them came an exciting and dynamic mix of walkers, marching bands, floats, motorcyclists, cars and other pipe bands. As the parade went ahead, flag-waving and thrilled folk cramming the footpaths called out and threw themselves emotionally into the pulsating occasion. On the right, we passed the 'Old Crown', a building that connects Birmingham to the time when it was little more than a market town and which means so much to me and other English Brummies. Brought back to life by the Brennans, an Irish family who spent a huge sum of money on its restoration, it is now run by the Hickeys, another respected Birmingham Irish family. Crossing the River Rea and beginning to walk gradually uphill, we came to the 'Big Bulls Head' on the corner of Oxford Street, at the other end of which runs Pickford Street in which William Bermegham had lived. Next was the 'Kerry Man', a major meeting place for the Irish and others thanks to Liam O'Connor, and then another popular pub and venue, 'Hennessy's', run successfully by the McDonnell family. Rising up from the corner of Allison Street, 'Hennessy's' and the 'Kerry Man' provide a clear link between the Irish of modern Birmingham and their forebears in the nineteenth century, so many of whom lived in Allison Street. Then the great throng went beyond the 'Royal George', on the corner of Park Street. Formerly 'Mary Donleavy's West of the Shannon', this belonged to two remarkable Irish Brummies, Mary and Seamus Donleavy. Seamus was a popular wrestler before he became a successful businessman and Mary is from a respected Sparkhill family. The name of their pub could not have been better, given the strong connection from the 1820s between the west of Ireland and Park Street.

Approaching the Bull Ring, the parade came back on itself, heading down from Saint Martin's, in which are the tombs of the de Berminghams. Prominent on this side of the road is Pat Finn's bustling pub the 'Dubliner', and Dubliners have had a marked presence in Birmingham along with the folk of Roscommon, Mayo and Galway since the 1820s. Then it was on to the Irish Club, recently saved from closure and a symbol of the vitality and significance of the Irish in modern Birmingham as well as a crucial centre of Irish culture. Through the work of the Irish Welfare and Information Centre, it also reaches out to those Irish folk who have not enjoyed prosperity and whose needs may have been forgotten and ignored without their work. Further along, the parade headed off into the Bradford Street area, now to be the focus of Birmingham's Irish Quarter. Dominated by the imposing structure of Saint Anne's Catholic Church, this is the site of pioneering work by Cara Housing and despite its appearance as a back-street district is a vital entertainment locality.

Many of us eschew the heaving crowds and the glitzy bars of Broad Street and head instead for the craic and music of clubs like Saint Anne's, invigorated by Helen Brennan and her sisters, and pubs such as "Cleary's" on Cheapside where singer Danny D'Arcy holds sway. And for the likes of me who enjoy the traditional Brummie drink of mild, the Irish gaffers of this quarter are an inspiration. Pushed out by big business from most city-centre pubs, mild is served properly by Roscommon-born Agnes Creaton of the 'White Swan' on Bradford Street and just up the way in the acclaimed real ale pub the 'Anchor'.

Now one of the biggest Saint Patrick's parades in the world, the 2002 celebration in Birmingham both reflected and stressed the importance of the Irish to Birmingham. With a population of over 38,000 they make up almost 4% of the city's people - a proportion which can be swelled greatly if the daughters and sons of emigrants are included as part of the Irish community. The statistical significance of the Irish is matched by the crucial role they play in the life of Birmingham. Three senior Birmingham City Councillors are Irish. They are Matt Redmond MBE, originally from Dublin, Mike Nangle, hailing from County Armagh, and Hugh McCallion from Strabane in County Tyrone. On the national political scene, Clare Short, MP for Birmingham Ladywood and Minister for Overseas Development, is proud of her Irish heritage; as is Baroness Christie Crawley, a former MEP. Similarly, Irish journalists like Maureen Messent are noted contributors to local newspapers such as the *Birmingham Evening Mail*.

Pat Malloy, right, with Pete Taylor on the harmonica.
Photo Kay Chinn

Culturally, the Birmingham Irish play a major role in the city. Brummie Irish musicians such as Pat Molloy who plays in the 'Antelope', Sparkhill, and Chris Stapleton of the 'Ceol Castle', Balsall Heath, have gained international recognition. So too have Irish dancers like Colin Dunne of Riverdance fame, whose parents come from Wexford. In education, Kerryman Bob Dowling, head of George Dixon School, has been knighted in recognition both of his contribution to education and his sterling work in building respect between various communities. Sir Bob's admirable efforts follow in the footsteps of Tom O'Loughlin, who was an esteemed headmaster in Hockley in the 1950s and 1960s and who turned part of his home into a youth club. Mary O'Donnell has also been honoured for her services to the community. Born and raised in her

early years near Kilcar, County Donegal, in the Gaeltacht, Mary joined her parents in Birmingham in 1958. She went to school at Saint Michael's, formerly Floodgate Street School and now part of the ambitious Digbeth Campus of South Birmingham College. In her adult life, Mary has devoted herself to helping children and adults with domestic and other difficulties to develop better, happier and more successful family lives. Her four sisters also work in the caring professions and 'we are all very proud of Birmingham and the opportunities the City has given us'. (Letter, 9 April 2000, *BirminghamLives Archive*).

Monica McDaid is another women devoted to doing good. Born in Derry, she later became a teacher at Saint Thomas Aquinas School and then went on to found the Romania Challenge Appeal charity. With Daniel O'Donnell as its patron, with the hard work of West Midland firefighters, and the commitment and drive of Monica and her supporters, this charity is striving to improve the lives of orphans of Romania. Like Monica, Danny Ryan has thrown himself into good causes. A second generation Irish Brummie raised in Balsall Heath by a mother and father who were imbued with notions of good citizenship, Danny has raised hundreds of thousands of pounds for charity. Most recently his efforts have focused upon the National Institute for Conductive Education in Moseley. For his good works, Danny was awarded the MBE.

Another key Irish Brummie is Paddy Doyle. Probably the greatest endurance athlete in the world, Paddy has a list of achievements in the Guinness Book of Records. He is one of a number of Irish Brummies who have made their mark on the sporting world, such as boxers Robert McCracken and Matt Macklin and footballer John Deehan. The list of high achievers amongst the Birmingham Irish extends into the business world. In the construction and related industries several people have made their mark

Paddy Doyle setting another record, with Danny Ryan MBE helping on the right and Tony Ryan of the Birmingham Irish Amateur Boxing Club on the left. Based in Lea Village, Tony has many exciting young prospects at his club and is backed strongly by Pat Finn of the 'Dubliner'. Pat had a good name as a boxer, holding the All-Ireland Super Heavyweight title, amongst others.

nationally. They include the Lynch brothers of Lyndon Scaffolding, Basil Burke of Burke's Masonry, the Gallaghers, Pat Kelly of DSM Demolition and Bill Cullen of Cullen Thermals. Indeed, Irishmen and women are prominent in every activity of the city's life. Amongst them are bankers such as Pat O'Neill, chair of the Birmingham Irish Community Forum; builders of quality like Alan Orton of Orton Building Services; building suppliers of note such as Liam Fallon; respected decorators of the type of Gerry Nicholl of Diamond Decorators, Kings Heath; and noted figures in the travel industry, foremost amongst whom are Maggie Roche National Accounts Manager of Stena Line and Martin Kilroy of Claddah Travel. In the licensed trade there are a number of prominent Irish people, including Rose McCann of the 'Bull', Angela Quinn of the 'Antelope' Sparkhill, Tom Mellett of the 'Bear' Sparkhill, Kevin McNamara of Saint Mary's and Saint John's Social Club in Erdington, and the Keanes of the renowned real ale house the 'Anchor' in Digbeth .

The visibility of the Irish in late twentieth century Birmingham heightens their invisibility in the nineteenth century. In the authoritative *History of Birmingham* by Conrad Gill and Asa

Briggs there is no reference to the Irish; whilst in the thoughtful studies of both Victor Skipp and Chris Upton they appear briefly either with regard to Catholicism or to the dire conditions in which many of them lived. Upton does comment also upon the notorious Murphy Riots of 1867 when serious disturbances broke out between Protestant English and Catholic Irish after the visit of the rabble-rousing Protestant preacher William Murphy, and it is this incident which provides the only mention of the Irish in older works such as that by Robert K. Dent.

This non-appearance of the Irish in the main historical works on the city is reflected in the meagre mention of them in the Catalogue of the Birmingham Collection. Brought out by the council in 1918 to assist local studies in the Reference Library by indicating the availability of primary sources it has only three headings under 'Irish'. Joe McKenna and other librarians have striven to address this lack of notice, but such historical inattentiveness is surprising given that the presence of the Irish in Victorian Birmingham was comparable statistically to that in the city today. In 1861 their numbers peaked at 11,322, making them 3.8% of the population. Both figures dropped in the following years and the Irish never formed as large a proportion of citizens as they did in Liverpool, Manchester and Glasgow. Yet they did constitute by far the largest ethnic minority in Birmingham and some of them had a considerable impact on local affairs.

Reverend Thomas M. McDonnell was one of those who gained the esteem of the people of Birmingham in general. When he took up his duties in 1824 at St Peter's Catholic Church in Broad Street he became the first Irish priest in the town. Swiftly he raised a repair fund and two years later enabled the purchase of adjoining land for a graveyard. Soon McDonnell gained a wider following for his determination to help the poor and from his fervent support of Daniel O'Connell's struggle for Catholic Emancipation.

An avowed opponent of bigots, the Saint Chad's Cathedral Records state that McDonnell was ever ready and most able to repel attacks on the church by Protestant firebrands. (Birmingham Archdiocesan Archives, *St Chad's Cathedral Records*, Vol. 1).

McDonnell also published a Catholic magazine for several years, but he did not restrict his campaigning to religious matters. He was a determined and forceful supporter of parliamentary reform and attended public dinners and political meetings that backed those in favour of reform. So popular was McDonnell that in 1831 he became the only Catholic on the council of the Birmingham Political Union, a body that through its massive public meetings and organisation did much to bring about the Great Reform Act of 1832. It was reported that he was a frequent and most acceptable speaker at the meetings of the Union and was a leading member of the council. In particular, his speeches 'always put the people in good humour, for while pointed and severe, they were embellished with sallies of wit that made him very popular'. A robust character, McDonnell was a prime mover for a scheme to build a church more glorious than either Saint Peter's or Saint Chad's. At a meeting in Saint Peter's he moved the motion 'that a commodious, and splendid Catholic church, bearing testimony to the increased liberality of our Protestant fellow-countrymen, and in some degree worthy of the dignity of Catholic worship, and to the sanctity and sublimity of the Christian mysteries, be erected in the town of Birmingham' (M. Hodgetts, *St Chad's Cathedral of Birmingham*, 1904).

However, McDonnell vehemently opposed knocking down the existing Saint Chad's church and replacing it with 'a noble temple' and preferred the new place of worship to rise up from a different spot in central Birmingham. In the ensuing controversy his superiors transferred him in 1841 to a quieter life in Torquay. Within

three days of his leaving over 7,000 people - many of them Protestants - had signed petitions asking for his return, whilst a number of other Protestants spoke up for him, declaring that the good relations between Catholics and Protestants in Birmingham were mostly the result of McDonnell's good efforts. Three years after McDonnell's departure, Daniel O'Connell, the acclaimed campaigner for the rights of Catholics, was given a public breakfast by English reformers. The 'Great Liberator' returned in 1846 when the Irish of Birmingham gave an address to him. (Eileen L. Groth, 'The politics of the Bible: radicalism and non-denominational co-operation in the Birmingham Political Union in R. N. Swanson (ed), *Unity and Diversity in the Church*, 1996; and John Denvir, *The Irish in Britain from the Earliest Times to the Fall and death of Parnell*, 1892).

John Frederick Feeney was a contemporary of the battling MacDonnell. He arrived in the city in 1835 to work as a journalist on a radical newspaper called the *Reformer*. Later he bought the weekly *Birmingham Journal* and through its columns in 1850 he appealed for tolerance when the Pope's decision to set up a hierarchy in England was accompanied by anti-Catholic outbursts. Seven years later Feeney started the *Birmingham Daily Post*, later the *Birmingham Post*, which continues to carry his name on its editorial page. For a man whose business was public life his personal life was deeply private. Indeed, very little is known about him and no business or family papers relating to the Feeneys have survived. There are no glimpses of Feeney's childhood, no hints as to his upbringing and no tantalising leads about his teenage years and early adulthood – other than a tradition that he had begun work as a compositor in a printing room. In fact, there's little hard information about him at all until he came to Birmingham, although it may be that he had been a journalist elsewhere as there were a significant number of Irishmen writing for newspapers in England. Whatever the case, Feeney took to Brum and stayed here for the rest of his life. In 1837 he switched to the staff of the *Midland Counties Herald*, where he worked for seven years until he bought the *Birmingham Journal*. This had been started in 1825 as a weekly and within a few years it had gained a reputation as an important radical publication that backed reform, but now it was in decline. The Irishman transformed its position and soon he had increased weekly sales to 12,000 copies.

John Frederick Feeney.

According to the 1851 Census, he was living at 145, Highgate – the Moseley Road neighbourhood. Aged 42, he was listed as a newspaper proprietor who was born in Ireland. His wife, Barbara, was fifteen years younger than he was and was local, having been born in Edgbaston. Living with them were his sister, Margaret White, and her son who had been born in New South Wales, Australia; his sister-in-law; two servants and three children. These were Peregrine (thirteen), Mary (eight) and William (six). All were born in Birmingham. Ten years later, Feeney had moved to the more affluent Church Road, Edgbaston where another son,

John, is noted. We do not know the surname of his first wife, Rebecca Sophia, who was the mother of all these children and all of whom were baptised in Anglican churches. Feeney married his second wife, Barbara, in 1850 according to the rites of the established Church of England in Saint Peter's and Saint Paul's, the parish church of Aston. Both of them are interred in a vault of the church beneath the Erdington chapel. Feeney was a great benefactor to Saint Peter's and Saint Paul's and it is thought that Frederick Road, Aston is named after him.

On his marriage certificate to Barbara, Feeney's father was named as John Feeney, bookseller, but what little else we know about the newspaper publisher comes from information gleaned from an obituary of his nephew Alfred Feeny – whose name did not include the final 'e' as with John Frederick Feeney. Alfred came to Birmingham in 1857 to work in the commercial department on his uncle's new venture, a daily newspaper. He stayed with the paper until his retirement in 1904. Alfred's father was Patrick Malvogue Feeny of Sligo, who was John Frederick Feeney's brother. Patrick was also involved in the newspaper business, having worked on the *Connaught Telegraph*, had a share in the *Mayo Constitution* and then taken a leading position on the *Morning News* of London, in which city Alfred was born. A major influence on the *Post* through the quality of his writing, his versatility and his journalistic flair, Alfred was also the Birmingham correspondent for the *Times* and was involved in the *Ironmonger*, which focused upon the hardware trades of Birmingham and elsewhere. A Liberal in politics, he was a staunch Catholic and was one of the best-known and most highly regarded members of the Edgbaston Oratory, attending mass daily at 8.30 in the morning. (*'Edgbastonians Past and Present. The Late Mr Alfred Feeny'*, Edgbastonia, vol. XXV, no. 289, June 1905; and H. R. G. Whates, *The Birmingham Post 1857:1957. A Centenary Retrospect*, 1957).

Alfred Feeny.

It may be speculated that John Frederick Feeney had also been a Catholic but had converted to Anglicanism – perhaps, as did others, to avoid difficulties at a time when there was marked anti-Catholic prejudice and when there were very few Irish Catholics in positions of authority. Whatever the case, it seems likely that he was from Sligo or Mayo, where the family had relatives in the early twentieth century, and he is an Irishman who has had a lasting effect upon Birmingham. Known as the 'Governor', for all he was self-effacing Feeney was a dogged and determined man who had successfully come through severe difficulties in the newspaper business and who was resolute in his belief in tolerance. He died aged 61 on 11 May 1862 and John Jaffray, his partner at the *Birmingham Daily Post*, used the columns of the publication to praise his colleague. He stated clearly that 'the history of Mr Feeney's career in Birmingham is indeed the history of the later developments of newspaper energy amongst us'. He was tactful, courteous, hard working and thorough in his business habits. Living a peaceful and uneventful life, he was 'one of the purest minds that God ever created, and as kind a heart as ever beat in human breast'.

After Feeney's death, his newspapers were run by his son, John Feeney, in partnership with Jaffray. The oldest son, Peregrine, had started work as a newspaperman but soon went to London to become an artist. One of his paintings, of Lyn Idwal in Wales, hangs in Birmingham's Art Gallery. John also had artistic leanings, especially towards industrial art, and profoundly affected the provision of art in Birmingham through his extraordinary generosity. It was John Feeney and Jaffray who established the *Birmingham Daily Mail* in 1870. Nineteen years later they set up the Birmingham Mail Christmas Tree Fund to raise money for 'toys and cash to brighten the lives of poor children in hospital'. In 1906, the fund began giving out Christmas dinners to poor families and boots to unshod children. Tens of thousands of English Brummies, my own Nan and aunts and uncles amongst them, owed the shoes on their feet to a charity set up by a second generation Irish Brummie.

John Feeney.

John Feeney had other positive and long-lasting effects on Birmingham. When the Art Gallery was opened in 1885, he gave the first instalment of an outstanding collection of works from abroad, in this case Japanese enamel, porcelain, lacquer, silver, armour and swords, and Chinese bronze, silver and lacquer. This was later supplemented by work from Persia, Turkey, Scandinavia, Germany, France, Spain, Austria and Russia. By 1899 the liberality of John Feeney had led to a collection of 1,693 pieces. Seven years later when he died, his generosity to the Art Gallery staggered the citizens of Birmingham by his bequest of 'the magnificent legacy of £50,000'. This huge sum was crucial for the building of a new Picture Gallery as an extension of the Council House in both Edmund Street and Great Charles Street. These Feeney Galleries were opened in 1912. Nobody who enters them should be unaware that they were paid for by a man whose father came from the west of Ireland. ('*Edgbastonians Past and Present.* Mr John Feeney J. P', Edgbastonia, vol. XXVI, January, no.296).

Feeney's will also left £20,000 to the University of Birmingham, adding to the £5,000 he had given whilst alive; £10,000 to the General Hospital, which swelled the £1,000 handed over previously; and £1,000 each to nine other hospitals and charities. His obituarist exclaimed that 'it is hardly possible to exaggerate the importance of this final and signal recognition on Mr Feeney's part of the true duties of citizenship'. Other philanthropic acts whilst he lived included donating £1,000 each to the Women's Hospital, the Coventry and Warwickshire Hospital and the Birmingham Bishopric Fund; and paying for the restoration of the Erdington Chapel and its monuments and the carrying out of the refurbishment of the entire chancel end of Aston Parish Church.

Daniel Joseph O'Neill did not have the wealth of John Feeney but he shared his good-heartedness. A Dubliner, he was called 'The Friend of the Poor' and was regarded as 'one of the most interesting personalities in the public and social life of Birmingham for upwards of half a century'. Residing in Charlotte Road, Edgbaston , 'from the first time he entered public life there were few movements with which Mr O'Neill was not

Daniel J. O'Neill.

connected in some way, or other. He was a friend to all, especially the "little prisoners in the slums" and was respected by all classes of the community.' O'Neill came to Birmingham in 1852 as a young man of twenty. A silversmith and art metalworker, he gained an important clerical position at R. W. Winfield's, one of the most important firms in the city. Five years later, he became involved in the campaign 'to endeavour to get Birmingham a Park worthy of the name; to save a grand historic building from being carted away, as so many thousands of old bricks; and to prevent the magnificent trees being felled for jerry-building and road-making'. The grand building was Aston Hall. ('*Friend of the Poor*', *Birmingham Gazette*, 21 July 1914; and Daniel J. O'Neill, *How Aston Hall and Park Were Saved*, 1910).

Birmingham was expanding rapidly in the 1850s and much of the parkland of Aston Hall had been built upon. O'Neill and others were resolved that what was left would be saved for the citizens of

Birmingham, a town that then did not have a park at all. Elected vice-chairman and secretary of a Working Man's Committee, O'Neill and others gave talks and arranged events to fetch in money to try to buy the hall and park. He then resigned his position at Winfield's and became full-time secretary to Aston Hall and Park Company Limited, which managed to secure the site, and in 1858 he was presented to Queen Victoria when she visited Aston Hall and Park. The queen thanked O'Neill for what he was doing 'in thus worthily providing for the physical and intellectual improvement of the people of Birmingham'. Later the town council took over Aston Hall and Park, but there is little doubt that O'Neill was crucial in saving them for his fellow citizens. In 1913 his efforts were recognised when he was presented with an illuminated address because of his work for the social and moral advancement of the people.

O'Neill was also concerned with the Association for Clothing Destitute Children and with the bad housing of the poor in a Birmingham that was proclaimed as the best-governed city in the world. Similarly, the hardships of the poor affected Dr E. R. Hennessy. Raised in Galbally, Tipperary, he came to Birmingham in the early 1890s where he began a good medical practice in Aston Street, Gosta Green. Soon he became involved in public life and in 1895 he was elected a councillor. During his six years as such he always commanded the full attention of the Council House through his fluent speech and 'he accomplished a lot of useful work, more especially on behalf of the poorer inhabitants of Birmingham, who always had in him a staunch friend'. Later moving to Rookery Road, Handsworth, Hennessy became active in the district's Education Committee upon the retirement of Rev. W. Ireland, rector of Saint Francis Catholic Church. ('*Our Picture Gallery*'. No 128. Dr E. R. Hennessy, Handsworth, vol. XI, no. 129, March 1904).

Education was a matter that pulled a number of Catholic priests firmly into the public eye in Birmingham. Prominent amongst them was the Reverend Canon O'Sullivan, Vicar General of St Chad's, who was 'deeply beloved by those of his own nationality and faith'. Born into a well-off Irish farming family, his father died when he was but three months old and his family was broken up. At the age of ten, an uncle placed him at Sedgley Park, then the foremost Catholic public school in England. Three years later he was sent to Oscott College to train as a priest and after a time at the English College in Rome, he returned to Birmingham in 1848 to assist at Saint Peter's Church. Within three years he was moved on to Saint Chad's where he took charge of the Catholic day schools and showed a keen interest in the Catholic night schools. His influence was great. When there was little education available for poorer children, 'Canon O'Sullivan, with a few voluntary teachers, was doing giant's work. Hundreds of poor fellows, after doing an exhausting day's toil in the workshop and the factory, were taught their first simple lessons in reading and writing. Many Catholic citizens today holding fairly good social positions have to thank Canon O'Sullivan and his few co-adjutors for those first lessons in knowledge which in after years, must have proved so valuable.' ('The Rev. Canon O'Sullivan', in *Birmingham Faces and Places*, vol. II, June 1889, no. 2, pp. 27-9).

Canon O'Sullivan's health was strained by his exertions and he was sent to a quiet country parish, before he was transferred to Stafford where again he threw himself into education work. In 1866 he came back to Birmingham to become Vicar General of Saint Chad's and five years later was elected at the head of the poll as a member of the first Birmingham School Board. Also on the board were some of the most significant men in the history of Birmingham, including Joseph Chamberlain, George Dawson, and Robert Dale. These three were opposed vehemently to any education that was attached to a particular form of Christianity. The most eloquent of speakers, they were adept at 'wit, sharp repartee, and much sarcastic word fencing', and their attacks on the churchmen on the board 'were also frequently interspersed with cutting raillery and biting sarcasm'. There was only one member of the board who had the ability to challenge them and to best them. That was Canon O'Sullivan and for that he gained the esteem of his protagonists. A staunch advocate of Home Rule for Ireland, he resigned his position in 1879.

Reverend Arthur O'Neill.

Reverend Canon O'Sullivan.

The contentious matter of Home Rule energised another of the leading religious figures in Birmingham. The Reverend Arthur O'Neill was a Protestant minister whose father 'had to fly from his native country'. Like Canon O'Sullivan, Reverend O'Neill grew up fatherless – for his parent died before he was born in 1818 in Essex – and it seems that he was raised in the army where he became involved in the medical field. As a young man he had a religious experience and decided to become a minister. Soon after he was drawn to Chartism, a massive working-class movement that was struggling to gain the vote for working-class men. Through an extension of the franchise they hoped to bring about social change that would benefit the working class.

Arriving in Birmingham in 1840, he started a small chapel in Newhall Street and became prominent locally both as a Chartist and as a member of the Peace Society, a body that sought to eradicate conflict. O'Neill was also concerned with advocating temperance and spreading education.

During 1842, agitation swept across England and O'Neill addressed two huge meetings of striking miners in the Black Country. The gatherings had been banned and O'Neill was arrested, charged with using seditious language and sentenced to twelve months in jail. A political prisoner at the age of twenty-three, O'Neill was not swayed from the cause of social justice. After the decline of Chartism he campaigned for the Reform League, which influenced the passage of the 1867 Reform Act, and he came out clearly against the Crimean War and other conflicts. Dedicated to working-class self-improvement he was involved in setting up a number of trade unions and was 'a staunch Home Ruler and a detester of Coercion Bills'.

As a result of the Tudor Conquest of Ireland, the Cromwellian invasion and atrocities, and the triumph of the Protestant King William over the Catholic King James II at the Battle of the Boyne in 1690, by the nineteenth century few Catholic Irish owned land. Amongst this small minority were Daniel O'Connell's family of Kerry and the O'Connors of Roscommon. Throughout the country great estates were owned often by absentee landlords. Many of these were titled through their Irish possessions and sat in the House of Lords and too many of them cared only for the rents they garnered from owning land that was tilled by others. Of course, there were improving landlords, but the attitude of too many was that of George Moore, of Moore Hall in County Mayo. He recalled that 'until the seventies Ireland was feudal, and we looked upon our tenants as animals that lived in hovels round the bogs, whence they came twice a year with their rents'. (Valerie Pakenham, *The Big House in Ireland*, 2000).

If tenants could not pay, then too regularly they were evicted and their families were left destitute. The bad winter of 1878-9 made the position of many tenants unbearable. The weather was exceptionally wet, crops failed, prices dropped and incomes plummeted. Unable to pay their landlords, farmers across Ireland were threatened with the loss of what they regarded rightly as their land. Faced with this dreadful situation, Michael Davitt founded the Land League. The son of a tenant farmer from County Mayo who was evicted after the Famine, his family had emigrated to Lancashire where Davitt lost his arm in a factory when he was eleven. Later becoming a Fenian, one of those who believed that independence for Ireland would only come through physical action, Davitt was jailed. Upon his release, he threw himself into activating the people of Mayo and breaking down what he saw as their economic ignorance and slavish social attitude towards landlords and agents. He succeeded 'by holding the landlord class, its arrogance and acts, up to opprobrium and contempt, as being the sordid beneficiaries of

legal injustice which had robbed the nation of its patrimony and industry of its right reward'. (Michael Davitt, *The Fall of Feudalism in Ireland*, 1904).

Supported by Charles Stewart Parnell, the leader of the Home Rule Party, and the Fenians, Davitt led a popular campaign against unbridled landlordism. Described by some as a land war, in reality it was a struggle for social and economic justice. T. W. Moody has declared it 'the greatest mass movement of modern Ireland'. Determined to win by moral force, the Land Leaguers focused upon civil disobedience and the wholehearted backing of those threatened with the loss of their homes and livelihoods. When bailiffs arrived to serve eviction notices, they were met with huge demonstrations; those forced from their homes were given succour by their neighbours; embargoes were placed on farms from which tenants had been thrown out; and those people who did not fall in with the Land Leaguers were boycotted. This term for social ostracism arose when Captain Charles Boycott of Lough Mask House, County Mayo and the agent for Lord Erne, defied the League. By the autumn of 1880, he and his family were isolated and ignored and their crop was only brought in because troops protected 50 Orangemen who had arrived from the north of Ireland. (T. W. Moody, *'Fenianism, Home Rule, and the Land War (1850-91)'*, in T. W. Moody and F. X. Martin, edited, *The Course of Irish History*, 1984, p. 286).

Gladstone's Liberal government was seeking to bring in land reforms but like later governments, its 'concessions' were accompanied by a coercion act, whereby powers of arrest and detention were strengthened. This followed legislation that extended the powers of the Lord Lieutenant to search and arrest and made the people in supposed 'disturbed areas' pay for the cost of extra policing. It was these coercion acts that were loathed by the Reverend Arthur O'Neill, who advocated that they be swept from the

Chief Constable Charles Houghton Rafter.

statute book and that Ireland be given Home Rule. The belief that Ireland should be self-governing within the United Kingdom was pushed forward by the Home Rule Movement, founded in 1870 by Isaac Butt. The next year Reverend O'Neill brought the Irish leader to Birmingham to explain his beliefs. For the cause of Home Rule, the battler for human rights 'spent his money and his time; on its behalf he has spoken with all the oratorical force which alone comes when the speaker is advocating that which he believes to be just and for the welfare of his countrymen'. ('The Rev. Arthur O'Neill', *Birmingham Faces and Places*, vol. II, no. 10, February 1890).

Interestingly, in 1899 the new chief constable of Birmingham, Charles Haughton Rafter, was a man who had wide experience of the land agitation in Ireland. A Belfast man, he joined the Royal Irish Constabulary as a gentleman cadet and went on to serve as a district inspector in various parts of Ireland for seventeen years. At the time of the subjection of Captain Boycott to 'moral Coventry', Rafter was given charge of the Ballinrobe area, where the landlord lived. He was

also involved in policing incidents in Athlone, Sligo and Tipperary. His work at this latter place earned him the admiration of Count Arthur Moore, a Home Rule MP. So high was the feeling locally that 'any want of tactic or judgement might have precipitated an encounter at a moment's notice between the two excited parties. During all that time Mr Rafter kept a cool, clear head, and got well through the troubles of that eventful period, handling large numbers of armed and excited men with unfailing good temper and tact.' ('Mr Charles Haughton Rafter', *Moseley and Kings Heath Journal*, vol. VIII, August 1899).

Knighted in 1927, Rafter was concerned deeply for the welfare both of his men and local children. Within months of his appointment, he put out an order and circulated to each chief superintendent a copy of the Prevention of Cruelty to Children Act 1894, drawing attention especially to sections on cruelty, employment and places of safety. He also pre-empted national legislation by insisting that juveniles should not appear in courts intermixed with adults. All juveniles were to be dealt with first and be removed from the courtroom before adult prisoners were allowed in. On occasion, he 'donned the robes of Santa Claus and came down the chimney at a police Christmas party for children to give a touch of realism to the distribution of the toys'. Praised widely for his excellent police work and for cleaning up the 'black spots of Birmingham', Rafter died in 1935 at his holiday home in Galway. Aged 77 and still chief constable, he was acclaimed as 'a great citizen' and as 'one of the finest police officers this country has ever known'. On the day of his funeral, a memorial service was held at Saint Martin's in the Bull Ring, after which he was interred at Saint Peter's, Harborne. Thousands of people lined the route to pay their respects, many of them out of admiration for Rafter's work in cracking down on the peaky blinder gangs. ('Not Allowed to Retire Though Aged 77', *Birmingham Gazette*, 24 August 1935; 'Unstinted Tributes',

Evening Despatch, 23 August 1935; and 'Funeral Route Thronged', *Birmingham Gazette*, 28 August, 1935).

Given the passion of Canon O'Sullivan and the Reverend O'Neill for the rights of the Irish tenantry and the fact that so many of the Irish in Birmingham had been forced from their country because of the landowning system, it is ironic that a member of one of the biggest Protestant landowning families was living in Edgbaston. The census of 1881 indicated that Sarah Pakenham, a widow aged 73, was residing with a companion, cook and servant at 3 Clarendon Road. Headed by the Earl of Longford, the Pakenhams' main estates were in County Westmeath around Pakenham Hall. In 1821, Maria Edgeworth exclaimed that Longford's newly refurbished and furnished 'big house' was 'now really a mansion fit for a nobleman of his fortune'. About this time it was the first country house in Ireland to have central heating so that 'the whole house and every bedchamber, every passage so thoroughly warmed that we never felt any reluctance in going upstairs or from one room to another'. Luxury such as this served only to highlight the poor living conditions and hardships of so many Irish tenants.

Mary Fraezer, another widow, also made her living from land in Ireland, where she was born. The head of her household, she lived at 57 Wheeleys Road, Edgbaston, with her sons, James and Edward, also from Ireland. They were partners in an iron founder fender and fire iron manufactory that employed eighty men, twelve women and six boys. The Fraezer household was made up by Mary's grandson, John, granddaughter, Margaret, a cook, and a housemaid. Nearby at 61 Wellington Road, William B. Dawson lived in even grander style. A thirty-seven-year-old from Dublin, he was an annuitant - that is, he received a yearly grant or annuity. His wife, Sarah, was from Birmingham as were their five young sons – all of whom were

served by a cook, nursemaid, monthly nurse and gardener.

Overall, the Irish middle class was small in nineteenth century Birmingham, but two people born in Ireland and living in Edgbaston have made a lasting impact upon the city. A longstanding business is that of the office supplier Osborne's. Begun in 1832 as a specialist stationer, it is the result of the hard work and drive of Edward C. Osborne. Born in Cork, he was just 21 when he set out on a successful business and social career, and by 1881 he had become secure in the local establishment as an alderman and magistrate. Living in Carpenter Road, he gave his occupation as a stationer and printer employing twenty-one men, ten boys and ten girls. One of the most important firms of solicitors in the city is that of Glaisyers. Having gone through various partnerships, it now carries solely the name of Henry Glaisyer, whose home was in George Road and who was born in Dublin. Though from an old Sussex family, he spent the first five years of his life in Ireland. ('City Registrar Succumbs After Operation', *Evening Despatch*, 19 December 1904).

Another notable middle-class figure was Michael Maher. A stationer and ink maker in New Street, he was also a journalist and became a town councillor, a member of the Board of Guardians and co-secretary of two charitable appeals to help the destitute in the 1850s. Michael Maher was involved deeply in helping the poor. The early part of 1855 was 'a sad time for the poor' as the weather was terribly severe and inclement, and trade was indifferent. As a result the mayor opened a subscription for the relief of extraordinary distress. The two honorary secretaries were James Corder and Michael Maher. It would seem that it was also Michael Maher's daughters who were 'eager to toil in the work of charity' and assist Father Bowen in his educational work with factory girls in Smallbrook Street. (J. A. Langford, *Modern Birmingham and its Institutions*. vol. 1, 1881; and 'Account of Father Bowen' in Fr H. Barnett, *The Story of St Catherine's in the Horse Fair*, 1971).

When Michael Maher died in 1862 The Town Crier paid tribute to him as 'emphatically a good man – honest and honourable in all his dealings, whether professional or private; a faithful friend, a loving husband and father; very tender and helpful towards the poor; and pious and God-fearing in the best of all "senses" in that he carried his religion into practice, and made it part and parcel of his daily life'. Never guilty of a shabby act or an unkind or spiteful word, 'in his own modest way' Michael Maher helped and comforted his poorer brethren. He had little wealth and his station was just that of a simple tradesman, still he 'was known by no title but the worthy name of Michael Maher'. His sons represented some of the Irish who were arrested in the Murphy Riots of 1867. ('In Memoriam. Michael Maher, *The Town Crier*, vols 1-5, 1861-66).

Although Birmingham was renowned for manufacturing and although so many Irish men and women were employed in the making of things, there were not many of their countrymen who were gaffers. Amongst those who were and whose houses were in Edgbaston were Joseph Wolf Salaman, manufacturing jeweller of Duchess Road; Charles Marcus, a Dubliner of York Road and a silversmith; and Edward Wootton, a manufacturer of brass from Beaufort Road. Associated with their number are Hugh McClelland from County Down, a hardware merchant in Calthorpe Road; Andrew Charles, of Carpenter Road and born in Derry, who was a hardware factor; and William H. Johnston from Wicklow, who was one of Her Majesty's Inspector of Factories.

Elsewhere in the city, Honora Langer of Bandon, County Cork was a widow based at 48 Dudley Street in the Bull Ring who employed four men

as a boot and shoe manufacturer; whilst in Cardigan Street, close to the modern Millennium Point, James N. Coghlan gave work as a stay busk manufacturer to fifteen women. In the Jewellery Quarter there were a number of men born in Ireland who appeared to be in a good way of business. William Sheppard from Athlone lived in Caroline Street and was an electroplater with four men, three boys and four girls in his employ; whilst his Birmingham-born wife was a silver plate burnisher as was their teenaged daughter. John McIntregart of Church Street was also married to a Brummie and as a brass founder had nine women, six men and two boys on his books; whilst in Vyse Street, Albert Ewen was a jewellery maker with three men and two boys working for him. To the list of these people could be added John F. Moore, born in Dundalk, also married to a Birmingham woman and a tailor with six men. However, there were two manufacturing businesses begun by Irish families that were to have a major impact upon Birmingham and its people in the twentieth century and which were essential in the city becoming one of the world's most important car making centres.

Sadly, Fort Dunlop in Erdington is no longer the hive of activity it was when thousands of people worked there, amongst them many Irish folk. But for much of the twentieth century the Dunlop was one of the greatest manufacturing firms based in Birmingham, sending its products around the world. That it did so 'is owed chiefly to the entrepreneurial flair of its founders and the meeting of two Irish families on the playing fields of Birmingham'. William Harvey Du Cros was a Protestant descendant of French Huguenots who had gained from King William's victory at the Battle of the Boyne in 1690. In the late nineteenth century, he became involved with John Boyd Dunlop, who had designed a pneumatic tyre that stopped the vibration of a bicycle when it was ridden. Through doggedness and flair, the Du Cros family overcame design difficulties, bought other patents and used their cycling expertise to gain the world rights to the first practical pneumatic tyre. After complaints about the smells from its Dublin factory, the operation was moved to Coventry but the family was faced with a problem: rubber was crucial for tyre production but knowledge about this product was slight. The company had no control over its rubber supply and its tyres were hand-made from components that were bought in. It was then that the Du Cros family came to know the Catholic Byrnes.

Frank A. Byrne.

To make the company's Irish staff more at home and help them forge a bond with their English fellow workers, Arthur Du Cros began the Anglo-Irish Social Club in Coventry and recruited several Irish international rugby players. In 1893, the team played Moseley, which included Frank and Fred Byrne, both of whom came to play for England. Their father, Thomas, had been involved in the rubber business since 1855. At first he was general manager of J. Kirby and Sons of New Street, manufacturers of gutta percha (a rubbery substance), but from about 1871 he went into business for himself with works in Charles Henry Street, Highgate and on the Lichfield Road in Aston. It appears that he prospered for

he raised his children at Penns, Warwickshire and sent Frank to Brampton College, Huntingdonshire. ('Mr Frank A. Byrne', *Moseley and Kings Heath Journal*, vol. V, no. 56, January 1897).

After their father's death in 1889, five of his sons became involved in various rubber concerns, one of which was the Byrne Brothers India Rubber Co. based at Manor Mills in Aston and in which Frank was involved. Through their association with the Byrnes, the Du Cros family acquired detailed knowledge about rubber making and Arthur Du Cros acknowledged that they served their apprenticeship at Manor Mills. In 1896, one of their companies bought that part of the Byrne Brothers' business that specialised in making India rubber tyres. Other premises were also purchased on the Lichfield Road, and were called Para Mills. Crucially, the deal involved the takeover of all associated machinery, including the British rights to the Doughty press. This American designed machine so speeded up the process of tyre moulding and vulcanisation that the time was cut from two hours to three minutes. The Byrne brothers carried on making general rubber goods at a new Manor Mills factory in nearby Salford Street. In turn this was bought out in 1901 by the new business of the Dunlop Rubber Co., of which Arthur Du Cros was managing director. (Joan Skinner, *'Dunlop in Birmingham: The Making of an Industrial Empire'*, Barbara Tilson, ed, *Made in Birmingham. Design & Industry 1889-1989*, 1989).

Through their tyre-making business, the Du Cros family became interested in the manufacture of cars and began an association with Herbert Austin. With the purchase of the works at Longbridge in 1905, the 'old man' as he was known started one of the biggest and most important factories in Birmingham. For that achievement he gave credit to the vital help of Harvey Du Cros, who 'joined my firm, and the family furnished the additional capital which

Mary Ratcliffe's father Bill Fenlon, right, came from Enniscorthy, Co. Wexford, during the war and worked at Dunlop from 1953 until he passed away aged 58. He was a foreman and travelled the world for Dunlop taking a group of men to open up and run the new factories. This photo of Bill was taken in the USSR. The men with him are Russian workers. They are carrying black bread, which is all that they had to eat.

enabled the Austin Company to expand'. Austin's very involvement as a pioneer of the car industry had begun whilst he worked for a firm set up by an Anglo-Irishman from Carlow, Frederick York Wolseley. He was descended from a Staffordshire family that suffered for its Catholic faith in the Reformation and then converted to Protestantism. In 1690, William Wolseley fought with King William and from 1725 the Irish branch of the family was settled at Mount Wolseley, Tullow in County Carlow.

In the nineteenth century two Wolseleys distinguished themselves. Sir Garnet rose from ensign to become the commander-in-chief of the British Army; whilst his younger brother, Frederick York, at the age of seventeen migrated to Australia and invented the mechanical sheep shearer. Not one of the great landowning families of the Protestant Ascendancy, the two Wolseleys grew up in Dublin in straitened circumstances following the death of their father. Sir Garnet

later wrote that their father had gone through hard times and 'full of charity, he felt much for the Irish poor, with whose misery in those days of high rents and high prices, he had the most real sympathy'. (Jimmy O'Toole, *Frederick York Wolseley, Mount Wolseley, Tullow, Co. Carlow*, 1995. Thanks to Ned Dunbar.)

After his apprenticeship, Austin became the manager of a small engineering business that carried out work for the Wolseley Sheep Shearing Machine Company. Noticing several weaknesses in the machinery, he pointed them out and suggested improvements in the Wolseley business that were acted upon. Impressed by the engineer's knowledge and ability Frederick Wolseley, the owner of the company, offered Austin the post of manager. The offer was taken up and Austin began to travel Australia, talking to sheep farmers and recognising the vital need for reliable equipment for those in the outback who were distant from suppliers and swift repairs.

This awareness led him to make significant changes to sheep shearing machinery, changes which had a major and long-lasting impact. Notably, Austin's trekking also impressed upon him the importance of good and fast means of movement.

Because of the difficulties with sub-contracted engineering work, Wolseley relocated his firm to England, but problems continued and thousands of defective machines were sold and then bought back. In an attempt to counter these pronounced aggravations, Austin was made manager of the British company and he and his family returned to England in 1893. Quickly, he turned his attention to the necessity of turning out high-quality goods that were inspected properly before they were dispatched. These were tasks that he was able to address more effectively after the company moved to premises at 58¹/² Broad Street, Birmingham. The transfer was encouraged by the fact that the city was the source for much of the company's machinery. But Austin continued to be unhappy with the standards of some suppliers, and he took the Wolseley to the larger Sydney Works in Alma Street, Aston, where the business could make more of its own parts.

At the Sydney Works, Austin started making other products, such as machine tools, textile machinery and bicycles. Perhaps affected by a visit to Paris, where he had examined the 'very crude internal combustion engines that were in existence at the time', he built a tri-car, which had two wheels at the front and one at the back. Finished in 1895 at his home, swiftly he took it out on the Coventry Road. The next year, the budding carmaker persuaded the board of the Wolseley to support his automobile venture and in 1896 he produced the Wolseley Autocar Number 1. This had two wheels at the rear and one to the front, and a year later it was followed by another three-wheeler. It was this vehicle that Austin ran to Rhyl and back in 1898. He averaged a speed of 8 mph, carried two passengers and had

no breakdown on the 250-mile plus trip. (*The Life Story of Sir Herbert Austin*, reprinted from the *Autocar* Issues 23 and 30 August and 6 and 13 September 1929).

By this date the ageing and ailing Frederick York Wolseley had resigned from active managership of the British company. But, although not having lived in Birmingham, still this Anglo-Irishman had a deep effect upon the city. Through his employment of Austin, Birmingham came to boast one of the greatest car plants in Europe, one that continues to produce top-quality products; whilst his own name was carried on by the Wolseley. In 1901, two years after his death, the motorcar side of his business was sold to Vickers Maxim. This company opened up the Adderley Park works from which it turned out an array of products from machine tools to motor cars, from commercial vehicles to marine engines and from airship engines to war work. Becoming the largest British carmaker, the company collapsed financially in 1926 – although the Adderley Park site then became known for Morris Commercials.

Men like Edward C. Osborne and Thomas Byrne, like Daniel O'Neill and John Frederick Feeney have left their mark on Birmingham. Drawn here by work, they strove for success and gained it. The great majority of their fellow Irish citizens in Birmingham did not prosper from their hard graft. They too were drawn here by the need to find work. Pushed from their own land by economic conditions beyond their control and not of their own making, they also came to make a decisive mark upon the city and exhibited to the full the true duties of citizenship.

Further Reading

Asa Briggs, *History of Birmingham. Volume II. Borough and City 1865-1938, 1952.*

Robert K. Dent, *Old and New Birmingham. A History of the Town and its People*, 1880.

Conrad Gill, *History of Birmingham. Volume I. Manor and Borough to 1865, 1952.*

William Powell and Herbert Maurice Cashmore (compilers), *A Catalogue of the Birmingham Collection Including Printed Books and Pamphlets, Manuscripts, Maps, Views, Portraits, etc*, 1918.

Victor Skipp, *The Making of Modern Birmingham*, 1983.

Chris Upton, *A History of Birmingham*, 1993.

Iestyn Williams, Dr Máiréad Dunne, Professor Máirtín Mac an Ghaill, *Economic Needs of the Irish Community in Birmingham*, 1996.

CHAPTER THREE
WE COULD NOT DO WITHOUT THEM

The interior of Saint Peter's, just off Broad Street. Thanks to Christine Goodall.

Sir Thomas Holte of Aston was a vain and ambitious man. His family's fortunes had been rising for several generations and it owned wide lands in what are now Aston, Lozells, Small Heath, Bordesley and Saltley. Sir Thomas himself had been sheriff of Warwickshire in 1599 but he was firm in his intent to reinforce his social standing and to receive the honour of a knighthood. Such an accolade would signal to all that not only was he wealthy but also that he was a gentleman of status. His opportunity came in April 1603 when he was part of a delegation that welcomed King James VI of Scotland, the successor of Queen Elizabeth I and who was to become King James I of England. A few days later Thomas Holte was knighted, but still his self-importance was not satisfied. A chance for him to further improve his situation came in 1611 when James I created the new title of baronet that ranked above that of a knight. This was a

hereditary title and it was exclusive. Only 200 were created and the chosen few were the elite of the gentry, owning land worth £1,000 a year. (Oliver Fairclough, *The Grand Old Mansion. The Holtes and Their Successors at Aston Hall, 1618-1864*, Birmingham 1984).

The aim of this novel honour was to raise money for the payment of the king's army in Ulster. Following the Gaelic resurgence of the fifteenth century, the Tudors strove to conquer Ireland and extinguish the semi-independent Irish rulers. Resistance was dogged and many of the Gaelic Irish remained unbowed, especially in Ulster where they were led by the O'Donnell and the O'Neill – whose English titles were the Earls of Tyrone and Tyrconnel. But following the decisive defeat by the English at Kinsale in 1601, and despite holding out for another two years, even these lords had to acknowledge the might of

Elizabeth. As Robert Kee put it feelingly, the O'Neill soon became 'weighed down with the sad realisation that he could no longer be master of his own house in Ulster in anything but name'. Harassed by English officials, suffering the imposition of English laws, having to endure the penalisation of Catholics, and beset by plotters seeking to implicate him as traitor, the O'Neill could take no more. On 4 September 1607 he and Rory O'Donnell, Hugh's heir, sailed into exile from County Donegal. Following the Flight of the Earls, their lands were forfeited to the Crown. In this manner, strangers from England and Scotland were given the best land and rights over the Catholic Irish in Donegal, Tyrone, Derry and Armagh, and also in Cavan and Fermanagh. This 'Plantation of Ulster' needed the high expense of a strong army to hold down the Irish. The price of £1,095 paid by Sir Thomas Holte for his baronetcy helped to pay that cost and, because of it, he was able to add the Red Hand of Ulster to his arms. (Robert Kee, *Ireland. A History*, London, 1981. Thanks to Jerry Kelleher.)

Ironies abound in history and a few years later in the English Civil War, Irish soldiers helped to defend Aston Hall for a man who had helped to pay towards the sweeping away of Gaelic Ulster. Sir Thomas was a lukewarm Royalist and tried to steer a middle course between the Cavaliers and the Parliamentarians, the latter of whom were strong in Birmingham and Coventry. However, in December 1643 he deemed it necessary to ask for a garrison to be sent to Aston Hall from the Royalist fortress of Dudley. In response, forty musketeers were sent. This action provoked a Parliamentarian attack. The first assault was on the parish church of Saint Peter and Saint Paul, where John Frederick Feeney was to be laid, and which lay below Aston Hall. The place of worship 'was defended by 40 stout French and Irish men who we took prisoner'. Soon after, Aston Hall itself fell. (Oliver Fairclough, *The Grand Old Mansion*).

The painstaking research of Joe McKenna into the Aston Churchwarden's Accounts indicates that these soldiers were not the last Irish people to come to Aston in the seventeenth century. In 1653, 4d was 'given awaie to Irish passengers', and at various other dates, money was given to Irish folk travelling through. Their number included 'nine poore Protestants that came with a pass out of Ireland' in 1689. The Kings Norton Churchwardens' Accounts also indicate similar payments. Still, there is no evidence of any Irish person taking up residence in the Birmingham area, other than that of a James Wright from Dublin in 1723, whose presence is indicated by Birmingham's certificates of settlement. He is a solitary figure until the early nineteenth century when the Irish in Birmingham become more apparent. (Joe McKenna, *The Irish in Birmingham*, unpublished manuscript, 1991; and W.H.B. Court, *The Rise of the Midland Industries 1600-1838*, London 1938).

On 12 May 1805, the Franciscans of St Peter's Church off Broad Street recorded the baptism of Lucia, the daughter of Bartholomew and Catherine Robinson of Ireland. Between then and 25 April 1826 the baptisms took place of a further twenty-four children whose parents came from many parts of Ireland: Carlow, Derry, Donegal, Dublin, Kildare, King's County (now Offaly), Leitrim, Limerick, Mayo, Queen's County (now Laois), Tipperary, Westmeath and Wicklow. Two couples appear twice, suggesting longer-term settlement: Thomas and Elizabeth Maccormick of Luxlip (as spelled in the records), Kildare on 19 May 1811 and 1 August 1813; and Michael and Catherine MacDonnel of St Jacob's, Dublin on 29 November 1812 and 13 November 1814. The registers of Saint Chad's also record Irish people: the marriages of Charles Mulligan and Joanna Dennison of Ireland on 6 June 1814, and of Thomas Hethering of Tipperary and Catherine Leary, County Wexford on 16 February 1819; and also the burial on 24 October 1824 of 'Thomas Rock (Irish)'. None of these people is listed in contemporary trades directories and, as the registers do not give occupations, there is no indication of their employment. Birmingham's directories do list a number of people who have Irish names, but it is unwise without further evidence to presume that such people were Irish or indeed second or third generation Irish. ('The Franciscan Register of St Peter's 1657-1830' in W. P. W. Phillimore and others (eds) *Warwickshire Parish Registers. Baptisms*, vol. II, London 1904; and *Registers of the Cathedral Church of St Chad, Birmingham Warwickshire, Baptisms, Marriages and Burials 1807-1837*, Birmingham 1994).

The Maccormicks, MacDonnels and others were part of a small community. Giving evidence to the Select Committee on State of the Irish Poor in 1834, the Reverend Edward Peach stated that he had ministered to no more than 100 Irish when he took up his post as priest of St Chad's in Bath Street in 1807. This position was transformed 'about 1826' when 'a vast increase took place so that my chapel could not hold my congregation by many hundreds'. Peach believed that there were now at least 5,000 to 6,000 Irish under his charge. The Reverend McDonnell of St Peter's disagreed with this figure. He gave the total Irish population of Birmingham as about 6,000 - of which between a sixth and a third came under the ministry of his church, St Peter's. McDonnell's lower estimate is supported by the comments of the acute French social observer Alexis de Tocqueville. In 1835 he wrote that 'at the most' there were 5,000 Irish in Birmingham. It is difficult to decide who is the more accurate. The lack of reliable statistics from the period is compounded by the likelihood that the Irish population of Birmingham fluctuated with the season. Yet the evidence would seem to favour McDonnell, especially as the 1841 Census counted 4,683 Irish in Birmingham. ('*State of the Irish poor in Birmingham*' in *Royal Commission on the Conditions of the Poorer Classes in Ireland*, Appendix G, *Report of the Select Committee on the State of the Irish Poor in Great Britain*,

Parliamentary Papers, XXXIV, 1836, p. 1.; and Alexis de Tocqueville, *Voyages en Angleterre et Irlande*, 1967 edition).

In contrast to the earliest Irish settlers, those who arrived in Birmingham from the mid-1820s tended to come from a distinct part of Ireland – Connacht, particularly its counties west of the Shannon. McDonnell himself declared that chiefly they arose from Mayo and Roscommon. This influx was prompted by the rapidly worsening rural conditions in Ireland. Following the Act of Union in 1800, Ireland lost its own parliament and was subjected to the United Kingdom parliament in Westminster. This led to the decline of most Irish manufactures because free trade allowed large-scale industries in England to export their cheaper products to Ireland without the payment of duties.

The pronounced weakening of Irish industry and loss of jobs was accompanied by other deteriorating conditions in the country, and in the west over three quarters of the people lived on and off the land. A steep population rise led to a sharp competition for land. In turn, this forced many families to till marginal places that were difficult to farm and gain a living from. They also had to contend with the hiking up of rents by landlords. With more money to pay on rent, the rural peasantry was squeezed and unable to invest in better farming methods. Their lives were blighted further by poor harvests that led to famine conditions in some areas in 1816-7 and 1822. Unhappily for those who became destitute there was no provision for paupers. Large numbers of troops returning home after they were demobilised at the end of the French wars in 1815 compounded the problems besetting Ireland. To this cauldron of hardship was added the attempts of landlords to introduce large farms that were worked by landless labourers. Agrarian warfare erupted in the west and south of Ireland, as working people banded together in secret societies to protect the oppressed. When landlords sought to seize the goods of tenants in rent arrears, large numbers of neighbours assembled by night with carts and horses to carry off the whole produce of the farm; whilst people combined to force landlords to employ local men and to try to keep up wages.

As an Irish priest exclaimed to the French visitor Alexis de Tocqueville before the Great Hunger, if a starving man sought help from his landlord he would be met by 'liveried lackeys, or dogs better nourished than he, who will roughly drive him away'. But if he presented himself at the door of a cottage, he would do so without fear and would be 'sure to receive something to appease his present hunger'. It was the poor who prevented the poor from starving to death in Ireland. These qualities of generosity, sharing and neighbourliness were much needed by those Connacht folk who were forced by economic necessity to leave their homes to find work in England. (Alexis de Tocqueville, *Voyages*).

Spinning wool in Cliffony, County Sligo.

The burdens of rural life fell most harshly upon two groups: the cottiers who rented about five acres and who had to take on paid work to make up their incomes; and the labourers who struggled to afford an acre of land, which gave them but a single crop of potatoes. They had no option but to graft for others if they and their families were to survive. It is likely that it was families from these groups that were prominent

in the Irish migration to Birmingham from the mid-1820s. By this time, ferry services were linking Dublin, Cork and Belfast with Liverpool and for 3d (just over one penny today), it was possible to get a passage on deck. When the winds blew fiercely and the waves of the Irish Sea rose powerfully, the sailings must have been frightening and upsetting but such considerations did not deter the pioneering men and women from the west.

No one knows who were the first Mayo and Roscommon folk to come to the English Midlands and the route they took is uncertain. Some may have trudged towards Sligo town and caught a boat there; whilst others may have slogged across the Irish Midlands to Dublin. Here they would have taken the cattle boat to Liverpool, thence to spread out across Lancashire, Cheshire, Staffordshire and Warwickshire in search of crops to bring in and cash to earn. Writing later in the century, John Denvir explained that 'the hardy Connaughtmen generally passed through Liverpool on their way to the English agricultural counties. It was a sight to remember – the vast armies of harvest men, clad in frieze coats and knee breeches, with their clean white shirts with high collars and tough blackthorns . . . marching literally in their thousands from the Clarence Dock, Liverpool and up the London Road to reap John Bull's harvest'. (John Denvir, *The Irish in Britain from the Earliest Times to the Fall and death of Parnell*, 1892).

The wearied and long-drawn-out journeying of the first Irish migrants is brought to life by Edward Price. Aged 63 in 1851, he was a coach spring worker. He and his wife, Bridget, had their home in Lichfield Street, close to the present Law Courts in Corporation Street. Their oldest child, John, a twenty-six-year-old gun finisher had been born in Liverpool, but his younger siblings starting with George aged seventeen were all Irish Brummies. Patrick and Mary Connor of Greens

Village had trod the same path more recently. A young couple, their four-year-old daughter was born in Liverpool, whilst their baby had arrived in Birmingham.

Irish emigrants aboard ship at Liverpool in 1846. Pictorial Times, 1846. Thanks to the Guildhall Library.

In total, the 1851 Census records fifteen Irish families who had children of various ages born in Liverpool. Unfortunately, the exact place of birth of only one set of parents is given. Dennis Mackay was a plasterer from Dublin and his wife, Catherine, was a servant from Queen's County (Laois) in the Midlands. They had two children aged five and three born in Liverpool, and a baby of eight months whom they had in Birmingham. Given the connection between Dublin and Liverpool, it is not surprising that the Mackays had made their way to Birmingham this way. However, a number of the other families lived in streets where there was a high concentration of people from the west of Ireland, and it is not improbable to believe that many from the west did arrive in Birmingham via Dublin and Liverpool. This belief is given support by the case of Honor Cusack. She applied for relief in 1851, and although she had lived in Birmingham for 22 years since she was four, she was returned to Ireland so that her own parish in Westport, Mayo could support her. Before this was done, she was asked 'what port would be nearest to the county of Galway, and she said Dublin'. This would have necessitated a trip from Liverpool. (*Report of the*

Select Committee on Poor Removal, Parliamentary Papers, vol. XIII. 1854-5).

Other Irish families seem to have made their journey from Waterford or Cork to Bristol and thence to the West Midlands. Nine families with at least one Irish parent had children born in Bristol. One of them was Thomas Mann who lived in a back house in Cecil Street, in the Summer Lane neighbourhood. A labourer married to a woman from England, he was from Athlone. This town straddles the Shannon, half in Roscommon and half in Westmeath. His presence would suggest that there were folk from Connacht who did traipse to those ports in the south of Ireland that were connected to Bristol. Finally, twenty families had children born in London. In two of them, there was a Dublin mother or father; whilst two had parents from Cork. One of them was the household of William and Mary Marrett, both of whom were glasscutters – as were their two older children who were born in London. Their younger children, from thirteen-year-old Hannah down, had arrived in Birmingham. There were close shipping ties between Cork and London, and again it is not surprising that families from the southern province of Munster should make London their arrival point in England, via Cork and Waterford. But it does seem that some west of Ireland people may also have travelled this route, as is indicated by the case of Patrick Grogan who lived in Ward Street, close to Summer Lane. A fifty-year-old oilcloth japanner from Mayo, his wife, Elizabeth, was from Roscommon – as was Charles, their oldest child at fifteen. His siblings aged seven and under were born in London.

In addition, these families are examples of step migration, as is that of the Lerrys. Headed by Bernard, this family makes plain the way in which many Irish families stopped for a while on their way to Birmingham from their port of entry. In 1851 the Lerrys lived at 15 Water Street, off Snow

Hill. A twenty-nine-year-old bootmaker from Tune (probably Tuam) in Galway, Bernard was married to Jane from Down in Ulster. They gave lodgings to Michael Miland, another bootmaker. He and his wife Alis were also from Tune (Tuam). There were two other lodgers: Patrick Farry, again a bootmaker, and his wife, Ann, both of whom came from Borle, Roscommon. Bernard and Jane Lerry had three children under five, all of whom had been born in Manchester. Indeed, it is likely that many Irish migrants found their way to Birmingham via Manchester and the Potteries district. Certainly, research into Irish settlement in Longton and Hanley indicates the preponderance of Connacht folk in the local Irish community. (Paul Daley, *Irish Settlement in the Potteries 1851-1891. Integration or Separation?* undergraduate dissertation, The University of Birmingham, 1995).

Numbers 9-12, Thomas Street, 1880s. In 1851 number 9 was a lodging house run by an Englishman married to an Irishwoman, Jayne Walker.

Michael MacCarthy, a bricklayer's labourer, apparently came that way. He lodged in Thomas Street, later to disappear for the cutting of Corporation Street, with his wife from Stoke and their children, all of whom were born in Birmingham. Others like Patrick and Catherine Grogan passed near to Stoke, coming via Newcastle under Lyme, Staffordshire. Living in Lower Tower Street, Patrick was a silk weaver

whilst their sixteen-year-old son, William, was an oilcloth japanner. His younger sister, Eliza, was six and had been born in Newcastle. Once again emphasising the manner in which the west of Ireland people looked after their own, the family gave lodgings to Daniel Fletcher, a sixteen-year-old labourer from Galway. Patrick Garvey, a bricklayer, and his wife, Mary, followed the same path. Finding a home in a yard in Cheapside, their oldest child, Patrick aged five, was born in Ireland, but they had his younger sister, two-year-old Maria, in Newcastle. Their baby, John, was newly born in Birmingham. Mary Angle, a hardware hawker from Bartholomew Street, must have stayed a while in the Staffordshire town because her husband was from there as were all their children.

Other families had obviously travelled further seeking work and opportunities, amongst them John and Maria Lawless, from Galway and Roscommon respectively. They had four children: John was five and born in Scotland; Richard was three and they had him in Lancashire; Martin was two and had been born across the Pennines in Yorkshire; and seven-month-old James was also brought into the world in Lancashire. Mary Hunter had travelled almost as far. Residing in a court in Queen Street, she was the head of the household and a dressmaker. Her three oldest children were born in Ireland, but the youngest arrived in Newcastle upon Tyne.

However they arrived, the spalpeens, seasonal labourers, soon made their presence felt locally. During the 1830s, for example, John Thomas had a farm four miles southeast of Birmingham town centre on the Warwick Road in the Acocks Green area. Each year he employed Irishmen at harvest time, after which they would move on to work the land in Staffordshire 'and get back in time for their own harvest'. Irish farm labourers were as noticeable in the 1851 Census. At a farm in Washwood Heath worked Mike Mccade and John McKade, two young men from Mayo, and other

Irish farm labourers were employed in Ward End and Alum Rock. But not all Irish agricultural labourers were from the west. The same census indicates that the farmer of Turf Pits, Erdington employed Thomas Farmer from Armagh and his wife, Ann. Their eldest child, James, was seven and had been born in Armagh, but the next son, Thomas, was born in Erdington, as was seven-month-old John. The family also had lodging with them Mary Gomon, a widow from the same county. At a nearby farm, there were a large number of young Irish farm labourers, three of whom were from Cork: Bawsey Cunningham, Thomas Nichol and Martin Shanon. ('*State of the Irish Poor in Birmingham*').

Other migrant labourers did not live on the farms; instead, they lodged in towns like Stafford, Wolverhampton and Birmingham and used these places as bases. In the course of his work for the Birmingham Town Mission, Thomas Finigan, a Catholic turned Protestant evangelist, met a group of such men on 27 August 1837. With their hooks in their hands they were ready to fight, as he put it, 'thoughtless young men who insulted them and cast reflections on these poor shillingless bogtrotters from Connaught'. These folk must have had to rough it for much of the time. In a period of prejudice against the Irish in general, the Connacht migrants had it tougher than most. Many people looked down upon them because they proudly spoke their own Irish language, they clung fast to their faith, and they stood by their culture – as Finigan showed. In October 1837, he witnessed an Irish wake in John Street. Although his strict religious principles and middle-class morality were offended by what he saw, still it gives us a rare insight into the popular culture of the Birmingham Irish. At the wake 'some were drinking – others singing – and others in wicked lewdness holding converse one with another – men women old and young – the corpse was laid in the coffin on a table before them with face and hair uncovered, a large crucifix at the head, and lighted candles round the

coffin – snuffing – smoking drinking'. A year later, Finigan commented on how the Irish celebrated Saint Patrick's Day in the local pubs. (Thomas Finigan, *Journal of Thos Augtn Finigan Missionary*. Birmingham Town Mission 1837-1838, Birmingham Reference Library 312749).

A lodging house in New Canal Street, 1904.

Unfairly derided by the majority, the Connacht labourers were valued as hard-working and intelligent men by farmers like John Thomas who were keen to employ them year after year. Those agricultural workers who stayed in Birmingham rented a bed in one of the town's many lodging houses in the poorest areas. Each day they would rise early and tramp out to their labour in the fields - for even though Birmingham was growing rapidly, the countryside was yet within walking distance of the town centre and potatoes were still harvested as close as Camp Hill. At night these Connacht men - and some women - would trudge back to dark streets and dismal rooms shared with many others. No doubt, they sang of their homeland and of the families that they had left behind, and no doubt, many of them slept fitfully, beset as they were with melancholic hearts. But even though they must have missed the bogs and peaceful lakes of Roscommon and the mountains and waters of Mayo, and even though they must have thought longingly of their friends and kin, still some of these folk made up their minds not to return home after bringing in the harvest in the English Midlands. Instead, they called for their families to join them in settling in a foreign land where nobody but they spoke Irish and where they were marked out further by their Catholicism and their culture.

A 'hand made turf' bog, Grange, County Sligo.

The 1851 Census confirms the continuing presence of agricultural labourers in the industrial city of Birmingham. There were 136 of them, making them one of the largest groups of Irish workers in the town. Only three gave their place of birth, but in each case it was Mayo - a county that was well known for its spalpeens. The census indicated that many of them were settled in Park Street and its continuation, Park Lane - on the corner of which now stands 'Brennan's' pub (formerly 'Mary Donleavy's West of the Shannon' and before that, the 'Royal George'). Kinship ties were obvious amongst these people, as was shown by the example of the MakDonals. As with many Irish folk, the English census enumerator may have spelled their last name incorrectly. The head of the household was Martin. Four lodgers who shared his last name and who were also agricultural labourers joined him. One of them was an elderly lady called Mary - and she was not the only female who worked on the land and who lived in Park Street.

By the 1881 Census, the expansion of Birmingham had made its poor central areas distant from farms and this may explain why very few agricultural labourers are present by this date. Another explanation is that Irish agricultural workers had moved on to find better-paid work

in factories or on building sites. However, such folk were evident in the rural parts of Edgbaston, around where the University of Birmingham and the Queen Elizabeth Hospital now stand. At the substantial Metchley Park Farm, all the farm workers bar two were from Roscommon: Peter Gilligan was the farm milkman; Edward Morris was the cowman; and Thomas Morris, John Giblin, Edward Giblin, James Merryman, Patrick Rogers and Martin Dorrihy were all labourers. James Brannan from Mayo was also a labourer, whilst his fellow Mayoman Michael Gauley was another cowman.

The tradition of Irishmen travelling to the English Midlands for work in the summer was remarked upon by Flora Thompson in Lark Rise to Candleford (1939), her book on rural life in the late 1800s. She recalled that Irish harvesters often had to be called in to finish the field. Amongst them were 'Patrick, Dominick, James (never called Jim), Big Mike and Little Mike and Mr O'Hara' and to the children they seemed 'as much a part of the harvest scene as the corn itself'. George Hewins, the central character of The Dillen (1981), worked with such men when he went pea picking outside Stratford-upon-Avon in the years just before the First World War. Along with the Romanies, the Irish lads had a round, 'see, they knowed where they could drop into work. They went to the same farmers every year . . . they was relying on them coming'. (Flora Thompson, *Lark Rise to Candleford*, 1973 edn); and Angela Hewins (ed), *The Dillen. Memories of a Man of Stratford upon Avon*, 1982 edn).

Growing up in Treanoughter, Mayo in the 1950s, Marrie Walsh was alert to the economic pressures that had assailed her people for over a century. As a child, each year she watched as her father and his friends did what the local menfolk had done for more than a century – leave for seasonal work. In her insightful book on her Irish country childhood she described how the land that they farmed was 'poor and little of it was suitable for growing crops, surrounded as we were by bogs, hills and water'. Consequently, each year many of the men went to England in the summer to earn money, leaving their wives and children 'to work the farms as best they could'. Marrie's dad always came home. Other agricultural labourers did not. Some of them stayed in England and sent for their families to join them. It was hard-working people like these who had founded the Irish community in Birmingham and the Midlands. (Marrie Walsh, *An Irish Country Childhood. Memories of a Bygone Age*, 1996 edn).

It is apparent that from an early date, large numbers of spalpeens did not return to Ireland and instead decided to stay throughout the year. Winnie Spence recalls that her grandmother often talked about the numbers of Irishmen who came over for farm work every year from Easter until late October after the potato harvest. She lived in Bloxwich and was born in 1857. Many of the men stayed and married and the number of Catholics so increased that her father and uncles gave land in the centre of Bloxwich for a church, a school, and a cemetery. The agricultural depression of the 1880s led to hard times and a loss of work on the land, 'but the Irish men soon found work in the building trade'. (Letter, 8 September 2002, *BirminghamLives Archive*, South Birmingham College, Digbeth campus).

One of those farm labourers who settled in Birmingham was Peter Lawless, a sixty-three-year-old widower from Killcommon, Mayo - as were his four adult children who lived with him in Henrietta Street on the edge of the Jewellery Quarter and running off Constitution Hill. The two daughters were button makers, whilst one son was a bricklayer's labourer and the other a spoon maker. In a court off Edgbaston Street, Patrick Jennings was another farm labourer from Mayo. His wife, Jane, was a washerwoman from Galway, whilst their son and daughter had been born in Birmingham. Aged thirteen and nine, both were wire workers. Former seasonal workers

such as Peter Lawless and Patrick Jennings were joined by their country folk who had left the west of Ireland intending a permanent settlement. Together they provided the core of the Irish in Birmingham.

A snatch of evidence about some of these early migrants is provided by the 1851 Census. It records a forty-year-old blacksmith called John Noon living at 24 Smallbrook Street with his wife, Jane, and two cousins. All were from Roscommon. Three other cousins lodged at the house: Mary Noon aged fifteen; twenty-eight-year-old John; and twenty-seven-year-old Thomas Noon. They were born in Birmingham, suggesting that members of the Noon family had moved from Roscommon sometime in the early 1820s and were amongst those who had provided the bridgehead for others to follow them. Margaret Wire of Alcester Street must have migrated in the same years. A forty-three-year-old widow and worker in bone buttons, she came from Galway and had a son aged twenty-four who was born in Birmingham. It is apparent that she maintained contact with folk from her county as she provided lodgings for John Cronin, a twenty-seven-year-old grate fitter also from Galway.

Following the great increase of the Irish in Birmingham in the later 1820s, it seems that their population stabilised until the late 1840s when it rose dramatically by at least 60%. In April 1847 alone, the town's poor law authorities reported that '1,761 Irish persons were relieved in the short space of 21 days'. There is no doubt but that the great majority of these were new to Birmingham, nor can there be any hesitation about the reasons for this sudden increase. Father Bowen was the priest in charge of a Catholic mission in the very poor Inkleys neighbourhood and in 1856 he wrote that the local 'streets, courts and squalid squares were densely packed with labourers', a large proportion of whom were 'sturdy Catholic emigrants, driven out by the late

"Potato Famine", from Mayo and elsewhere in Ireland'. ('*Select Committee on Poor Removal*'; and '*Account of Father Bowen*').

By 1845, although Ireland's population growth had slowed from the 1820s because of its desperate economic situation, the numbers in the island had soared to $8^{1/2}$ million. This led to an average density on cultivated land of 700 people per acre, one of the highest in Europe. Unhappily, there was also a marked swelling in the proportion of poorer people, many of whom lived on unyielding land. This great body of the deprived was made up of $1^{1/2}$ million landless labourers, for whom the potato was the most important source of food, and 3 million more smallholders and cottiers who were also largely dependent upon this staple diet. The potato was eaten three times a day, leavened with salt, cabbage or fish – when available – and buttermilk. A well-balanced diet, in the west and much of the south there was little or no alternative food if the potato crop failed – as it did at the end of 1845 and 1846.

Women digging potatoes in Roscommon, Illustrated London News, 1870.

By September of 1846, it was estimated that three quarters of the potato crop had failed, although the real figure could have been nearer 90%. Up to 4 million people were faced with starvation by what is rightfully seen as a crop failure unprecedented in the history of modern Europe. Food prices escalated dramatically and there was no sign of the government acting to bring in wheat – at a time when Irish landlords still exported meat and other produce. Filled with arrogance towards all those who were poor, too many in the British establishment blamed the Irish peasantry for the famine. They damned them as idle and viewed the calamity as an opportunity whereby the peasants would be forced to help themselves and adopt modern

Bridget O'Donnell and her children of Kilrush, County Clare, were amongst those tens of thousands evicted during the Great Hunger. Illustrated London News, 1849.

farming techniques. Such insensitive and almost inhumane reactions ignored the fact that Ireland's rural problems arose from the iniquitous ownership of the land by a foreign elite.

Suffering from malnutrition, the Irish poor fell victim not only to starvation but also to fatal diseases that preyed on them because their resistance was lowered by hunger. Too tardily the British government acted. Relief works provided employment for some and soup kitchens helped feed others, whilst private charities, the Quakers and the Americans all sought to help. But the government's response was woefully inadequate and in the summer of 1847 all help was ended. The famine was declared to be over, because that year's crop had not failed. Nobody in power seemed to have had the intelligence to realise that because of the catastrophe of the previous year little seed had been available for planting and so the potato crop was meagre. Hunger and disease once more stalked the land, especially in the west. With so many people seeking poor relief, the poor rates rocketed. Landlords were obliged to pay the rates of holdings worth less than £4 a year. These were the tenancies of those who were most affected by the Great Hunger and with so many unable to pay their rents, landlords grasped the chance to evict the cottiers and save the poor rate money. What little hope the poor had was stolen from them. Other landlords saw the famine as a means to change the system of farming on their estates and so encouraged the emigration of their tenants. (Peter Gray, *The Irish Famine*, 1995).

In 1847 itself, Alexander Somerville toured Ireland. In Roscommon, his emotions were harrowed by what he saw:

"The people are going about, those who can go about, with hollow cheeks and glazed eyes, as if they have risen out of their coffins to stare upon one another. A woman told me yesterday she was starving, but it was not for herself she begged for food; she prayed for Heaven to let her die and give her rest, 'But, oh!' said she, 'if you would take pity on my poor child, for it is dying, and it does not die.' May Heaven have mercy on such a mother and such a child! They were literally skin and bone, with very little life in either of them, and food. And they were but a fraction of a population wandering to and from a fertile land which they are not allowed to cultivate." (Alexander Somerville, *Letters from Ireland During the Famine of 1847*, 1994 edition).

The poor were swept from the land, especially in the west. In Mayo, Lord Sligo issued thousands of notices to quit, trying in vain to justify his actions by stating that he was under 'the necessity of ejecting or being ejected'. His neighbour Lord Lucan 'cleared' 2,000 folk from the parish of Ballinrobe alone – where Birmingham's Chief Constable, Charles Haughton Rafter, would serve later as a district inspector at the time of the ostracisation of Captain Boycott. The land robbed of its people was given over to pastoral 'ranches'. The evicted families, as elsewhere, put up makeshift scalpeens, cabins made from debris; or else dug scalps – holes less than a yard deep and covered with sticks and turf. Even in these miserable homes the poor were persecuted by evictions, so that in Mayo many died by the roadside. (Peter Gray. *The Irish Famine*).

The thrusting out from their homes was a terrible thing for families. Asenath Nicholson movingly told of one near Newport, Mayo.

"Perhaps in no instance does the oppression of

A family evicted from a cottage tumbled, Illustrated London News, 1848.

the poor . . . come before the mind so vividly, as when going over the places made desolate by the famine, to see the tumbled cabins, with the poor, hapless inmates, who had for years sat around their turf fire, and ate their potatoes together, now lingering and oftimes wailing in despair, their ragged, barefoot little ones, clinging about them, one on the back of the weeping mother, and the father looking on in silent despair, while a part of them are scraping among the rubbish to gather some little relic of mutual acquaintance . . . then, in a flock, take their solitary, pathless way to some rock or ditch, to encamp supperless for the night." (Asenath Nicholson, *Lights and Shades of Ireland*, 1853).

One of those who must have seen, if not experienced, such ordeals was Patrick Cion. Twenty-two years old in 1851, Patrick was a bricklayer's labourer from Ballinrobe. His wife, Margaret, came from Kennelle, Roscommon and their two-year-old child was born in Birmingham – suggesting that the parents had arrived soon after the Famine. Like so many of their fellows, they were given lodgings by others from the west. They lived at 20 Henrietta Street with Michael Monagan, also a bricklayer's labourer, and his wife, Mary, both of whom were from Roscommon. The Monagans' twelve-year-old son had been born in Yorkshire, but their daughter aged 23 had been born in Birmingham, suggesting that this family was also amongst the pioneers of the west of Ireland migration to Birmingham. Their other lodgers included Catherine Clinton, a widow from Roscommon town who was a hawker; and Michael Igo, another bricklayer's labourer, from the same place - as was his wife, Mary. The Igos' seven-year-old son was born in Birmingham, indicating that they had moved just before the Great Hunger afflicted Ireland.

Corner of Thomas Street and Dale End, 1880s.

Evicted folk having to traipse the roads looking for work, The Graphic, 1880.

The potato blight came back with a vengeance in 1848, and once more the west and south were ravaged by hunger and pestilence. All parts of Ireland were affected badly and horrors were everywhere, but the depredations of the famine were at their worst in rural areas, especially in the western counties of Mayo, Sligo, Galway and Roscommon – from the latter of which emigration was especially high. By 1851, so terrible had been the deaths from the famine and so great had been the emigration that Ireland's population had dropped to 6,600,000. If estimates of natural growth are taken into account, then something like 2,400,000 people, or a quarter of the population was missing. Scarred by their terrible experiences of starvation, illnesses, death and evictions, many Irish people fled their island. As refugees, the slightly better off sailed for America whilst the poorest tended to cross to England, Scotland and Wales.

Because Birmingham was so far inland it did not become one of the biggest centres of Irish settlement, as did Liverpool, Manchester and London, but still it pulled many. According to the tabulations of Irish-born people living in the principal British towns, these fresh migrants boosted the Irish population of Birmingham to 9,341 by 1851. I have scoured the census for that year and found 7,981 Irish living in Birmingham and that part of Aston within the borough of Birmingham. This added Deritend, Nechells, Bordesley, Highgate, parts of Sparkbrook, Small Heath, Nechells, Duddeston and Ashted to the town. Excluded from Birmingham's population were the rest of Aston, including Lozells; Balsall Heath; Saltley; Ward End; Erdington; Harborne; Northfield, which embraced other districts such

A woman and child desperately searching for potatoes after the land had been gleaned for the crop. Illustrated London News, 1849.

as Weoley Castle; Kings Norton, which also included areas such as Moseley; and Yardley, which took in places like Sparkhill and Stechford. It is certain that I have missed some people in my count, whilst I did not look at the returns for Edgbaston or at those Irish people who were in the workhouse, Winson Green Prison and the Asylum. Still it is unlikely that all of the discrepancy between the two

TABLE 1. **Streets of Highest Irish Population**

Street	total population	Irish population	% Irish
Edgbaston	574	214	37.5
Green's Village	372	189	51.0
Henrietta	466	131	28.0
John	748	261	35.0
Livery	1592	394	25.0
London Prentice	768	357	46.5
Myrtle Row	150	118	78.5
Old Inkleys	708	228	32.0
Park	842	388	46.0
Slaney	688	356	51.5
Water	451	117	26.0

(Source: Census of Great Britain, 1851)

numbers can be accounted for by these factors. I do not believe I have overlooked more than 1,300 people; whilst it is improbable that such an amount of Irish people lived in Edgbaston, a prosperous middle-class area that was never associated locally with the Irish and had a total population of only 9,269.

Accordingly, whilst not dismissing the figure of 9,341 Irish in Birmingham in 1851, my analysis is based on my own count of 7,981. This research stresses that whilst Irish people were found in all parts of the city there were pronounced differences in their concentration. In Aston within Birmingham, there were 854 Irish, representing 1.7% of the people; whilst in the more recently urbanised western wards of All Saints and Ladywood they totalled just 242, or 0.7% of the inhabitants. It is difficult to ascertain the exact Irish presence in the rest of Birmingham's wards as in the most populous, central part of the town the 1851 Census returned figures for parishes that overlapped municipal boundaries. Together these had 140,190 residents, amongst whom there were 8,873 Irish. At 4.9% of the total they were a more obvious

presence here than in outer Birmingham. Despite the difficulties of interpretation, within the large central area further differences are clear. In the newer, northern streets that radiated from Summer Lane there were 578 Irish, and in the freshly laid out streets off Holloway Head there were 249. Both were expanding districts and it seems that in each of them the Irish would have made up the same low proportion as they did in Aston within Birmingham.

If the Summer Lane and Holloway Head localities are included, there were 1,923 Irish in outer Birmingham or 24% of the total. Their fellows were packed into the older, over-crowded and central localities of the town: 1,106 Irish lived in the neighbourhood north-west of the Town Hall and in the Jewellery Quarter - although 642 of these were found in Livery Street and two small streets which ran off it; 787 had homes in just fourteen streets of the Gun Quarter; 134 made their base close by across Lancaster Street; 1,138 gathered in a small stretch of streets, alleys and courts east of Bull Street, the main shopping thoroughfare of Birmingham's middle class; 1,089 focused on streets flowing down the hill southwest from the Town Hall, around Hill Street itself; 912 were drawn nearby to the markets' quarter in the Bull Ring; and 892 had their dwellings across the way in the streets south-east of High Street around Digbeth. Within this central area, eleven streets stand out as having a major Irish presence, as is made plain in Table 1.

In these streets, as elsewhere, the Irish community could be expanded significantly if the English-born children of migrants were included. For example, in Water Street this exercise would raise the Irish from a quarter of the residents to over a third; whilst in London Prentice Street it would increase them from almost a half to near two-thirds.

Greens Village and the corner of John Bright Street, 1880s.

Father Sherlock explained the preponderance of the Irish in these streets. He was praised by John Denvir as 'one of the finest characters Ireland ever produced'. Indeed, 'no man – priest or layman – in England has done nobler service for the Irish cause'. Responsible for converting the Unitarian chapel in Moor Street to Saint Michael's Church, Father Sherlock felt that:

"the formation of the large Catholic population here dates from the commencement of the famine in Ireland. As the great majority of them on arriving here were destitute, they fixed their habitations where they could get them cheapest,

and at the same time near their employment. The elder members of the family worked at buildings, while the younger and females are employed in factories." (John Denvir, *The Irish in Britain*)

An astute observer who was aware of the move of the younger generation into what had been regarded as 'English trades', nevertheless Father Sherlock underestimated the importance of the pre-famine Irish community that provided a focus for refugees from the Great Hunger. These earlier migrants from Mayo and Roscommon provided a link and a base for their fellows seeking a life away from discrimination and death. The support given in this way is indicated in Greens Village, which was to be demolished for the cutting of John Bright Street later in the century. At number 12 lived James Moran, a labourer aged 35 and his wife, Margaret, a domestic (servant). Both were from Roscommon. However their children, all twelve and under, were born in Birmingham. The couple gave lodgings to several people all of whom, bar one, were labourers and were from their county: Catherine Moran and Mary Brennan, both of whom were relatives; John and James Gannon; and Michael and Catherine Galvin, who was from Mayo and was not recorded as having an occupation.

Migrants from other parts of Ireland also showed such communal solidarity. Patrick Barnwell ran a lodging house at 31 London Prentice Street. He and his wife were from Queen's County. Their daughter, Sarah, was twelve and was born in Birmingham and they gave a bed to Thomas Wareing, a labourer from their county. Better-known by its Irish name of Laois, this area in the Irish Midlands had also been devastated by the famine. W. S. Trench, an Irish land agent in the county, tellingly recounted the coming of the potato blight to his property in August 1846. There was a fearful stench 'from the rotting of such an immense amount of rich vegetable'. But his own losses and disappointments, 'deeply as I felt them, were soon merged in the general desolation, misery and starvation which now rapidly affected the poorer classes'. In Laois and elsewhere in the Midlands, not many people were found dead on the roads or in the fields from a sudden deprivation of food as in the west, rather 'they sank gradually from impure and insufficient diet; and fever, dysentery, the crowding in the workhouse or hardship on the relief works, carried thousands to a premature grave'. (W. Steauart Trench, *Realities of Irish Life*, 1868).

There was also a significant gathering of folk from the Irish Midlands in Water Street, close to Snow Hill. In number 2 court was a household from 'Mismeath' (perhaps Westmeath) and the Gavacon family from Marmade, Longford. Patrick and Bridget's oldest child was six and was born in their county, but their two younger children had arrived in Birmingham. Close by in number 4 were Patrick and Mary Richard, both of who were bricklayer's labourers and their three young children, all of whom were also from Longford. This was a county in which Catholic tenants were turned from their lands because of their religion, and where the landlords replaced the many previous tenants with one who was Protestant. There were also two families from Westmeath in Water Street: the Evans family and the Scotts. Again, the birthplaces of their children indicate that they had come during the Famine years. (A. Somerville, *Letters from Ireland*).

Of the total Irish population in Birmingham in the 1851 Census, enumerators recorded the county of birth of 1,312, or 16.5%, of them. The results are striking and corroborate the impressionistic evidence from the 1830s about the conspicuousness of folk from Connacht. People from Roscommon accounted for 24% of the total; those from Mayo came to 13.5%; and migrants from Galway and Sligo made up 7.5%; and 5% respectively. With just two people, Leitrim was the only county from the province that had no impact. In all, Connacht folk made

up 50% of the Irish, the birthplace of whom was noted. This province was the stronghold of the Irish language and migrants from the west continued to speak it in Birmingham. Early in his missionary work, Finigan went into the back streets of Birmingham and 'addressed one woman in her native language, & we instantly obtained not only a hearing, but this woman went out unto her neighbours and informed them that an Irish Clergyman was in the court. The consequence was that my friend and I were received with civility in every house and with marked attention even to tears in many of them.' Later that day Finigan conversed with a woman 'near 80 years of age who could scarce understand a word of English'.

A short while later, Finigan's area was changed so that now he covered Lichfield Street, Stafford Street, Dale End, Lower Priory into Old Square, 'with the cross of streets, as Thomas St - John St - London Apprentice St then including all the courts'. Irish people were noticeable in this quarter, much of which was cleared in the later 1870s and early 1880s for the cutting of Corporation Street. On Wednesday 26 July, Finigan went down a narrow passage into a court where, 'the first house I entered was inhabited by three Irish families and a group of women were assembled in idle gossip whom I addressed in the well known Irish salutation whenever any of them enter a strange house, the English of which is "God save all here". I was received with a "tá fáilte romhat" – "you are welcome." These Irish speakers were reinforced after the Great Hunger. John Denvir described how Father Sherlock had been taught colloquial Irish by his old nurse, a knowledge which helped him when ministering in the Black Country to west of Ireland migrants 'who could speak nothing but Irish'. Such a skill must have been as useful to him when he moved to the Well Street mission in one of Birmingham's poorest neighbourhoods where Connacht people were widespread. (Thomas Finigan, *Journal*; and John Denvir, *The Irish in Britain*).

The older, central parts of Birmingham were overcrowded, unsanitary and filled with decaying properties, but here the poor from the west had no choice but to gather. According to the 1851 Census, Greens Village, a collection of decrepit houses that had few drains, had 189 people who were born in Ireland. They formed 51% of the population and if their English-born children were added to the total then the Irish community in the street rose to well over 60%. The places of birth of forty-one of these folk are recorded: twenty-six were from Roscommon - five of whom originated in Strokestown; eight came from Mayo; and three had roots in Galway. Strokestown was a place whose people suffered grievously in the Famine. Here as in much of the west, casual or seasonal labourers made annual agreements with landlords to occupy a portion of manured ground to grow one year's crop of potatoes. Rents were often twice as high in this conacre system as they would have been for leasehold property. Sometimes a number of small-scale farmers would come together, form a type of collective, and lease a townland that was on poorer soil. These tenants lived in clusters of houses called clachans. They put their resources together and farmed communally. These rundales, as they were known, were tightly packed with people and usually lay next to townlands of richer soil that were used for grazing and were almost empty of people. With three quarters of Roscommon's farms consisting of less than five acres, the burden of the poor law rates fell on the major landowners. One of them was Major Denis Mahon of Strokestown. Faced with massive bills because of the unprecedented call for poor relief, his agent persuaded him to pay for the emigration of more than 1,000 Strokestown tenants. Their departure would cut costs and allow their land to be given over to the tillage of oats. This needed a larger acreage than for tilling potatoes and so meant that fewer families could live on the land.

Scores of those evicted and compelled to emigrate died on the journey to Canada, and others

perished soon after they arrived. In Strokestown anger welled. Tenants went on a rent strike and secret societies thrived. In the summer of 1846, a petition of local men exclaimed to Major Mahon that:

"Our families are well and truly suffering in our presence and we cannot much longer withstand their cries for food. We have no food for them, our potatoes are rotten and we have no grain . . . and Gentlemen, you know but little of the state of the suffering of the poor . . . Are we to resort to outrage? Gentlemen, we fear that the peace of the country will be much disturbed if relief be not more extensively afforded to the suffering peasantry. We are not for joining in anything illegal or contrary to the laws of God, or the land unless pressed to by HUNGER." (Stephen J. Campbell, *The Great Irish Famine*. Words and images from the Famine Museum Strokestown Park, County Roscommon, 1994).

In November that year, Major Mahon was shot dead. The murder led to a new coercion act and to the billeting of police and troops at Strokestown House. Today, the house is fittingly the site of the Famine museum, one of the most moving and evocative living museums in Ireland or Britain.

It is likely that two couples in Greens Village, Birmingham, had lived through the trauma that beset Strokestown. They were William Graham, a thimble maker, his wife, Honorieth, a servant, and their four-year-old child who was born in Birmingham; and Patrick Gannon, a young blacksmith, and his nineteen-year-old wife, Margaret, a warehouse woman. Dorothy Greary was also from Strokestown. She worked as a servant and her husband, Patrick, was a metal roller from Loughrea in Galway. A similar pattern of settlement was apparent in London Prentice Street where 357, or 47%, of the inhabitants were Irish-born. There is information about the origins of 116 of them: 44 came from Mayo, 34 from

TABLE 2. **Presence of Connacht People in Streets of Highest Irish Presence**

Street	No. of Irish-born	No. with county of Birth	No. from Connacht	% from Connacht
Edgbaston	214	24	24	100
Green's Village	189	41	36	90.5
Henrietta	131	111	88	79
John	261	133	97	80.5
Livery	394	0	0	0
London Prentice	357	116	103	86.5
Myrtle Row	118	0	0	0
Old Inkleys	228	0	0	0
Park	388	7	5	sample too small
Slaney	356	18	15	sample too small
Water	117	89	47	51.5

(Source: Census of Great Britain, 1851)

Roscommon, 22 from Sligo and three from Galway. Just thirteen had moved from other parts of Ireland. As is seen by referring to Table 2, folk from Connacht were dominant in the streets of highest Irish concentration and from which there is information about counties of birth.

In only one Birmingham street did the enumerator note the actual parish of birth of a significant number of Irish migrants. This was Henrietta Street, just to the north-west of the city centre, which had 131 Irish-born residents. They accounted for 28% of the total population and of these five were from Galway, thirteen hailed from Mayo and seventy came from Roscommon. Amongst these latter, people from Elphin, Jalsk, Kilkeevin, Oran, Rathcarn, Briarfield, Westfield, Mill Town, Cargans, Ballintubber, Lanesboro and Roxboro were noticeable. Number 3 house, number 4 court Henrietta Street exhibited a powerful example of the connection between county, township and kinship networks. This was the home of Batly Keegan, a thirty-two-year-old bricklayer's labourer from Roscommon. His wife, Margaret, was from Castlerea, Mayo, but their seven-year-old eldest daughter had been born in Kilkeevin, Roscommon. This was also the place of birth of Batly's cousin and lodger, Patrick Haban, a shoemaker. Other lodgers included Edward Pathan, another cousin; John Greyham, an uncle; John and Ann Nigan; and Catron Carney, a servant. The three men were bricklayer's labourers whilst all five were from Oran, Roscommon.

Kinship was as vital in the emergence of an Irish community in other parts of central Birmingham. At 131 Howard Place lived Michael Kelley, a farm labourer, his wife Catherine, their six children and two male relatives who were also farm labourers. Nearby at 19 Norfolk Street, the labourer James Quirk, his wife and two children were joined by five of his Flynn cousins and two other lodgers; whilst at 5 Greens Village the labourer Bryan Gerarty and his Roscommon wife, Mary, who was thirty-eight, gave lodgings to Michael Gerarty, a relative from the same county.

Greens Village is a first-rate example of a

community bonded by kinship, for out of thirty-nine Irish households there were seven in which the lodgers were related to the head. In other parts of central Birmingham there is also an indication of larger gatherings of kin, such as in

Register No. 75.

Name—MARTIN GIBLIN.
Residence—Newtown Row, Birmingham.

Place of business or where employed—
Age—27.   Height—5 feet 5 inches   Build—Medium.   Complexion—Sallow
Hair—Brown.   Eyes—Brown.   Whiskers—None.
Moustache—None.   Shape of nose—Ordinary.   Shape of face—Ordinary.
Peculiarities or marks—Mole left cheek near ear and near chin ; mole centre of left cheek ; scar left of forehead and scar back of head ; mole back right forearm ; scar front of right forearm.
Profession or occupation—Polisher.
Date and nature of conviction—4th July, 1905.   Drunk and disorderly. Placed upon the Black List and Discharged.
Court at which convicted—Birmingham City Police Court.

N.B.—Should any known Habitual Drunkard attempt to purchase or obtain any intoxicating liquor at any premises licensed for the sale of intoxicating liquor by retail or at the ... that the law may be enforc... licensed person or the person ...ormation of such attempt to

To the Licensee of the
To the Secretary of the Registered Club

Whose special attention is called to above.

Special attention is also directed to paragraph 4 of the Watch Committee's regulations, viz. :—

Martin Giblin, The Habitual Drunkards Book.

15 court Edgbaston Street. Here were two households of Drurys, both of which were headed by labourers from Mayo; and four families of Tulleys living in two households. Similarly, in 14 court could be found Thomas and Bridget Welch next door to James and Ellen Welch. The same situation was evident in 25 court Livery Street. Thomas Clark, a twenty-three-year-old farm labourer, was joined by his wife and ten adults and children with the same name; whilst further up the terrace was Michael Clark. A grocer's porter, he and his wife gave

accommodation to seven other Clarks.

Many Brummies know of an ancestor who came over in the famine from the west of Ireland. One is Helen Butcher, whose maternal grandmother told her that her grandfather and grandmother were Patrick and Elizabeth Carroll née Devaney from County Clare. Patrick was a labourer and in 1839 their daughter Elizabeth was born when the family was living in Moor Street. She married a Charles Hudson and it seems that their offspring became Church of England, although the memory of Patrick and Elizabeth was passed on. Still, very few people have researched fully the connection with an Irish ancestor. One is Louise Newton, whose father is a Giblin.

"In the beginning of the nineteenth century, Richard Giblin had two sons, Jacob and Richard. The potato famine hit Roscommon in the 1850s, after their father's death the two brothers decided to leave their country to look for a better life. They travelled to England by boat and made their way to Birmingham.

The 1850s census shows a family of Giblins in Birmingham, and two of Giblen. The brothers came to live in Steelhouse Lane. Jacob married first on 16th October 1859, he married Anna Meakin, the daughter of Patrick Meakin. Richard married on 3rd July 1860 also at St. Chad's. Richard's bride was Ellen Cain, the daughter of John and Bridget Cain. Ellen also came from Roscommon. They had three children, Mary Ann in 1861, Thomas 1863 and Helen in 1867. Ten months after Helen's birth, Richard remarries. Richard was working as a labourer and all three children were baptised at St. Chad's." (Letter, February 1998, BirminghamLives Archive).

Interestingly, the 1851 Census reveals that a John and Bridget Giblen were living in a yard in Livery Street. Amongst their thirteen lodgers in a small two-bedroomed home were four people called Cain or Kain.

Gordon Carr's ancestors lived in 4, house number 8 court Dale End. The home was headed by John, a brick labourer who had been born in Ireland, as had his wife, Mary, and their four children. Living with them were Timothy Healy, another brick labourer, who was from Cork, as were his wife and six children; and Peter Mullony, also a brick labourer. Peter's wife, Jane, was from the same county. Their oldest child had been born there, but the youngest had arrived in Staffordshire. The household was made up by a visitor, Charles Medearman, a teenaged brick labourer from Roscommon. Gordon Carr points out that:

"the other families quite clearly give their country of origin, whereas my Carr ancestors give their birthplace as 'Myory', which doesn't appear to exist! It makes you wonder what was actually said (and heard) on the doorstep on that particular day back in 1851! I suspect they came from 'west of the Shannon'.

In November of that year, my great-grandmother, Ann Carr, was born in nearby Thomas Street, the first of my Irish ancestors to be born in Brum. The family remained in that area of the city, close to St. Chad's Cathedral, where several marriages and baptisms have been found. They took up japanning in quite a big way, actually appearing in directories. In Hulley's Directory of 1881, Dennis Carr of 36 Lionel Street is described as a 'maker of japan and every description of varnish'. My grandmother, Ellen Benton, was admonished by the nuns at her school for having dirty hands, which occurred as a result of her japanning work!

However, in spite of their apparent skills, drive and industry, they still had their fair share of hardship. Like other families of the time, they suffered both infant and premature deaths, and John (senior) actually died in the Birmingham Workhouse in 1889, a sad end considering that he had brought his family out of Ireland to escape the Famine." (Letter, 28 February 1998, *BirminghamLives Archive*)

If kinship, township and county ties were vital in the emergence of the Irish community in Birmingham, then so too were the occupational networks made plain by the Carr household. In John Street there were two households of hat makers, one of which was headed by Edward Groke of Mayo. His two teenaged children were born in the same county and were also hat makers - as were his lodgers, the Killasan family from Sligo. At the head of the other household was Edward Carr, a hawker also from Sligo. So too were his wife, Mary, and their two daughters, all of whom were hat makers. Running off John Street was London Prentice Street. Charles Miller, another Sligo hat maker, lived at number 44 and gave lodgings to three others in the same trade. The two men were from his county, whilst the wife of one of them originated from Mayo. In the rest of the street there was a single female hat maker from Galway and seven more hat-making families: five were from Mayo and two from Sligo.

John Street was cut across by Lichfield Street where the occupations of eighty-one Irish people were noted. Nineteen of them were shoemakers. One of them lived in a lodging house and another was a woman whose husband was in the gun trade. The other shoemakers belonged to nine households. Unfortunately, there is no indication as to their counties of origin, but other evidence does suggest that occupational ties could overlay those of county and kin. This was exemplified at 10½ Rope Walk where Michael Farrey, a tailor from Sligo, rented rooms to a tailor from Wexford and another from Tipperary; and also at 32 Henrietta Street, the household of which was headed by Patrick McGover, a nailmaker from Ballurbet, Cavan. Lodging with him were nailmakers from Castlebar, Mayo and from Cork, Tipperary town and Gory, Wexford.

The corner of Lichfield Street and John Bright Street, 1880s.

The significance of occupational networks was as marked amongst the Irish of outer Birmingham as it was for their fellows in the central areas. In a court yard in Ward Street, close to Summer Lane, lived the Patrick Grogan who had come to Birmingham via London. He was an oilcloth japanner from Mayo. His wife was from Roscommon as was their oldest child, also an oilcloth japanner. With them lodged Elizabeth Perry, an unmarried table cove dealer from Mayo. The household next door was headed by another Patrick Grogan, a linen weaver from the same county. His teenaged son shared his place of birth and was another oilcloth japanner. Not far away in Saint George's Street were John and Mary Sherlock, a button turner and button cutter. Both came from Dublin - as did their neighbour Joseph Maker, who made metal buttons. In the same neighbourhood there were two more households of Dublin button workers at 2 court, Great Hampton Street. Kinship ties were also apparent amongst the Dubliners of Birmingham, as with Thomas Moffitt of Dartmouth Place. A twenty-eight-year-old glass blower married to Sarah from Shropshire, he gave lodgings to his brother and another person from his town of birth. Across the town in 8 court, Cheapside, James Drisdall was also married to a Shropshire woman. He was a brushmaker, like his lodger David Drisdall.

Aston within Birmingham was distinguished by other collections of workers. The largest number were 111 soldiers, most of whom were based at barracks in Vauxhall with the 4th (The Queen's Own) Regiment of Light Dragoons. The regiment's headquarters was in Dublin and in 1854 its men took part in the Charge of the Light Brigade in the Crimean War. One of the survivors was Private Henry Keegan, who received a sabre wound in his leg. Born in Kildare, after his discharge he settled in Birmingham where he died in Adderley Street in very poor circumstances. Further out towards Saltley and the railway carriage works of Joseph Wright were nineteen men involved in coach making, two of whom were from Belfast; whilst there were twenty-three brickmakers and brick labourers. Most of these were part of family groups and worked in the clay pits close to Garrison Lane and Highgate Street. In the Holloway Head area and the western wards of All Saints and Ladywood, the most remarkable set of workers were glass cutters. They lived in six households, five of which were headed by men from Cork City or from the County Cork towns of Douglas and Riverstone. (I thank John Bourne for the details about the 4th Regiment and Robert Steele for the information on Henry Keegan, 'Death of Balaclava Man in Birmingham', *Birmingham Daily Mail*, 16 February 1892).

In particular, Irish policemen were bonded by their job. There were thirty-six of them in the 1851 Census, for eight of whom the enumerators noted the place of origin. They came mostly from counties whose people had a tiny numerical presence in Birmingham: two were from Wicklow with one each from Clare, Donegal and King's County (Offaly). One more originated in Dublin and the two others in Down. Three of the men were sergeants. Out of a force complement of twenty-six sergeants (in 1852), this represented 11.5% - the exact proportion of the thirty-three Irish constables to the total of constables in the town. Remarkably, this figure was almost four times that of the Irish in the general population. Irish police officers continued to be prominent in Birmingham. Amongst them was Inspector Kelly, who distinguished himself by his attempts to keep the peace during the Murphy Riots and their tense aftermath; and Michael McManus.

McManus had an outstanding and remarkable career. Brought up in Newfield, Mayo and formerly a labourer, he joined the force in 1873 and retired in 1918 as deputy chief constable. For several years he was attached to the Duke Street Division, which covered mostly English streets and was 'then by far the roughest in the town'. A tough and determined man, McManus once took on a gang of highway robbers on his own. Kicked, stabbed, and beaten with belt buckles, McManus was mauled severely, but 'he had some consolation as the ruffians had to accompany him to hospital'. Popular both with the members of the police force and the public, McManus did 'splendid work in connection with various hospitals and other charitable institutions'. Well-known for riding a large white horse around Birmingham, McManus and many other Irish police officers passed into local working-class folklore. ('Demonstration in Birmingham', *Birmingham Daily Post*, 25 November 1867; 'Half-Century of Police Service', *Birmingham Daily Gazette*, 6 March 1918; and 'Michael McManus Warrant Number 4754, PC 197', Record of Service, 30 June 1918. Thanks to Dave Cross of the West Midlands Police Museum)

Throughout Birmingham in 1851, 5,231 Irish were recorded with 765 occupations. They ranged in economic status from John Ryland, an Armagh accountant who lived in prosperous Ashted Row with his family and a servant, to James Foy of 6 Park Street. He, his wife and their five children aged three and upwards were all beggars. Overall, few Irish could be regarded as middle-class. Depending upon the interpretation of jobs and without any knowledge of income, at most they formed 2% of the total. This small group included professionals, clerks, teachers and actors amongst others. More discernible were those who sold things. Although there were just fifty-eight

Deputy Chief Constable Michael McManus.

retailers, there were also ninety-nine dealers, ninety-five hawkers, twenty-eight travellers and twelve merchants. Together they constituted 5.5% of the Irish noted with occupations. Once again, there are problems with assigning them to a class, although most lived in poorer streets. Some were well off, like Robert Twinem. A provision dealer at 69 Digbeth, he had a wife and two young children and employed Joseph Harvey as an errand boy/servant with eleven-year-old Jane Harvey as a general servant. In contrast to him were two middle-aged widows, Bridget Haley and Catherine Carly, who gathered old clothes and lodged with the Flanagans in Carey's Court, Castle Street.

The great number of jobs in which the Irish were involved reflects both Birmingham's multiform industrial structure and the large number of sub-divisions in certain trades such as button making, in which forty-three types of job were mentioned with regard to Irish people. Similarly the census enumerators listed twenty-seven kinds of

TABLE 3. **Chief occupations of the Irish in Birmingham**

Occupation	Number
Labourers	1769
Metal Trades	697
Servants, Charwomen, Launderesses, Housekeepers, Washerwomen	616
Manufacturing, various	450
Selling	292
Clothes Making	290
Button Trade	246
Shoemaking	191
Building Trade	163
Soldiers and police Officers	152
Miscellaneous trades	115
Others	250

(Source: Census of Great Britain, 1851)

labourers, in addition to which were errand boys, porters, excavators, navigators and coal heavers. Taking these sub-divisions into consideration and excluding those who were retired, pensioners or on the parish, then the Irish of Birmingham can be regarded as taking part in 334 distinct occupations. These have been grouped under relevant headings in Table 3. Although they were spread across a wide range of trades, there were 1,393 Irish working in metal, the button trade and other manufactures. They comprised 26.5% of the total. Another 9% were involved in shoemaking or the manufacture of some form of clothing, with 2% finding employment in miscellaneous trades.

Contemporary observers disregarded the variety of occupations with which the Irish were involved. In 1834, George Redfern, prison keeper and Deputy Constable of Birmingham, reported that most Irishmen locally 'are employed as builders' or plasterers' labourers'. His opinions were supported by William White, a builder, and James Holmes, a plasterer who praised his Irish employees for their hard work, honesty and

ingenuity. During the winter, he paid them between 12s and 13s for a six day week, a sum that could be increased in the longer days of the summer. Twenty-one years later, and as clerk to the poor law guardians of Birmingham, James Corder told the Select Committee on Poor Removal that very few of the Irish locally were artisans. He believed that they were generally employed as hard-working labourers. It was a view held strongly by A. M. Sullivan in 1856 when he wrote in *The Nation* that the Irish of Birmingham 'are poor to a man, and chiefly bricklayers' labourers'. ('State of the Irish poor in Birmingham'; *Select Committee on Poor Removal*; and A. M. Sullivan, *The Nation*, quoted in John Denvir, *The Irish in Britain*).

They and their fellow labourers did make up the largest group of workers amongst the Irish locally, but they were not the majority. The 1851 Census recorded that 1,769 of them, or 34 %, were labourers, errand boys, porters and others in similar jobs. There is good ground to suppose that seasonal agricultural labourers who began to settle in Birmingham from the 1820s moved from farm work into labouring on building sites. There was plenty of opportunity to do so, for in that decade the number of houses in the town increased spectacularly by over a third from 21,345 to 29,397. Again the 1851 Census provides some support for this proposal. For example, at 12 Slaney Street there lived Mrs Clane, a fifty-two-year-old widow from Mayo where spalpeens were so common. She was joined by her two teenaged daughters and several lodgers, all of whom were from Mayo. Three of them were day labourers.

Excluding errand boys, porters and others, actual labourers totalled 1,647 and were divided by the enumerators into twenty-seven types. However, the great majority could be assigned into three main categories: 1,022 labourers (including day, general and jobbing labourers); 321 bricklayer's, building, mason's or plasterer's labourers; and 135 agricultural labourers. Such workers tended to be less numerous in outer Birmingham. In the Holloway Head district they made up 11.5% of the total of Irish people for whom occupations were recorded; in the western wards they were 21.4%; and in Aston in Birmingham they were 17.7%. The occupational heterogeneity of the Irish of these outer areas was equalled by the variety in their place of origin. Such information is available for 280 of them from a combined population of 1,212. In a sharp contrast to the Irish of central Birmingham, only 19% were from Connacht. Interestingly 16.5% came from Ulster, four times the proportion in the rest of Birmingham; 17% hailed from Cork; and 21% from Dublin. Overall, people from Ireland's capital were well-represented even in central Birmingham where they made up 14% of the total Irish population.

The incidence of labourers was at its highest in the 'most Irish' and 'most Connacht' streets, as is made plain in Table 4. The exception was London Prentice Street.

Although censuses consistently under-recorded women workers, their presence is marked wherever the Irish lived and female servants made

TABLE 4. **Presence of Connacht People and Labourers in Streets of Highest Irish Presence**

Street	% Irish-born	% Connacht-born	% Labourers
Edgbaston	37.5	100	41
Green's Village	51	90.5	42.5
Henrietta	28	79	39.5
John	35	80.5	41.5
Livery	25	ncr	42
London Prentice	46.5	86.5	31
Myrtle Row	78.5	ncr	48.5
Old Inkleys	32	ncr	49
Park	46	sample too small	48
Slaney	51.5	sample too small	43
Water	26	51.5	37

(Source: Census of Great Britain, 1851) ncr: no counties recorded

Number 9 Court, Thomas Street, 1880s. In 1851 two mixed Irish/English families lived in this yard, whilst a number of Irish men lodged in an overcrowded lodging house.

tantalising in raising the possibility that such women may have been as influential in the origins of the chain migration from Connacht as were male agricultural labourers.

Just under half of the females giving their occupations as servants either lived with their families or were in lodgings with other Irish folk. The circumstances of some of those living away from their families is heart-wrenching. Ann Jones was at the tender age of six and was given as a house servant with an English family in the Upper Priory; whist the ten-year-old Margaret Burns and Hannah Kelly were house servants with strangers at 10 Little Hampton Street and Upper Tower Street respectively. Four twelve-year-olds were also recorded as house or general servants with English employers: Margaret Melyourne in John Street; Mary Makin from Dublin in Lower Hurst Street; Mary O'Hara in Lancaster Street; and a girl given only as Hannah in Livery Street. The fears and upset of such youngsters away from home and family hardly bears thinking about.

up one of the largest sectors of employment. In total, 461 were in some form of service. Of these 251 were single women 'living in' with English or other non-Irish employers. Excluding four females for whom the relevant information is not noted, their average age was twenty. The place of birth is given for forty-nine of them. At 19% of the total this is a slightly higher proportion than the equivalent for the general Irish population. Interestingly the results are similar: 51% of the women came from Roscommon, Galway and Mayo and 20.5% were from Dublin. Unfortunately, it is impossible to ascertain how many Irish in the 1820s and 1830s were single, female servants and if so, where they were from. Still, the evidence from the 1851 Census is

Twelve Irish women were teachers of some sort, five of whom were unmarried and were based at the Catholic school in Bath Street. A few single females were also employed as shop assistants, but the greatest number of young, working women were involved in the manufacturing trades of Birmingham. According to Father Bowen, many were in factories doing jobs 'mostly of the laborious and uninviting kind, such as "screw works", "umbrella wires", japanning the same, or enamelling saucepans etc'. The 1851 Census indicated that they were also well represented as burnishers, polishers, spoon makers, filers, gilt toy workers, makers of hooks and eyes, japanners, penmakers, screw workers and press operators. In particular, they were obvious in the button trade. Altogether, 246 Irish worked in some aspect of this industry: 113 of them were unmarried women under 30. ('Account of Father Bowen').

Many of these occupations were harmful: the lacquering of metal objects was recognised as very unhealthy; the use of pumice stones, sand and lime dust in spoon polishing caused respiratory problems - as did the dust from the drilling of pearl and the use of mercury in the gilding of buttons; whilst the fumes from japanning made it one of the most injurious trades to women. Equally, the wages were low and often intermittent. In 1837, Finigan wrote of the plight of John Hannon who lived in 5 court, London Prentice Street. For eighteen months he had been afflicted by sickness occasioned by overworking himself and was confined to his bed. He and his wife were supported by their two daughters aged fourteen and thirteen who were pin headers, 'but for the last four or five weeks they got nothing to earn - in consequence of the bad state of the trade'. (Thomas Finigan, *Journal*).

There were numerous younger children at work, and it is heartbreaking to see how their childhood had been stolen by an unjust and unfair economic system that blamed the poor for their poverty and then punished them for being poor. Mary Flynn was just four and was recorded as a penmaker with her older brothers and sisters in the Park Street lodging house of her father. It is likely that she helped her siblings in fetching and carrying – as would have done Henry Durr, a seven-year-old button shanker in Lancaster Street; whilst as an errand boy William Lynch, aged six, must have been running messages for his father who was a master shoemaker. However, there is also strong evidence of the full-time employment of young children outside the home, as with eleven-year-old Peter Dunavan of Park Street. The son of a hawker in lodgings, he was a factory boy. Two years his junior, Barbara Flin of Bull Street was in a button works, earning money to supplement her father's income as a labourer.

Bull Street was close to London Prentice Street, which had been associated strongly with the Irish since the inflow of the 1820s. Short and narrow, it

ran between two more important roads and was close to the middle-class dwellings of Old Square. Unlike them, the properties of London Prentice Street were old and decaying. Many were lodging houses, five of which were operated by Irish. Two of them were women - Eleanor McNally and Mary Kielty, a sixty-nine-year-old widow. Of the three others, John Ratakin and his wife were a young couple from Roscommon who had eight lodgers, five of whom shared their name; Thomas Doherty was a widower from Tubercurry, Sligo; whilst Patrick Barnwell was from Queen's County (Laois) and, judging by the age of their daughter, he and his wife had been in Birmingham for at least twelve years. Together they rented accommodation to forty-three Irish folk, yet a focus on these official lodging houses masks the prevalence of lodgers in the street. Of a further fifty-one homes headed by someone Irish, only twelve were occupied by single families. The remainder had a substantial number of lodgers, visitors or relatives. Excluding two houses in which adult English lodgers were also present, 325 Irish and their English-born children were crowded into thirty-seven dwellings - an average of almost nine people to each. The most overcrowded was 7 house, 10 court where James Garry, a general labourer, his wife and five children gave lodgings to Mary Crosby and her two adult children; Patrick Keely; Thomas and Bridgett Morton and their two youngsters; and Bridget Farrall, a fifty-year-old widow and her four daughters.

London Prentice Street was in the area assigned to Finigan and his comments emphasise that the dire situation of too many packed into too little space was longstanding - and not just for the Irish. On 15 September 1837 he commented that the street had 'on the whole 119 or 120 houses' in the majority of which 'there are from 12 to 16 persons lodging or living, in others it is less, but I never found it any under six - except in two or three cases'. He estimated that the population was at least 850, of which half was Catholic and by inference Irish. Despite his sometimes disparaging comments about Catholicism, Finigan recognised that poverty forced many of the Irish into dreadful living conditions. In early February 1838 he passionately wrote of how throughout his area the 'human misery, wretchedness and want even to almost starvation were truly appalling'. Everyone was affected by the bad winter yet 'the English poor were not wholly left without some small assistance from the Parish officers - but the unfortunate natives of Ireland who had the temerity to present themselves and crave even a mouthful of bread at the workhouse door were spurned away with contempt and inhuman scorn'. (Thomas Finigan, *Journal*).

Numbers 3-6 London Prentice Street, 1880s.

This was a recurring theme in Birmingham. Normally, someone could claim relief from the poor law union after five years residence. This relief was either outdoor, in that tokens for bread and coal were given to poor families and they carried on living in their homes; or else it was indoor. This meant that the family had to go into the hated workhouse. Despite the residential qualification, it was the practice in Birmingham to return to Ireland all Irish people who applied for relief. Complaints were received about this practice from the authorities in Cork, Galway and Dublin North. This matter was brought up at the Select Committee for Poor Removal in 1855. Part

of the evidence was a statement in writing from Michael Benson, a labourer of Dale End. It is not known whether this was written by Michael Benson himself, yet it does emphasise the way in which Birmingham Irish families maintained links with Ireland:

"My son, Michael Benson, who formerly lived in Vail-court was sent by me to Ireland about three years ago, to his uncle, Bartholomew Kerans, at Ossey, in the County of Galway. ; he was then about 14 years of age, and was sent at his uncle's request who promised to provide for him. I paid the fare myself . . ." ('Select Committee on Poor Removal').

From the 1850s, the Birmingham Guardians of the Poor seemed to have adhered to the residential qualification, and in the early part of the year, they were forced to give outdoor relief to thousands of Birmingham Irish. Their hardships had been caused by severe weather that had led to no work for building workers. James Corder, the clerk to the guardians, stated that 3,000 orders of admission to the workhouse were offered. Hating the thought of seeing their families split up and their independence torn from them by the workhouse regime, many of the Irish applicants tore up the orders and trampled them under foot. Indeed, not one person would go into the 'house'. In these circumstances, it was deemed inadvisable to try to return all these people to Ireland 'to prevent riot and disturbance' and so outdoor relief was given. In the following years, Irish people found it more difficult to obtain outdoor relief. This deterred many from applying, but those that did were more likely to be placed in the workhouse than were English applicants. Throughout the 1860s and 1870s, there was a higher proportion of Irish Brummies in the workhouse than for the population of the town as a whole. As late as 1894 it was stated that 'we find in Birmingham that, compared with the natural population, the Irish take a very large percentage of relief in the house'. (*Report of the Royal Commission on the Aged Poor*, Parliamentary Papers XV, 1895).

James Corder was a contradictory witness. He claimed that the Irish made frequent fraudulent claims for relief but also stated that the fear of removal stopped them from applying. He also acknowledged that 'as soon as the frost broke up, the great bulk of Irish paupers ceased to apply for relief, having, as I believe, returned to their labour'. The inconsistencies in James Corder's attitudes towards the Irish were shared by large numbers of middle-class English people. Still, he did have some sympathetic leanings: he did not think that England could do without Irish labour; he appreciated that Irish labourers did work that 'our own labourers would not undertake'; and he thought that the Irish, 'are, generally speaking, a morally conducted people; and this I should state, that if a single Irishwoman here had the misfortune to become pregnant, she would have a very great reluctance indeed to be sent to Ireland; the disgrace attached to it in Ireland would be so great, that she would have an aversion to appearing there. (*Select Committee on Poor Removal*).

Dr John Darwall was not bothered by contradictory feelings towards the Irish of Birmingham and there is no way that he shared Finigan's insight and sympathy. This medical man blamed the Irish poor for the terrible environment in which they had no choice but to live. As the 1820s ended, he acknowledged that few of them were employed in manufactories and instead were mason's labourers 'or follow whatever other casual occupation they can obtain'. Yet his understanding of the precariousness of their earnings did not stop him from declaring that there was 'a large class of Irish, who are said to be seldom less than 5,000 in number, but who are perpetually changing'. It was amongst them 'that fever mostly prevails, and their habits, morals, and conditions are very far inferior to those of the native artisans'. Badly

clothed, miserably fed and miserably lodged, they 'exhibit a striking contrast to their more fortunate neighbours'. (John Darwall, 'Observations on the medical topography of Birmingham and the health of the inhabitants' in *Midland Medical and Surgical Reporter* and *Topographical and Statistical Journal*, vol. 1,1828-9).

Darwall's derogatory opinions were mirrored by those of John Mouchet, surgeon of the General Dispensary and the Town Infirmary of Birmingham. In 1836 he commented on the overcrowding of the Irish locally and decried them as 'the very pests of society' who 'generate contagion' through fevers and other infectious diseases. He exclaimed that this ill health was caused 'not by poverty' but by 'the want of ventilation and the cleanliness of person'. Such an attitude betrayed an ignorance of the vile environment in which all poor people lived. Those in poverty did not open the windows of their homes because they were desperate to keep in what heat there was; whilst they were unable to clean themselves effectively because of polluted wells, a lack of running water in dwellings, an inability to afford utensils and no changes of clothing. ('*State of the Irish Poor in Birmingham*').

In his major report of 1849, and without judging them, Robert Rawlinson graphically laid out the severe difficulties faced by all the poor in Birmingham. He explained that there were 'about 2,000 close courts undrained, many unpaved and where privies exist they are a source of nuisance'. Of those he had inspected personally, large numbers had 'a want of water, privies and cesspools which were crowded against the houses and a deficiency of light and ventilation'. Joseph Hodgson, a surgeon, submitted a statement to Rawlinson in which he pointed out that privies were too few in the poorest parts of the town, and where present they were too conspicuous and missing doors. This meant that 'ordure' was often kept in households and emptied anywhere at nightfall. Elsewhere, such as the Inkleys and other Irish quarters, 'the door is opened, and it is thrown out without the least reference to the spot where it falls, or anything else'. (Robert Rawlinson, *Report to the General Board of Health on the Sewerage, Drainage and Supply of Water and the Sanitary Condition of Birmingham*, 1849).

Dreadful unsanitary conditions characterised most of the streets of heavy Irish settlement. Rawlinson's report included evidence from James Russell, one of Birmingham's two unpaid Medical Sanatory Inspectors. This brought to the fore the lack of clean water, drainage and sewerage in much of central Birmingham. In Henrietta Street, where so many Irish lived, there were two courtyards with raw sewage on their surfaces. This was also the horrible situation of one courtyard in the markedly Irish Park Lane. Elsewhere, in the New and Old Inkleys, Park Street, London Prentice Street, John Street and Weaman Street there were many houses in disrepair and with no availability of clean water. This latter problem was severe in Myrtle Row, in Greens Village, where there was one water pump for 53 three-roomed back-to-back houses. This was brought to notice by the correspondent of the *Morning Chronicle*. He noted that the pump that drew water from a well was 'at the extremity of the row. There had been a second pump at the other end, but it rotted away, and the property of these fifty-three dwellings being divided between three owners who could not agree amongst themselves, the pump had not been repaired.' Between 300 and 400 people lived in Myrtle Row and the water they pumped up was 'of a greenish colour, and smelling strongly of gas as if a gas-pipe had burst, and were emitting a stream through it'. A woman told the reporter that the water was filthy stuff and there was not enough of it to wash the house. For drinking, she had to buy water at a ha'penny a can. (C. Mackay, 'Birmingham. Sanitary Condition', *Morning Chronicle*, 1851)

It was the Irish poor of streets such as these

whom medical practitioners condemned as having an aversion to vaccination against smallpox. Given the contemporary middle-class preoccupation with public health and the fear of the spread of disease, the Irish mostly featured negatively in sanatory reports. In 1841 local physicians and surgeons stated that there were three kinds of lowest lodging houses in Birmingham: mendicants; prostitutes; and Irish - of which there were 252 known to the police. In some of these Irish lodging houses the inhabitants were 'beggars and trampers, but the majority of them are resident labourers, employed by the builders and in various occupations'. Such premises were found 'principally in the old streets of the town' but especially in Slaney Street and London Prentice Street. The latter was 'almost occupied by the low Irish' and was rated as 'one of the filthiest streets in the town'; whilst Slaney Street, 'which furnishes the largest amount of febrile disorder, is inhabited by the lowest class of Irish'. A few years later, Joseph Hodgson felt that typhoid had increased partly because of overcrowding and perhaps from an influx of Irish. (A Committee of Physicians and Surgeons, *Sanatory Inquiry - England. Report on the Public Health in the Borough of Birmingham*, 1841; and Robert Rawlinson, *The Sanitary Condition of Birmingham*, 1849).

If the Irish poor were castigated by many commentators for their bad housing and unhealthy environment, then the streets with which they were associated were condemned as dangerous. One author welcomed the late-nineteenth-century disappearance of London Prentice Street as the sweeping away of a 'nasty, dirty, stinking street' in which children could learn lessons of depravity. In 1863, a reporter from the *Birmingham Gazette* damned the people of the street as a mixture of the worst class of Irish and regular thieves. In an almost unique voice from the Birmingham Irish of this period, J. Goffey responded to this slur. He was resident at

13 London Prentice Street and explained that there was no more than one house harbouring thieves. J. Goffey went on to object to the condemnation of 700 Irish for the evil doings of a few. It is likely that this man was the James Gafey, a second generation Irish Brummie, who was recorded in the 1851 Census. His father, Patrick, had been born in Ireland and was a labourer and huxter, a small shopkeeper who sold everything. The mother of James was Susannah, who had been born in Birmingham. (T. T. Harman, Showell's Dictionary of Birmingham. A History and Guide, 1885; 'The Night Side of Birmingham. No. 1. A Bird's Eye View', *Birmingham Daily Gazette*, 30 October 1863; and 'The Night Side of Birmingham. No. 2. London Prentice Street', *Birmingham Daily Gazette*, 5 November 1863).

Other writers were as disparaging of Irish neighbourhoods as was the *Gazette* reporter. Writing in 1885, John Thackray Bunce was delighted by the cutting of the new John Bright Street and other alterations behind New Street Station for 'they swept away a series of narrow streets, close courts and confined passages, shut out from fresh air, imperfectly lighted, fetid with dirt, ill-supplied with water, and so inhabited that at one time - in the flourishing days of the Inkleys and Greens Village, and the like - the police could not venture into them single-handed; while no family could dwell there without destruction to the sense of decency, or peril to health and life'. (John Thackray Bunce, *History of the Corporation of Birmingham with a Sketch of the Earlier Government of the Town*, Vol. 2, 1885).

Yet it was the supposedly notorious Greens Village that was the focus of the county and kinship networks of the 'sturdy Catholic emigrants' from Ireland mentioned by Father Bowen. To those who lived there, it may have been dirty and smelly, but also it was a place of refuge and support. Nearby in Smallbrook Street, Father Bowen set up Saint Patrick's day school in

Thomas Street, 1880s.

'a large and lofty upper room with unsealed floor up steep and dark wooden steps over a storehouse for vegetables with skylight and 2 small windows behind'. Getting hold of 'primitive desks and a huge gallery', he was helped in his efforts by the Sisters of Mercy from Alcester Street who had since 1846 run a Sunday school in a loft in Park Street. In the charge of priests from Saint Chad's, there were also schools for the Catholic poor in a seven-roomed warehouse in London Prentice Street. Rare accounts such as this give us an opportunity to pull back the curtain of middle-class prejudice and disdain and to see the poor of Greens Village and other quarters as people in their own right doing their best to get by in trying circumstances. (*Account of Father Bowen*').

Finigan's writings further emphasise the humanity of the Irish poor and their hardships. In a back house in Weaman Street, he came across a man who was dangerously ill in bed. A poor, miserable fellow, he was in great bodily pain and had a high fever. There was no food or kindling in

The Gullet was another street whose people were vilified. In reality, the Irish and English who lived here were some of the poorest in the city. Most of them were women, children and the elderly.

the house for the wife and three children, whilst no medicine could be had 'and being from Ireland they had no claim on parochial aid'. A few days later, the missionary went into number 3 London Prentice Street. It was 'wholly inhabited by Irish pedlars and mendicants, many of such character I have heretofore found, as in the present instance to possess much shrewdness – keen intellect and argumentative faculty'. These people discoursed with Finigan on religion and defended their Catholicism against his Protestantism by referring to Henry VIII, Queen Elizabeth, Luther and Calvin. Despite his abhorrence of drink and the like, Finigan's sensitivity towards the Irish led to him becoming known as the Irish Parson. Differing strongly from his Catholic fellows in religion, still he perceived that the 'poor countrymen and women are but too often looked at with eyes jaundiced by prejudice'. (Thomas Finigan, *Journal*).

The ignorance of outsiders towards the realities of life amongst the poor in general was blatant, but concerning the Irish, such insensibility was affected deeply by racist attitudes. Few brought to public notice the generosity of the Irish poor towards each other; of how they took in folk from their townlands, counties and provinces even if it led to overcrowding – for such was better than seeing a fellow destitute; of how they sought to find work for each other; and of how they strove for a better life for their children. Instead, cartoons in leading publications like *Punch* slurred the Irish as ape-like, whilst too often those who should have known better reinforced negative stereotypes. In 1834, Father Peach of Saint Peter's denounced many of the Irish in his parish. He damned them as reckless with money, as not aspiring to live comfortably and of living for the present moment. Completely insensitive to the dreadful economic pressures that they had been assailed with in Ireland, Peach believed that many of them had come to Birmingham because they had been engaged in disturbances and breaches of the law. Noisy, drunken and brawling, for Peach their saving grace was that 'they give money to one another when in distress and sickness and they send money to their parents and wives and poor relations in Ireland'. Giving evidence to the same report on the 'State of the Irish Poor in Birmingham', William White, a builder, put forward a more favourable picture, stressing how his Irish workers sent money to their families in Ireland and their steadiness at work. Similarly, James Holmes, a plasterer, made it plain that his Irish workers were honest and valuable. Indeed, 'we could not do without them'. ('*State of the Irish Poor in Birmingham*').

Holmes was right. Birmingham could not have done without Irish labourers. The massive physical expansion of Brum from the 1820s was made possible partly because houses and factories were provided by builders who relied overwhelmingly on the hard work and skills of Irish labourers - the majority of whom came from Roscommon, Mayo and Galway. As Holmes highlighted, the English poor preferred factory work and that if it were not for labourers from Ireland 'we could not get the work done'. This building work was vital. Birmingham's population in 1821 was about 107,000. By 1841, including Edgbaston and those parts of Aston in Birmingham, it had swollen to 178,000. Twenty years later, the numbers had gone up so significantly that the population had increased by 63%. Given these figures, the impact on Birmingham's prosperity and growth by those who had been forced to flee from oppression, hunger and disease cannot be underestimated. The Irish labouring poor had made their mark on Birmingham – and so had those who were factory workers and traders.

The corner of Silver Street and The Gullet, 1880s. In 1851 there were two overcrowded Irish households in Silver Street and three Irish households and a number of Irish lodgers in The Gullet.

CHAPTER FOUR
FUSED TOGETHER BY A CERTAIN FIRE

Park Street, 1904.

William Murphy was a bigot. An Irishman himself, his father had converted the family to Protestantism and to a vehement hatred of the Catholic Church. After stirring up trouble in Ireland, Murphy came to England in 1862 and began work as a travelling anti-Catholic speaker for the Protestant Electoral Union. Not only was he a bigot, but also Murphy was a liar. He asserted that Catholics had stoned his father to death in front of his family. This was an untruth for his father had died of a heart attack. The unsavouriness of Murphy was heightened by concerns as to what happened to money he collected for his proposed Protestant Hall in Birmingham and, most of all, by the salaciousness of his speeches. Filled with sexual themes and unsubstantiated sexual allegations, the lechery of

Murphy's meetings was made worse by the sale of a sordid publication called 'The Confessional Unmasked'. It was too obscene for newspapers to take quotes from.

Wherever he went, the vileness of Murphy's words and his antagonism to all things Catholic led to demonstrations by the local Irish and often clashes with his English supporters, so that sometimes troops had to be called out. Unfortunately, his rantings found a ready audience amongst those who feared the Catholic Church and the impact of large-scale Irish migration. And despite Birmingham's reputation as a liberal town, tolerant of all religious beliefs, Murphy found his adherents as well as those who abhorred him and his prejudices. Patsy Davis argues strongly that the anti-Irish riots that broke out in Birmingham in 1867 because of Murphy did not emerge in a vacuum. Instead, they exploited pre-existing tensions. Those tensions were longstanding. Finigan mentions quarrels between Irish Catholics and Irish Protestants – although I have found no evidence of any significant number of this latter group in Birmingham. In 1850, there was uproar when the Pope re-established the hierarchy of the Catholic Church in England. Agitators proclaimed this to be 'Papal Aggression' and 8,000 people met in the Town Hall to protest. Feeney's *Journal* stood out for tolerance and although sales dipped, many good people in the town were proud of the paper's stance. The next year 6,000 people turned up to a meeting of the Birmingham Protestant Association to hear a speaker denounce the 'Infamy of the Inquisition and True Policy of England in Resisting Papal Aggression'.

Since then, the Orange Order had grown in Birmingham and the evidence collected by Patsy Davis suggests that the police targeted the Irish. For many years, generally negative opinions of the Irish held sway. They were regarded as almost innately criminal and prone to fighting and rioting. In fact, the alleged criminality of the Irish was based upon the determination of many of them not to bow down to landlordism and to assert their independence. Nevertheless, in Birmingham as elsewhere, the undeserved reputation for violent behaviour by the Irish ensured that some of the police were likely to be ill-disposed towards them. In particular, this was the case in the poorest streets of the town where the Irish from the west had gathered.

Oft-times the supposed danger of an Irish neighbourhood arose from the fact that, as with the English poor, their dreadful living conditions led them to live more of their lives on the street. The middle class were fearful of the boisterousness of poorer people and of their gathering in large numbers in the public space.

Accordingly, pressure was brought on the police to bring 'respectability' and 'order' to the street. This led to many petty convictions for playing football, gambling, urinating in public places (not surprising given the total absence of water closets) and fighting. And again as elsewhere, the Irish were more likely to be sent to prison for any misdemeanour. Patsy Davis's detailed research has revealed that in 1861, almost 10% of the prisoners in Winson Green Prison were Irish. This was two and a half times as great as their proportion in Birmingham as a whole. In other years, the number of Irish prisoners was 300% more. (Patsy Davis, 'The Irish in Birmingham in the 1860s', unpublished thesis, 2003).

The rapid growth of the Irish in Birmingham in the 1850s to 11,332 Irish-born, nearly 5% of the population, gave Murphy the opportunity to exploit the stresses in the town. During 1867, he 'lectured' in the West Midlands and then decided to set up his base in Birmingham. Religious tension was already high because of the High Church of England practices of the Reverend J. S. Pollock in Saint Alban's, Highgate. According to a contemporary historian, J. A. Langford, this agitation 'was fanned into open flame by the arrival of Mr Murphy'. But like others, Langford blamed the resulting serious riots on 'the violent conduct of the Irish Roman Catholics in the town'. In fact, whilst some of the Irish cannot be exonerated from any wrongdoing, it was the Irish of Park Street who were invaded by huge gangs of English 'roughs', led by a former bare-fisted knuckle fighter, and whose homes were destroyed. (J. A. Langford, *Modern Birmingham and its Institutions*, vol. 2, 1881).

The vicious disturbances known as the Murphy Riots began on Sunday 16 June when Murphy gave his first inaptly named 'lecture'. His proceedings were 'so repugnant to the feelings of Christian charity one to another, that on his application to the Mayor of Birmingham for the use of the Town Hall it was refused by the

Park Street two days after the Murphy Riots, 1867.

'service', another misnomer, he fumed that he 'would prove to the people of Birmingham that every Popish priest was a murderer, a cannibal, a liar and a pickpocket' and that 'if ever there was a rag and bone carrier in the universe, it was the Pope himself'. Stirred up by Murphy and his associates, the next day a massive English mob attacked Park Street. The Irish defended themselves staunchly against this 'band of roughs'. As described by a more sympathetic observer to the riot, this was made up 'principally of pugilists, pick-pockets, garroters, and that grade in social life termed the "dangerous classes."' However, helped by the police, this wrongly called 'party of order' forced out the Irishmen who protected the street and gutted the houses of the Irish living there. Eventually the mayor called out a squadron of the 8th Hussars from the barracks in Ashted and magistrates read the Riot Act.

Park Street was so devastated that almost all the houses 'were wrecked, every window broken, the frames generally torn out, the contents of the shop thrown out amongst the mob, and the furniture taken and destroyed'. With no protection, Irish women and children 'huddled in corners and mourning over the absence of the male portion of the family, and the wreck of their little all in a silence only interrupted by some half frantic wail of lamentation or the bursts of crying from the children'. An eyewitness who wrote to *The Nation*, an Irish newspaper, supported this informed account written soon after the event in Birmingham. The robbers and police 'broke into the Irish houses, beat women, children, old men, and old women, stole their goods, their clothes, their food, and everything they had in the world, broke everything they could not take, and drove the people into the streets almost naked.' So many of those Irish people had endured hard lives and tragedy in the west of Ireland. It must have been very bitter for them to have to go through yet more calamities after struggling to set up homes and establish themselves in Birmingham.

sensible advice of the stipendiary and other magistrates'. Undeterred, Murphy's supporters put up a wooden tabernacle on waste ground in Carrs Lane. The siting was calculated to incite the outrage of the Irish who lived nearby in the Park Street quarter. When Murphy arrived in the afternoon, a large number of Irish people gathered to hiss, groan and throw stones. The numbers of those opposed to Murphy increased and a battle with the police ensued. By now Irish men and women of the Park Street locality had come together in what was described by Langford as 'an immense mass, mad with excitement'. There was another mass brawl with the police. In all 26 people were arrested. Most were Irish. Late that afternoon, Irishmen smashed the windows of the house of John Ashton, the father of T.H. Ashton, the secretary of the Birmingham Protestant Association, which had brought Murphy to Birmingham in the first place. (J. A. Langford, *Modern Birmingham*).

Protected by bodyguards – some of whom brandished revolvers – Murphy did that which he did best. He fomented trouble. At the evening

Assaults were also made on Saint Michael's Catholic Church in Moor Street and the home of Father Sherlock. (T. Underwood, *The "Murphy" Riots and Demolition of Park Street, Birmingham June 16th and 17th 1867*'; and John Denvir, *The Irish in Britain*).

To prevent further outrages, police armed with cutlasses and troops were stationed in the Irish parts of Birmingham. This led Reverend William Cattell, a Wesleyan minister from Walsall, to proclaim in Murphy's tabernacle that Birmingham's authorities had given in to 'their friends from the Emerald Isle'. He warned that the Protestants of England would demolish the Oratory Church, Oscott College and nunneries. Murphy followed him and exclaimed that he would lead in a 'war to the knife' against popery. Yet, although it was the Irish who had suffered grievously, they were blamed for reacting to Murphy and thus for the riots. John Thackray Bunce was firm in his interpretation that the trouble was caused when 'a crowd of infuriated Irishmen assembled round the building. One of these, in a drunken state, being arrested, a general riot was provoked, stones being thrown in all directions, and many persons being injured'. Similarly, Robert Dent decided that the riot originated in the weakness of the chief magistrate in refusing to grant Murphy the right to 'lecture' at the Town Hall, 'thus tacitly giving the rough element in the town to understand that Mr Murphy was not to be protected from any attacks by such of the said roughs as might feel themselves aggrieved by the - certainly intemperate - language of the lecturer. (*Birmingham Daily Post*, 19 June 1867; John Thackray Bunce, *History of Birmingham*; and R. K. Dent, *Old and New Birmingham*, 1880).

Having seen their property mangled, the Irish were not only made culpable for the riots but also they were punished for them. Barbara Weinberger stresses 'the fact that a majority of those appearing in court after the riot bore Irish names

and were charged with throwing stones at the police from inside their houses makes it very obvious that the police sided with the anti-Irish rioters and were seen to do by the inhabitants of the quarter'. It is also apparent that Irish rioters were treated more harshly than were those who were English. Of the twenty-five people charged with riot, fourteen of them came from Park Street; whilst when the Irish sought recompense for the destruction of their property, the magistrates disallowed all claims bar two. (Barbara Weinberger, *The Police and the Public in mid-nineteenth century Warwickshire*', in Victor Bailey ed, *Policing and Punishment in Nineteenth Century Britain*, 1981; and Joseph McKenna, *The Irish in Birmingham*).

Disturbances continued and in July an Irishman, Michael McNally, was shot and killed when he and two friends went to the Dale End pub of Morris Roberts – the prize fighter who backed Murphy and who had led the English mob. One of those arrested for demonstrating against Murphy, McNally was twenty-four and lived with his mother in London Prentice Street. Although the evidence conflicted over whether Roberts was attacked or not, a Coroner's Inquest found that he had committed 'justifiable homicide'. Subsequently, he was found not guilty at his trial in Warwick. Many Birmingham people were appalled and disgusted by the violence of Roberts and others and the hateful talk of Murphy. The *Birmingham Daily Post* gave them a lead. On 18 June, its editorial declared that the riots were an 'irredeemably disgraceful affair' that discredited the town. The only satisfactory thing was that 'no person of respectability or position in Birmingham has in any way countenanced or taken part in the proceedings which have led to this lamentable exhibition. All the mischief is due to the intervention of strangers to the town; no local clergyman or minister, or laymen of note, having hand or part in the doings of Mr Murphy and his associates. It is also due to the Roman Catholic clergy to say that at no slight personal risk they have done their utmost to restrain their people; and but for their exertions much more serious disaster would doubtless have occurred.'

New Vale Court, Park Street, 1904.

This leader also regretted that Murphy and his associates would not be punished for their proximate and moral responsibility for the riots. Without naming the Irish rioters and without exonerating them, the *Post* acknowledged that 'the indiscriminate circulation of indescribably filthy books, the use of language unparalleled for violence, incessant attacks upon everything which Roman Catholics hold dear – the doctrines of their Church, the honour of their clergy, the purity of their wives, their sisters, and their daughters – what are these but direct and almost irresistible means of provocation to forcible retort?' It should also be noted that no attacks were made by the local English poor on their Irish fellows in London Prentice Street, Greens Village and in other streets where there were many Irish. It seems that neighbourhood solidarity maintained a peace, albeit uneasy at times.

Tension remained high in Birmingham. Murphy continued with his scurrilous talks from his base in Birmingham – as he did until his death five years later. In October 1867, further attacks were made on Saint Alban's Church, the centre of Anglo-Catholic worship in Birmingham; and on 20 November, a large meeting of Irish folk was held by the Town Hall. At this calls were made for the remission of the death sentences on the four Fenians convicted of killing a police constable in Manchester. Decried by Langford 'as a foolish act' that 'added fuel to this religious excitement', the 'anti-Fenian spirit of the people was roused, and a large number assailed the speakers, and broke up the meeting'. This English mob then marched on Saint Alban's again and tried to attack Irish areas and the Catholic churches of Saint Chad's, Saint Peter's and Saint Michael's. They were defended by the Irish. (J. A. Langford, *Modern Birmingham*).

Then on 24 November, the day the three Fenians were executed, a service of remembrance was held at Saint Joseph's churchyard in Nechells. The *Birmingham Daily Post* reported that 'there were many women present, and the greater part, both men and women, wore green ribbons on their hats'. It seems that about 2,500 people were there and, as Patsy Davis points out, this amount was 'about a quarter of Birmingham's Irish-born population and was supported by non-Irish residents'. The high state of agitation in the town was exacerbated by the arrest of Rickard Burke for buying arms in Birmingham for the Fenians. Purporting to be a representative of the Chilean government, Burke purchased a large supply of percussion caps, revolver caps, rifles, bayonets, revolvers and bullet moulds. Much of these munitions were bought from the Birmingham firm Kynoch's and were used in the Fenian uprising of 1867. This failed, but Burke returned to Birmingham under an assumed name. He was arrested on 27 November in London. (Patsy Davis, 'The Irish in Birmingham in the 1860s', unpublished thesis, 2003; John Denvir, *The Irish in Britain*; and Joseph McKenna, *The Irish in Birmingham*).

Sectarian and ethnic divisions continued to lead to conflict. In 1868, as part of his attempts to recognise the grievances of Irish Catholics, Gladstone and his Liberal government introduced a bill to disestablish the Church of Ireland. The church of a minority of Anglican Protestants, this was the official church in Ireland. Meetings were held to discuss the proposal – which did become law - at some of which there was violence. The worst event was on 16 April at the Town Hall when 'most disgraceful scenes of violence occurred. For some time the proceedings were completely interrupted by "free fights" on the floor'. At the same time, the Fenians carried on buying guns from Birmingham. Michael Davitt himself came to the town in 1868 and set up contacts with Birmingham gunsmiths. Ironically, many of these relied upon Irish workers. In 1870, the police intercepted a consignment of guns from Birmingham and a watch was put on the gunsmith who had supplied the guns. He was John Wilson of Steelhouse Lane. Another consignment was sent to Davitt's base in Leeds, where the Fenian leader was arrested. Wilson was also tried and although Davitt pleaded the innocence of the Birmingham gunmaker, he too was sentenced to jail. (J. A. Langford, *Modern Birmingham*; and Joseph McKenna, *The Irish in Birmingham*).

Thirteen years later, Birmingham was once more the scene of Fenian activity. A dynamite factory was set up in Ledsam Street, Ladywood, by John Cadogan-Murphy, an Irish American who called himself Albert George Whitehouse. Pretending he had a paint and wallpaper shop, he bought glycerine and nitric and sulphuric acid locally. With this, he began to make nitro-glycerine. Through the sharpness of an assistant at Harris and Co., the wholesale chemist in the Bull Ring, the police were alerted. One of Murphy's Fenian associates was Thomas J. Clarke. Both he and Murphy were arrested and imprisoned. Later released, Thomas Clarke went into exile in the United States of America. He came back to

Ireland and was one of the leaders of the 1916 Rising who was executed.

The trial of John F. Egan.

John Daly was another Fenian with an association with Birmingham. In August 1883, he visited his boyhood friend, James Egan, who lived in Kyotts Lake Road, Sparkbrook. A few days later and because of an informant, Daly was taken into custody and a search was made of Egan's house. Papers were found linking Egan to a former Fenian and a bottle was dug up in the garden. Tests revealed that this had traces of nitro-glycerine. Egan was sentenced to twenty years in prison and Daly to life. Soon after, the main magistrates' chief clerk told Alderman Henry Manton that the police had placed the bottle in Egan's garden. Birmingham's Chief Constable Farndale later confirmed this to Manton. The matter was taken to government circles, but Farndale now backtracked. Alderman Manton then went to John Redmond, the Home Rule MP for Wexford North and later leader of the party. It transpired that the entrapment of Egan had the sanction of high authorities, and it was apparent that Daly had also been set up through agents provocateurs. Redmond made the case known in Parliament and eventually Egan was let out of jail. Alderman Manton strove for the release of Daly as well, who had gone on hunger strike and avowed his innocence. Daly was given his freedom in 1896.

The 1860s were hard times for the Irish in Birmingham. Over-represented in those arrested and imprisoned, they had been subjected to the provocation of the indecently abusive speeches of William Murphy and one of their main localities had been sacked. Nothing is known about the reaction of the Irish in outer Birmingham, but it would seem that for a few years the Connacht folk clung even faster to their own neighbourhoods in central Birmingham. Patsy Davis has examined in detail three centres of the Birmingham Irish by way of the 1861 Census. The first was Hospital Street. She found that most of the Irish lived below Buckingham Street, in older houses closer to the town centre and to the earlier areas of Irish settlement in Henrietta Street, Water Street and Livery Street. Even in this lower part of Hospital Street, the Irish gathered in certain courts – as with number 27. There were eleven Irish households in this yard with 72 folk living in them. This averaged 6.5 people per house. Few of the households were made up of nuclear families and half had extended families within them. This pattern was the same for the Irish across Hospital Street, for out of a total of 72 households only 26 consisted of nuclear families.

Importantly, three families in 27 court had been living there since at least 1851. John and Mary Trimble were both from Roscommon and had living with them Mary's mother, Margaret, a widowed charwoman from the same county. Their next-door neighbours were the Dunns, as they had been in 1851 when the Trimbles had also given lodgings to people named Dunn. Also in the yard but now in a different house was the Maguire family. James was the head. Born in Westmeath he had lodged with his mother and father with another family of Maguires in 1851, when he was twelve and recorded as an errand boy. Now he was a gun implement maker. Further stability in the Irish parts of the street was provided by the Woodwards and Smiths, still in court 1 – as they had been in 1851; and the

Buckleys and the Hughes's who had moved houses within the street since then.

Numbers 99-101, Hospital Street, 1904.

Patsy Davis also looked in depth at London Prentice Street, where there were many lodging houses. Narrow, dark and forbidding because of gloomy big houses packed closely, it now forms part of Dalton Street – as does Rope Walk. In 1863, the journalist who wrote 'The Night Side of Birmingham' articles for the *Birmingham Daily Gazette* described dark passages that led off the street to courts crowded with little houses. As in Finigan's day, many of the dwellings were lodging houses in which lodgers shared a kitchen. Each bedroom held two or three beds, and sometimes two married couples with their children slept in such a small space. For this accommodation, each person was charged 3d per week, although long-term residents paid less and nothing was taken for young children. This payment also gave lodgers the use of the kitchen, fire, frying pan and soap and towel. Interestingly, the houses had a good supply of water and hot water was always available in the boilers.

It was stated that most lodgers were day labourers, rag and bone gatherers, hawkers and vagrants, but Patsy Davis has shown that, in fact, the majority were young families. These would be paying over three shillings a week in rent, more than that paid by the Irish of Hospital Street for their houses. This situation indicates that these young families found it difficult to rent homes. By 1861, the number of Irish in London Prentice had increased, so that there were 75 Irish households compared to 68 a decade before. In all the 568 residents of London Prentice Street lived in 80 houses, giving an average of 7.1 per dwelling. If only Irish households were taken this figure rose to 7.4. This contrasted sharply with the Birmingham average of 5.1. As in Hospital Street, households of extended family were common and several families were longstanding. The widow Bridget Gray was still at number 6, a three-storey house that was now an official lodging house with twelve lodgers, as she had been in 1851; whilst Eleanor McNally also continued renting accommodation. Both the Barratt and Miller families had been present a decade before, whilst the Sword family had moved the very short distance from Rope Walk.

The youngest working person in the street was John Garay. Aged seven he laboured at wire drawing with his ten-year-old brother, James. Their mother, Ellen, was a widow. Overall, the Irish of the street were working in more varied occupations than in 1851, but were not as strongly represented in manufacturing as were the English. Patsy Davis makes another telling point. The Irish community in the street was probably greater than the 1861 Census indicated. This was not only because Birmingham-born children of Irish parents needed to be included, but also because it is difficult to identify second-generation households. An example of this phenomenon is James Gaffey, who wrote to the *Birmingham Daily Gazette* in 1863. He was the son of an Irishman but because he and his household were all Birmingham-born, their Irish identity would have been overlooked.

The final street examined by Patsy Davis was Park Street, which was to be so devastated in 1867 in the Murphy Riots. There were 79 Irish households in the street, and overwhelmingly they were in that part between the 'Phoenix' inn

and Bordesley Street. Their occupancy averaged 8.4 per house as opposed to 7.2 in non-Irish households. Just two Irish residents owned their premises. John Murphy had a marine store at number 79, next door to his brother and his family, and Patrick Hawkins, a beerhouse. John Murphy had prospered. In 1851, he was a dealer living at number 30 Park Street and had shared this premises with his brother and his family. It was obvious at that time that John Murphy and his wife were recent arrivals. Their oldest child was five and had been born in Ireland, whilst the two younger children had been born in Birmingham. Other families who had been present since 1851 were those of Higgins, Wynne, Loftus and Carney. This latter family had managed to improve its situation, moving from lodgings into a house.

Lodging houses were noticeable in the street, and there was a mix of Irish, English, Germans and Russians in them. Overcrowding was marked in some. Catherine Brown was a widow from Roscommon. Her home was 192 square feet and it was shared with her two sons and thirteen lodgers. Once again, Irish households were likely to be made up less of nuclear families and more of extended families. In a marked change from 1851, when the street was the scene of an occupational network of farm labourers, there were now only 10 such people compared to 58 a decade before. However, labouring did remain the occupation of just over 50% of the men – yet there was evidence of a number of skilled building workers. Hawking and dealing were well represented, especially amongst women, and there were 25 Irish-run businesses in the street. Most of these were services. Few of the local Irish were in the metal trades of Birmingham, but there had been a pronounced fall in the numbers of shoemakers and servants. Although there were Dubliners and people from Laois locally, it seems that most of the Irish in Park Street were from Mayo and Galway.

Rightly, Patsy Davis stresses that her research does not support interpretations that the Irish were restless and transient. Of course, many Irish people moved in and out of Birmingham and within Birmingham. But this was true for English people as well. Residential mobility was high generally, especially that which was short distance and within a neighbourhood. My own English family, the Chinns, moved home eight times in a ten-year period from the late 1890s – almost all of those changes of residence being around the Ladypool Road, Sparkbrook. Patsy Davis also highlights that whilst there was no single Irish area in Birmingham, there were small areas of Irish concentration. These were where more than 20% of residents were Irish-born and where the addition of their English-born children could swell that proportion to 50% or more.

With regard to work, Patsy Davis extended her areas and took a sample of 3,244 Irish-born folk and their 2,138 immediate English or elsewhere-born children that lived with them. A third of Irish women were recorded as in employment. As with the English poor this was almost certainly an under-estimate as the taking in of washing and like work would not have been recorded. The three largest groups of employment for Irish women were domestic service at 27%, footwear at 24% and metal work at 23%. The general Birmingham figures for these occupations were 40%, 26% and 12%. Interestingly, there were ten nurses amongst the Irish women of the town. A higher proportion of Irish women worked outside the home and in jobs that were not regarded as women's work – some of which were unsafe.

In 1870, an explosion at an ammunition factory in Witton killed twenty young women. Five of them were Irish. Mary Ann Bradley was seventeen and lived in Princip Street; Sarah McKenna came out of London Prentice Street; and Mary Ann Concannon, aged just fourteen, was from Lichfield Street. At their gravesides, 'the

"coronach", a monotonous kind of song for the dead, was given by the mourners, the effect of which upon Protestants, unaccustomed to the Irish mode of burial, was peculiarly strange'. The fourth funeral was that of Margaret Burns, aged sixteen and from London Prentice Street. Thirty-six girls of the Sacred Heart Confraternity of Saint Michael's followed her cortege. They were dressed in black with white crosses and hoods. About 500 people walked with the funeral to Witton Cemetery, and the end of the procession was made up of the Saint Michael's young men's society. Margaret Ward was the last of the tragic young women and she was buried at Saint Joseph's Catholic cemetery. ('Scrapbook of Newspaper Cuttings collected by the Reverend William Greaney, 1866-67', Archives of Saint Chad's Cathedral, Birmingham. Thanks to Patsy Davis)

Compared to the population as a whole, Irish men were over-represented in general labouring work and building, two forms of employment that were notoriously casual and irregular, and in the poorer paid sections of the clothing industry. In all, 28% of Irish males were general labourers, six times the percentage for all Birmingham men; and 14% were involved in construction, as opposed to 8.5% generally. With a figure of 16% in contrast to that of 25%, Irish men were less likely than all Birmingham males to be engaged in metal working; and 10.6% could be categorised as involved in skilled metal work compared to 13% of all men. Crucially, the correlation between Connacht-born people and labouring was declining. In both Edgbaston Street and Henrietta Street, 79% of those whose counties were given came from the west. However, in Edgbaston Street only 25% were labourers, although 48% were in this work in Henrietta Street. In Slaney Street, London Prentice Street, Rope Walk, and John Street, the majority of people gave their county of birth. The figures for Connacht people were 54%, 44% and 66% respectively. With regard to work, around a third of men in each street were labourers. (Patsy Davis, '*The Irish in Birmingham in the 1860s*').

Little is known about the formation of trade unions and other organisations amongst Irish workers. In 1838, a Michael Hare was reported as a spokesman for the 'Irish mechanics'. Four years before, the president of the Leamington Lodge of the Irish Labourers Conjunction Union had been arrested in Birmingham. Trade union activity was banned and trade unionists of all kinds had to be secretive and so developed rituals. From a letter found on the president, it was obvious that he reported to a Grand Lodge that oversaw his union. Given the numbers of Irish workers in Birmingham there may well have been a local lodge. Certainly, in 1864 there was a strike in the building industry and one of the labourers' representatives was T. Carroll. He was reported as saying that the request of the men was so small 'it was scarcely worth coming to "ax" in a public place.' The journalist emphasised Mr Carroll's accent by putting quotation marks around the term ax. (*Birmingham Journal* 17, February 1838 and *Birmingham Advertiser*, 20 March 1834 both cited in Clive Behagg, *Politics and Production in the Early Nineteenth Century*, 1990; and Patsy Davis, '*The Irish in Birmingham in the 1860s*').

Through two young Irish workers, we gain rare voices from the Irish labouring poor of Birmingham. Aged eleven, William Morris lived with his parents in a yard in Edgbaston Street. Born in Huntingdonshire, his father was from Mayo and was a labourer - as was the father of another young worker, Harry Feeny. Born in Roscommon and thirteen-year-old, Harry worked at R. and W. Aston, a gun and gun implement maker.

"(I) blow bellows at a forge . . . It's very hot, but I don't sweat much; am hoast (hoarse) and have been for a week . . . can't speak with it at times. . . . the iron when being struck flies and burns the clothes, arms, and face, but not to hurt. The

finger was cut in striking." (*Children's Employment Commission: Third Report with Minutes of Evidence*, 1864).

On Sundays, Harry went to Catholic church and Sunday school, but was too tired to learn. William worked for the same firm. The government inspector described him as 'wretchedly pale and weak looking'. He had been at the forge since he was eight and worked from six in the morning until seven at night, although sometimes the day went on until nine in the evening. He told the inspector, '(I) blow and strike . . . The work here is very hot and wets the shirt. Get 4s 6d a week; pay it to the mother . . . Can spell some words. Go to school Sundays.'

37 Weaman Street, 1904.

A number of writers have asserted that in the 1870s gang warfare raged in parts of Birmingham between English and Irish 'roughs'. I have found no evidence of this. There is no doubt that there were serious disturbances in this decade, many of which involved 'sloggers' (hooligans) attacking the police. Many of these outbreaks of violence occurred in the Bordesley Street area. This included streets such as Park Street and Allison Street, where there was a high Irish presence, and many others where the people were mostly English. In such disorder, some second generation Irish Brummies were involved, but it would seem they were alongside English troublemakers and not part of Irish gangs. One of the most notorious riots took place on 13 July 1874, and a number of writers have taken this as their grounds for ethnic gang warfare. They are wrong to do so.

Numbers 1-5, number 3 court, Allison Street, 1904.

The *Birmingham Daily Mail* stated that between 500 and 600 people caused such an affray that 'one has to go back to the time of the Murphy riots to find anything like a counterpart of last night's al fresco revels'. The trouble was a revenge attack on a local man who had come forward as a witness for an attack on the police a few days previously. The culprit was apprehended and sentenced to six weeks imprisonment. As a result, on the night he was sighted, the unfortunate witness was hunted 'through a labyrinth of streets'. Desperately seeking refuge, he ran into a house which was then stoned. With the land wars in Ireland at their height, the editorial of the *Mail* exclaimed that 'No informer in Ireland ever had a harder time than did the poor fellow'. A force of fifteen constables and a sergeant 'traced the rioters to Allison Street'. When the police got to Coventry Street 'they were brought to a stand by the stones hurled by the mob and resembling a

hail storm'. The police charged and arrested four ringleaders, three of whom were from Allison Street. James Riley was aged 64 and a labourer; William Moran was a 25-year-old labourer; and Henry Manning was a striker aged twenty.

In the 1881 Census there is a 30-year-old William Moran, and although there is a slight discrepancy over what age he should have been by then, it should be noted that the age of many people is given inaccurately in censuses. William Moran was born in Birmingham, the son of Thomas Moran, a hawker, and his wife, Mary. Both were from Ireland. The family lived at 71 Allison Street. A James Riley of number 14 court Allison Street is also given in 1881 – although his age is recorded as 61 then, seven years younger than the age given in the newspaper four years before. A general labourer from Ireland, he and his wife had one teenager born in Wolverhampton and another in Birmingham. They gave lodgings to five people. The only Henry Manning I can find was aged 24 and lived in Holloway Head. He was the son of an Irish widow.

The other ringleader was given as George Davis aged 20 from Gibb Street. . There were a number of men carrying such a name in 1881. All of them were sons of English couples. One stands out. He is the George Davis who lived at 47 Fazeley Street, not far from Gibb Street and in the same neighbourhood. Aged 25 and an iron plate worker born in Birmingham, he was married to Bridget. She was born in Ireland, as were two of the couple's three adult lodgers. A number of others were also charged with riotous conduct. Julia Giblin was a fifteen-year-old umbrella maker from New Canal Street. In 1881, there were ten households of Giblins in Birmingham, nine of which were headed by people born in Ireland. Of these, two came from Roscommon. There is no trace, however, of a Julia. Charles Hemming, a 30-year-old labourer of Dartmouth Street, and James Keegan, aged sixteen and a brass caster of Barford Street, made up the arrested. In 1881 a

23-year-old James Keegan who was born in Birmingham was in Winson Green Prison; as was a 34-year-old Charles Hemming, also born in Birmingham. ('Our Roughs' and 'A Warning to Street Rioters', *Birmingham Daily Mail*, 14 July 1874).

Councillor Chamberlain, a witness of the fracas, spoke of the frequency of these riots in the district and mention was made of the Park Street and Milk Street gangs. On 26 September, the *Mail* also reported 'Incidents of the "Slogging Gang"'. In this, it was stated that a Thomas Joyce was the 'Captain of the Allison Street' slogging gang. According to the 1881 Census, a Thomas Joyce lived nearby in a back house in Park Lane, the continuation of Park Street. Aged 26, he was a tinsmith and both he and his wife were born in Birmingham, as were their three children, They had lodging with them an old woman who was born in Ireland. Joyce may have been of Irish descent, for there are a number of Joyce families in the 1851 Census. It is not possible to verify this. The other person involved with Joyce was an Andrew Toy of Bordesley Street, of whom I have found no trace. ('Incidents of the "Slogging Gang"', *Birmingham Daily Mail* 26, September 1874).

The next year another violent disorder took place, this time in Navigation Street. This was close to the Irish settlement in Greens Village, but the streets around were predominantly English. The Navigation Street riot took place after police arrested William Downes, a man suspected of involvement in a robbery in the 'Bulls Head' pub in Wharf Street. As two police officers marched him along Navigation Street they were attacked by a large group of men. Two other policemen went to help and were also assaulted by the growing mob, of which about twenty were causing the trouble. One of these policemen, PC William Lines, was stabbed. Sadly, a few days later he died in the Queens Hospital. A Jeremiah Corkery, alias Corcoran, was charged,

found guilty of the murder and was hanged. No mention is made in any reports of whether or not Corkery was Irish, although in 1881 a John Corkery was living with his Cork-born mother, Mary, in the New Inkleys. Four men were found guilty of rioting. They were John Creswell, Thomas Whalin, Thomas Leonard and Charles Mee; whilst William Downes and Thomas Carey were sentenced to imprisonment for their burglary of the pub. In 1881, a 24-year-old William Downes was in Winson Green Prison. He was born in England. The others are not given in the 1881 Census for Birmingham and presumably, they were serving their sentences elsewhere. ('The Murder of Police Constable Lines', *Birmingham Daily Post*, 31 March 1875).

In the years following the Murphy Riots, it would seem reasonable to presume that many young first and second generation Irish men and women were justifiably alienated from the police. But it is as apparent that many young English men and women were also disaffected. Although the Irish were prominent in certain localities, their centres of settlement were amidst streets that were overwhelmingly English, and in all but a few Irish streets there were large numbers of English people living alongside Irish folk. As the tension following the Murphy Riots waned, it seems increasingly likely that neighbourhood loyalties were emerging that overrode ethnic differences. This development was shown by the involvement of Irish and English youths in certain gangs. The emergence of this neighbourhood loyalty is also given credence by looking at intermarriage. Writing about the Irish in Britain in 1891, John Denvir was of the firm opinion that there were few places where the Irish were more intermixed and intermarried into the general population than in Birmingham. This meant that 'it is no uncommon thing to come across people bearing names such as Butler, Riley, Crowley, Larkin, Burke, Gorman &c. who are neither Irish nor Catholics. Some years since they were not so ready to admit it, but if you enquire closely now, as a keen politician only can, you will find there is an Irishman in the pedigree – either father, grandfather, or great-grandfather and even further back than that.' Denvir went on to notice the opposite effect: 'the English names brought in by an English father or grandfather married to a thorough-going Irishwoman, who has transmitted to her descendants the faith of Saint Patrick, and sometimes made them "more Irish than the Irish themselves"'. (John Denvir, *The Irish in Britain*).

Of course, it would be foolish to presume that everyone born in England was or regarded themselves as English, whilst the same principle would apply to persons born in Ireland. Still, it is possible to gain an impression of mixed marriages because of the great number of married couples in Birmingham in which one or both partners were born in Ireland. An analysis of the 1851 Census figures shows a marked difference between the Irish living in outer Birmingham and those in the most Connacht dominated streets. In Aston within Birmingham, excluding the soldiers in the barracks at Ashted, there were 199 such marriages. In 70 of them, a man born in Ireland married a woman born in England. Of these 41 were born in Warwickshire. In a further 44 marriages an Irish woman had an English partner, of whom nineteen were born in Warwickshire. Together, these mixed marriages were 57% of the total. The same pattern was evident in the western and newer areas of Ladywood and Holloway Head, where 64 Irish men and 49 Irish women had a partner born in England, representing 62% of the total. The Jewellery Quarter did not buck this trend, for out of 32 marriages 59% may be seen as mixed. A similar picture prevailed in the Summer Lane, Hockley and Saint George's areas to the north of the city. In 87 marriages, an Irish man had an English-born wife; and 53 Irish women were married to a man born in England. Together this was 54% of the total. However, within this area, the situation differed in Hospital Street. Here out of 35

relevant marriages, 71% were Irish-born only couples.

Within the central parts of Birmingham, the proportions were closer to those of Hospital Street. In the streets around the Bull Ring and the markets, there were 136 marriages in which husband and wife were born in Ireland, making 67% of the appropriate total. Inside this district, in the very poor Edgbaston Street all bar seven marriages out of 51 that were applicable were Irish-only. This was 88% of the total. Across the way in the neighbourhood of Allison Street and Floodgate Street, the Irish-born were also more likely to marry within the Irish community. In all, there were 75 relevant couples, 77.5% of which were in this category. Park Street, excluding Park Lane, had 69 marriages in which one partner was Irish. In 76%, both husband and wife were born in Ireland. The figure for such marriages dropped a little to 64%, from a total of 142 applicable marriages, in the streets behind this area; whilst in the neighbourhood of Lancaster Street, out of 31 couples, 61% could be viewed as intermarried. However, nearby in the Gun Quarter, Irish-only marriages prevailed once more. Taking into account 131 couples, 80% included partners both of whom were born in Ireland. This was exactly the same percentage as in Water Street, Henrietta Street and Livery Street, based on a total 130 marriages – as it was around the Inkleys and Greens Village on the same number of couples. Similarly, with reference to 250 marriages in London Prentice Street, John Street and Thomas Street, 80% again were Irish-only unions. Elsewhere in the city centre, there were 142 relevant couples, of which two-thirds were non-mixed.

Comparisons with married couples in the 1881 Census are difficult for, fifty-odd years after large-scale Irish migration to Birmingham began, it is hard to ascertain whether a husband or a wife born in England was of English descent or was second or third generation Irish. One example where this can be done to prove a mixed marriage is that of Joseph and Martha Bates of Allison Street. Joseph was born in Redditch and Martha in Birmingham, but her mother, who lived with them, was Elizabeth Simpson and she was an Irish-born hawker. The living in of a mother-in-law can also indicate where an apparently English couple had a strong Irish connection. Peter Eagan, a general labourer, resided with his wife Mary, a housekeeper, in a yard in Bordesley Street. Both were born in Birmingham, but Catherine's mother was Mary Doyle, a 68-year-old widow who was born in Ireland. Even considering such concerns, still the figures collected are suggestive of more intermarriage than 30 years before. In the Floodgate Street area and Park Street area, out of 169 marriages where one partner or both partners was Irish, 38% included an English-born partner. In 1851, in the Floodgate Street and Park Street areas, taken separately, such marriages had comprised 22.5% and 24% respectively.

With regards to the Greens Village and Old and New Inkleys neighbourhoods, another relationship leads towards a cautious interpretation of marriage evidence. Patrick Conlon, a bricklayer's labourer, lived in a yard in Hill Street. He was born in Roscommon but his wife was born in England. However, her mother, Mary Neary, was also Roscommon-born, indicating that her daughter was second generation Irish. Yet again, there is another couple that also infers a mixed marriage. John Kiley was also a bricklayer's labourer. He lived in Greens Village but was born in Cardiff. His wife, Catherine, was a hinge maker and was Birmingham-born. Her mother, Mary Conlin, was a Roscommon woman, and her younger sister was also born in Cardiff. Bearing in mind these concerns, the relevant marriages locally are again suggestive in that 34% may be seen as mixed in 1881 compared to 20% in 1851. The figure in the Gun Quarter, including Weaman Street and Slaney Street, is remarkably similar at

34%, again in contrast to 20%. Finally, and as might be expected, mixed marriage appears to

The corner of Allison Street and Coventry Street, 1904.

continue to have been more common in outer Birmingham. In Ladywood, 58% of marriages with an Irish partner included an English husband or wife. This was down slightly on the 1851 figure of 62%.

Pete Millington is a proud Brummie who is descended from a long line of Irish-English marriages. His Irish forebears arrived in the city before 1871, yet a sense of Irishness has been passed on to him and his children. This pattern of intermarriage has not, as one would presume led to the watering down and disappearance of the Irish aspects of his family, for in virtually every generation there have been new unions where either second and third generation Brummie Irish people marry one another or where new first generation Irish people re-enter the increasingly diverse equation. Both Peter and his father have married second generation Irish women. In this way, the long-term effect of intermarriage over several generations has compounded 'an enduring sense of both cultural and genetic "Brummie Irish" identity and heritage'. This phenomenon means it is important 'to recognise the concept of 'diaspora' rather than merely looking at immigration studies purely in terms of just first and possibly second generation immigrants.

Court 17, Hospital Street, 1904.

Peter's great-great grandparents, Alice O'Hagan and John Millington, were married at Saint Matthew's Church, Duddeston on 13 June1870. Alice was born in Bromsgrove in 1845, the daughter of a traveller named Patrick O'Hagan and she was an Irish Catholic. Still, the ceremony took place in an Anglican church. It seems on the surface that Alice 'did not retain much of her Irish Catholic heritage, her five children all married local people from Established church backgrounds and all subsequent baptisms, weddings and schooling took place outside of the Roman Catholic tradition' – although her sister, Mary, lived nearby and remained a devout Catholic. However, Peter's grandmother's ancestors, the Flynns and the Finns, maintained their Irish identity more strongly. As their descendant surmises, the 'O'Hagans seemed to find themselves in a minority situation in Lee Bank with their Irish Catholic identity gradually being reduced through constant contact with the prevailing host culture all around them. The Finns and Flynns on the other hand became part of a close knit community where the Roman Catholic tradition established itself more firmly and actually dominated the family for at least the next 4 to 6 generations – in fact, even to the present day.'

Pete's great-great-great-grandmother was a Mary Flynn born in Galway in about 1821. Fifty years

after she was living in Smith Street, Hockley. By then, her one daughter, Bridget, had married Thomas Finn. He always lived very close to his older brother, James, and both men worked as labourers for most of their lives. Thomas and Bridget Finn had six children in total, all of whom grew up in and around Hockley and married Brummies. Pete's great-grandmother was Mary Helen Finn. Contrary to family anecdote, she was born in Birmingham.

"My father's generation had always believed that she herself had been born in Ireland and I think that this demonstrates the prominence of the family's Irish characteristics back then. In contrast to contemporary Irish culture which actually seems very rich in distinctive Gaelic tradition (i.e. Gaelic theatre, literature, music, language, sport, art, dance, etc), the culture of the humble and unpretentious immigrants of the 19th century seemed to be dominated by the hard labouring and hard drinking tradition of the men-

The procession of the Virgin Mary outside St Peter's School in Ladywood in the early 1950s. Geoff Millington is on the back row, furthest right. Peter writes that 'This was a great annual event for Catholic schools and there are some good stories about this procession to St Chad's. Apparently the headmistress kept a huge pile of white dresses and shoes for the girls who couldn't afford them. Crowds lined the side of Broad Street to watch the children on their way from St Peter's. Again, I think this one demonstrates how the traditions became deeply ingrained, most of these kids were actually Brummie-born and bred but of Irish ancestors, like my old man.'

folk tempered by the religious devotion of the women. Their 'Irishness' is described mainly in these terms with a strong emphasis placed upon their devotion to the Blessed Virgin Mary, the various saints and all the associated rituals.

My great-grandmother is described as being very Irish in character, mainly in terms of her devotion to the Roman Catholic religion. My aunts also describe how she would tune in to Radio Athlone and on St Patrick's Day would dance vigorously around her home in Garbett Street in Ladywood.

Peter's great-grandmother had a cousin who was born in the same year as herself in Hockley and was also named Mary Finn. This girl was the daughter of James Finn, the older brother of Peter's great-great-grandfather, Thomas, and the two women were very close throughout their lives. After marriage this cousin became Mary Payne and ran a coach company in Aston called Danny Boy Coaches during the 1920s and 1930s. She was a strong matriarch, dedicated to her family with high moral values, devoted to the Catholic religion."

Interestingly, there are no stories of anti-Irish sentiment toward the nineteenth-century Irish immigrants in Birmingham. Rightly, Peter is proud of his ancestors.

"The character of people like my great-grandmother, a 2nd generation born Irish Brummie whose parents fled from post-famine Galway in the 1850s, may have been humble and unsophisticated, but she was also almost 'larger than life' in people's memories. These people were certainly not hiding away from an alien host society, but playing a very central role in their local communities, there can be no question about their strong Brummie identity as well as the pride they had in being Irish.

The 19th century Irish fitted well into the close-knit communities of the old courthouses, they added their shoulder to the proverbial wheel and earned respect from their neighbours. It was a commitment to their new home country that

continued into the next few generations and many men of my grandfather's generation fought in the Great War and just about everyone in the family was affected by the air raids of the 2nd world war. I do not know if people felt bitterness back then about Ireland's traumatic history under

Peter Millington explains that this is 'one of those great street party shots from the Coronation of 1937. I'm always intrigued as to wahy there do seem to be so many of these floating about. Did working class people suddenly fork out on cameras for this event, or was someone going around taking pictures of all the parties? Anyhow, this lot includes my grandmother Florence Millington on the right of the fron row and her mother, Mary Helen Clayton, nee Finn is the large lady behind her. Most of the other folks are close relatives and neighbours in their court in Garbett Street. I like this one because it is indicative of how people all got on together. The fact that they were Anglo Irish Catholics didn't stop them having a knees up with everyone else.

the long rule of her English neighbours, but it seems that once people were in Birmingham the politics of their troubled homeland were put aside and the family were very quickly establishing themselves as fully-fledged Brummies.

Perhaps the biggest legacy left by the 19th century immigrants I believe was their commitment to the local churches of Birmingham. My father's family were brought up firstly in Garbett Street and later in Monument Road, and were practising Catholics at St Peter's church near Broad Street. In spite of his admiration for the redevelopment of the canal area and the building of the International Convention Centre, my dad still mourns the disappearance of his old school, St Peter's RC, which he tells me backed onto the canal near the

Register No. 1.

Name and alias—ANN MORAN (*alias* McCUE).

Residence—28, Bordesley Street.

Place of business or where employed—Hawker.

Age—43.

Height—5 feet 2 inches.

Build—Proportionate.

Complexion—Fresh.

Hair—Sandy (Curly).

Eyes—Blue.

Whiskers—

Moustache—

Shape of nose—Sharp Pointed.

Shape of face—Oval.

Peculiarities or marks—Right eyelid cut ; slight scar on left cheek ; long scar on left temple.

Profession or occupation—Hawker.

Date and nature of conviction—5th January, 1903. Drunk and disorderly. One calendar month.

Court at which convicted—Birmingham City Police Court.

N.B.—Should any known Habitual Drunkard attempt to purchase or obtain any intoxicating liquor at any premises licensed for the sale of intoxicating liquor by retail or at the premises of any registered Club it is requested that the licensed person or the person refusing to supply the liquor will, as soon as practicable, give information of such attempt to the Police of the District, in order that the law may be enforced.

To the Licensee of the } 79 Monument Road Off License

To the Secretary of the }
Registered Club }

Whose special attention is called to above.

Special attention is also directed to paragraph 4 of the Watch Committee's regulations, viz. :—
"4. The Licensed Persons and the Secretaries of Registered Clubs on whom notices are served shall keep them readily available for reference, and shall in the event of the licensed premises being closed for business, or the Club ceasing to exist as a Registered Club, deposit such notices at the Police Station of the District."

Annie Moran. Habitual Drunkard's Book.

foot bridge which links the ICC to Brindley Place." (e-mail, 12 January 2003, *BirminghamLives Archive*).

The rise of mixed marriages reflects a community that was well settled and which would appear more at ease within Birmingham following the outbreak of anti-Irish violence in 1867. I have scoured the 1881 Census and found 6,258 Irish-born people in Birmingham. The official returns give a figure of 7,086. For my 1881 research I have included Edgbaston, as I did not for 1851, but I have excluded all those Irish people living in the workhouse, Winson Green Prison and the Asylum. Even so, there is a significant discrepancy. However, I have stuck with my figures for the resultant analysis. By 1881, it is clear that a greater proportion of the Birmingham

Irish were now living away from the older and central parts of the town. In Edgbaston, there were 213 Irish inhabitants out of 22,760 people. They were 3 .5% of the Birmingham Irish total. The population of Aston within Birmingham had expanded hugely to 131,661 with the development of Bordesley, Highgate, Sparkbrook, Small Heath and Nechells. Within this area lived 1,240 Irish, or 20% of the Birmingham Irish total.

In Bordesley and Sparkbrook, Irish people were present in 44 streets. Bordesley High Street had nine Irish households, and nearby Adderley Street and Sandy Lane had seven each whilst Upper Trinity had six. Across the High Street, there were six Irish households in Alcester Street, where Saint Anne's Catholic Church was located, seven on the Moseley Road, six on Camp Hill and five each in Cheapside and Warwick Street. Given the large populations of these streets, these tiny clusterings could not suggest even a small Irish Quarter. A further 50 Irish households were spread out across 35 streets. Across Birmingham, the western wards of Ladywood and All Saints (Brookfields and Winson Green) had also experienced massive growth to 119,620 people. In all 1,000 Irish folk lived here, or 16% of the Birmingham Irish community. They lived in 51 streets, and with ten Irish households, Camden Street was the only one remotely approaching a cluster. Again, this must be put into the perspective of the street's high population. Finally, the Summer Lane and Saint George's area had 668 Irish people, almost 11% of the total for Birmingham. Here there was a marked gathering of Irish people in Hospital Street and Tower Street. With a total of 262, they made up 40% of the Irish of this area and 4% of all the Birmingham Irish. If Hospital Street and Tower Street are discounted, then 43% of the Irish of Birmingham now lived dispersed in overwhelmingly English neighbourhoods. This compared to 24% in 1851.

A second generation Irish Brummie from

Hospital Street was to gain fame for himself and his city. His name was Owen Moran. The Morans were numerous in Birmingham, and had been since at least 1851. Thirty years later, there were twenty families with this name and a number of individuals who held it and lived as lodgers. The Morans were spread across the city, with families in Farm Street, Summer Lane, Hospital Street itself, Weaman Street, Cecil Street, Cross Street, Allison Street, Inge Street, Greens Village, Lionel Street and Camden Grove. The Morans of Greens Village hailed from Roscommon, those in Weaman Street came from Mayo and those in Camden Grove originated in Cork. Owen's father was John Moran, from Mayo, and his mother was Catherine, formerly Kelly, and born in Wolverhampton. In his life story, it was stated that he 'came of great fighting stock, his maternal lady being a lady who could on occasion, if necessary, wipe the floor with any two ordinary men'. Owen's sister, Annie, was also a noted fighting woman in the Summer Lane area and is still remembered as such in folklore. (*The Fighting Career of Owen Moran. The Famous Birmingham Boxer*, no date. Thanks to Danny Bateman).

His great-nephew, Nick Moran, tells of how Owen started on the road to boxing renown.

"Born in 1884 in Hospital Street, off Summer Lane, a tough area, he was a small kid (he was only 5'4" as an adult and weighed 8 stone 6lb). He quickly learnt to take care of himself. He liked nothing better than to be in a scrap. He was discovered in a travelling fair boxing booth by a noted boxing writer, Harry Cleveland, who advised him to turn pro which he did at the age of 16. . ."

Owen Moran was a fearless boxer and would take anyone on. Soon he came to the attention of the Americans and was reported as 'one of the toughest, roughest fighters of his weight and very courageous. One of his three visits to America

lasted five years, during which he fought the top talent and beat our most formidable fighters.'

Probably the best pound-for-pound boxer ever, Nick Moran proudly recounts how Owen Moran fought America's top names, 'including two titanic battles against the world featherweight champion, the American legend Abe Attell'. The first bout was over 25 rounds and the second, a few months later, over 23 rounds. Because of the scarcity of bantamweights in America, Owen Moran had to fight featherweights and lightweights 'who were taller and heavier than he was. He drew and beat a lot of them'. On one occasion in the States, 'Owen was sent the word by some mobsters to go easy on their boy. He did for a couple of rounds then k.o.ed him. In the

Owen Moran.

dressing room afterwards one of his friends said "they're after you Owen". He asked where they were, "In the bar". Owen walked in and said, "I'm Owen Moran what are you going to do." Nothing happened.' (Letter, no date, *Birmingham Lives Archive*).

It is likely that Owen had between 180 and 190 fights before he retired in 1916. He then became a racecourse bookie. He died in 1949 and was elected to the boxing hall of fame in 1965. In his later years, Owen Moran lived in Sparkbrook, where my dad and granddad were bookies, and as a teenager, I spoke to a number of people who had met him and told of his toughness. Through them, I was touching a man whose father had been one of those many forced from the west of Ireland for work and a future.

Another famous Birmingham Irish boxer and Summer Laner was Charlie Mitchell. He was born on 26 November 1861 at the Sydenham Medical College, Summer Lane, and was proud to be a 'Brum'. Both his parents were Irish, his father having served 29 years in the British Army before he became a medical curator in Birmingham. Charlie Mitchell received his education at an Anglican school and then went to King Edward's Grammar School in Gem Street (it later moved to Aston). Becoming a prize-fighter when it was illegal, Charlie Mitchell drew the notice of the American manager of the great John L. Sullivan and went to the States where he fought bravely and gained a great reputation. He took on John L. Sullivan three times and Jim Corbett. Charlie Mitchell died in 1918. (Lawrence Mahon, 'Charlie Mitchell – He Feared None', *Boxing News*, 2 October 1946. Thanks to Sammy Gregory).

It is noteworthy that both Charlie Mitchell and Owen Moran were proud to be Brummies and saw themselves as such. Owen himself was born in Hospital Street three years after the 1881 Census showed that the Irish were now spread out along the street and no longer dominated

number 27 court. In central Birmingham, the streets with the highest Irish presence were on the cusp of pronounced change. Park Street had lost many of its buildings and would continue to do so and now had 92 Irish-born residents and 44 Irish households. This was down from 388 Irish people in 1851. As in the past, those numbers could be swollen significantly if English-born children and grandchildren were added. In the case of Park Street, this would give another 77 to the total of the Irish community. I have also included as Irish households those where the mother but not the father was Irish-born, as for many people identity is passed on via the mother. Another 195 Irish people lived close to Park Street in Allison Street and parts of Meriden Street and Coventry Street.

Across Digbeth, there were 159 Irish folk in and around the Bull Ring, where in 1851 there had been 214 in Edgbaston Street alone. The markets area had also been the scene of clearances of houses and other property, and within a few years, a number of central streets with a traditionally high Irish presence would be swept away. Greens Village, Myrtle Row and the Inkleys were to disappear for the cutting of John Bright Street and the extension of New Street Station. In 1881 Greens Village had 43 Irish-born people compared to 189 forty years before, although there were 78 second generation Irish in the street. They lived in 21 households. There were eight apparently English households and one mixed Welsh and Irish household. The people in these numbered 55. This meant that 70% of the street was Birmingham Irish. In Myrtle Row, there were nine Irish households with twelve Irish born and 29 second generation Irish. They lived with three English households comprising 23 people. In 1851, this had 118 Irish-born out of 150, and if children were included, it had been almost exclusively Irish.

The same pattern of population decline in the street as a whole was noticeable in London

Erin's Hope Hurling Club, 1907.

Prentice Street, John Street and Thomas Street – although London Prentice Street remained overwhelmingly Irish, as did nearby Rope Walk. These were to be cleared soon after for the cutting of Corporation Street. There were also major falls in the Irish population in Water Street, Henrietta Street and Livery Street where railways had caused a severe loss of living space. However, nearby Northwood Street had a marked Irish presence and further into the Jewellery Quarter so did Camden Drive, off Camden Street.

John Denvir recognised 'that there has been a great change within the last few years in the location of the Irish in Birmingham' and they were 'more dispersed than formerly'. He identified that this was the result of redevelopment and civic schemes. These adversely affected many of the poor in central Birmingham, but especially the Irish poor. The great majority was forced to move and to abandon the ties of neighbourliness built up over the previous 60 years. With the numbers of newcomers from Ireland declining and the Irish-born an ageing group, the second and third generation Irish from this area had to move into nearby streets that were predominantly English. This shift aided intermarriage and the rise of cross-ethnic neighbourhood loyalties, and consequently it quickened the decline of specifically Irish streets or parts of streets. Still, the large and growing proportion of the Irish in outer Birmingham, where rents were higher, suggests also that a significant number of the Irish may have moved

because of a slight but important rise in prosperity. (John Denvir, *The Irish in Britain*).

There did remain a noticeable Irish presence in the Gun Quarter, which was little affected by physical changes and which had a population of 635 Irish-born. In New Summer Street, number 4 court was an Irish yard with ten Irish families. One of them was that of Biblin. Michael and Margaret, the parents, were both born in Ireland, as was their eighteen-year-old daughter. However, their son aged twelve had been born in New Jersey, United States of America. In nearby Cecil Street, Princip Street and Hanley Street, there was also a significant number of Irish families. In the latter, one family was so poor that its members lived in a room above the brew-house, the communal wash house in a yard. Peter Coine was a bricklayer's labourer aged 48. His wife, Kate, was 38 and their twenty-year-old daughter, Lize, was a spoon polisher. The family was made up by Ellen aged two.

Of course, the Gun Quarter included Weaman and Slaney Street, where the Irish had long been established. The number of Irish-born in Slaney Street had fallen sharply from 356 in 1851 to 68 thirty years later. Yet the large number of English-born children of Irish families indicated a very high Irish presence, as it did in Weaman Street. In number 9 court Weaman Street, all bar one house out of ten was headed by someone Irish. Of those Irish people in the yard, and for whom a county of birth is given, ten were from

Galway, seven were from Mayo and one was from Roscommon. Number 11 court was exclusively Irish with eight houses headed by Irish people, two of them from Tipperary. There were also a number of Dubliners in the Gun Quarter, but this remained a Connacht neighbourhood, with 74% of those who gave their counties of origin hailing from that province. Of the total, 70 were from Mayo; 39 hailed from Galway; and 20 originated in Roscommon. To their number could be added three people from Athlone, which was half in Connacht and half in Leinster, and one person who stated Connaught. The example of

Daniel O'Farrell.

the Gun Quarter highlights that a large minority of the Irish continued to live in small neighbourhoods where county and kinship ties remained important as a coping strategy against poverty.

Throughout Birmingham in 1881, there lived Irish people born in all 32 counties of Ireland. Of

the 6,258 Irish counted in my research, 1,956, or 31%, gave the counties or places of their birth. As in 1851, folk from Ulster were represented weakly, with just 7.5% of the total, of which almost half were from Belfast. With 15.5%, Munster made a stronger showing, although this was mainly because of the 192 Cork-born people who made up two thirds of this figure. Folk from Leinster constituted a third of the Irish in Birmingham. This was due largely to the 427 Dublin-born people, who alone were 22% of the Irish-born of Birmingham. Westmeath and Queen's County (Laois) each provided 2% and the other counties of Leinster together constituted 5%.

As in 1851, the largest number of the Irish-born came from Connacht. With numbers from Sligo and Leitrim insignificant (2%), this meant that folk from Galway were 11% of the total; those from Roscommon were 14%; and those from Mayo were 15.5%. To their number I have added the 3% of people who gave their birthplace in Athlone. In all, the Connacht figure was 45%. This was 5% down on the proportion for 1851. However, it is likely that these figures underestimate the Connacht numbers. This is because the enumerators were more likely to give the county of birth in outer Birmingham where the Irish were fewer, and were less likely to do so in the central parts of the town in which the Irish were more populous. For example, of the 159 Irish-born in the Bull Ring area, none had their county of birth recorded, but the 1851 Census had shown that this was a strongly Connacht neighbourhood. This factor would explain the big drop in Roscommon-born folk from 24% to 17% (including Athlone). Importantly, there is evidence to suggest that Connacht people were moving into outer Birmingham. In the Holloway Head area they made up 16% of those Irish people who recorded their county of birth; in Brookfields and Winson Green they constituted 32%; in Ladywood they came to 34%; and in the Summer Lane neighbourhood (excluding Tower

Street and Hospital Street) they came to 24%. This movement was made up of families rather than the young, single women from Connacht who were so apparent as servants in outer Birmingham in the 1851 Census

Apart from seven Irish-born folk in Birmingham's central business district and those in Edgbaston, the Irish in Birmingham in 1881 were made up by those in two other areas: the Lancaster Street and Gosta Green neighbourhood; and the Hurst Street and Sherlock Street locality. In this latter area there were 305 people born in Ireland. They were dispersed amongst 35 streets in a populous and crowded area. The only clustering was in Charles Henry Street where someone born in Ireland headed six out of the ten households. Interestingly, two families lived in 14 court, Inge Street. A bricklayer's labourer, John Moran, and his wife, Ann, headed one of these. Their children, aged from thirteen down, had all been born in Birmingham. The oldest, Mary, was a tailoress. Inge Street was in one of Birmingham's two small Jewish Quarters and tailoring was a major occupation locally. John's aged father, also a bricklayer's labourer, and two English lodgers made up this household. The other family was that of Burn. This exemplifies the trend to intermarriage. Thomas was a railway porter born in Birmingham – as was his wife, Ellen, a cook. However, living with the family was Ellen's mother, Ann Flinn. She was a charwoman born in Ireland, as was the family's 80-year-old-lodger, Ellen Hopkins. A woman born in Derbyshire and her child lived with the family. The Burn and Moran families lived next to court 15. This is the site of the last of the back-to-backs in Birmingham. Thanks to the Birmingham Conservation Trust, Heritage Lottery and English Heritage they are to be restored and opened as a living museum that will reflect all of Birmingham's peoples, including the Irish.

The final locality was that of the neighbourhood

The back of 37 Weaman Street.

of Lancaster Street and Gosta Green. It had 232 Irish-born residents. This was a densely packed area and there is no evidence of significant clusters of Irish people locally. Close to where Corporation Street was cut, it is likely that it was this area to which would come many of the displaced Irish inhabitants of London Prentice Street, John Street and Thomas Street. Annie Middleton was born in a yard in Lancaster Street in 1906. She recalls that:

"My mother's parents were Irish. Her father was Daniel O'Farrell and her mother Ann O'Donnell. Her father used to follow the boom for work, going from town to town. They had 7 children, 4 daughters and 3 sons. Born in Redditch and some in Coventry. Her father died in the General Hospital aged 42. Her mother died 2 years after aged 40, leaving 6 orphans. My aunt Ann was the eldest. She was in service in London. So that left my mom at 16 to look after the rest. The older members of the family came from Ireland to the funeral, and decided with the priest, that they should be put in a home. But my mother chased them out. not giving the priest time to get on his bike. They were living in Moland Street and she kept the family together but they were very poor. The ones at school were given Daily Mail boots. And one night when Mom came home from work Detective Inspector Daniels was in the house. It was spotlessly clean, and the lads had got a good fire for her to come home to. She asked the inspector why he was there. He said he had come because the children were not wearing the D. Mail clothes, 'if you have sold them you will get in trouble'. 'Go and get them Dan', she said, 'They are orphans not paupers and they are not going to look like them so we do not want them.'" (unpublished manuscript, no date, *Birmingham Lives Archive*).

Annie's Uncle Dan, a second generation Irish Brummie, joined the British Army when he was sixteen. His niece remembers him 'as a very clever man, and he was handsome in his red coat with the black ribbon on the back. I used to ask him to let me polish his buttons.' When the First World War broke out, he was called up as a reservist. Sadly, he was killed, as was his brother, Charles.

The locational changes of the Birmingham Irish were accompanied by a marked shift in occupations. Between July and November 1872 a series of articles on the Irish in England was published by *The Nation*, an Irish nationalist newspaper printed in Dublin. They were written by Hugh Heinrick. A Wexford-born schoolteacher, Heinrick lived in Birmingham. He reckoned that the Irish population here was 30,000, and obviously, he included second generation Birmingham Irish in his figures. He was deeply concerned by the drift away from the Catholic Church of a significant proportion of these folk and by what he felt were the bad effects of so many having had to live in the poorest parts of the town. With the insight of

someone close to the local Irish, he explained that locally:

"there is to be found a larger percentage of the Irish people who are trained to skilled and artistic workmanship than in most other English towns; and here, as in all other cases where Irish taste and genius are cultivated, their peculiar adaptability for the higher kind of manual arts is evident. However, the great body of the people earn their bread by the severest toil. Chiefly the young have been trained to skilled labour; and the numbers of those who have worked their way into middle-class positions, though considerable, bear no proportion to the great toiling many." (Hugh Heinrick, *A Survey of the Irish in England*, 1872, ed Alan O'Day, 1990).

Twenty years later, John Denvir agreed with the assessment that the second and third generation Irish were improving their positions economically and in the work place. He acknowledged that 'the hod carrier' was 'not altogether extinct', but that his sons 'will be found among the artisans of Birmingham, and making fair progress in various other occupations. His daughters still find employment in the manufacture of the multifarious articles fashioned from brass, iron, and other materials for which Birmingham is world-famed'. This trend had been noticeable even in 1851 and had become more marked in the succeeding decades. There is a mass of evidence in the 1881 Census to corroborate Denvir's view. (John Denvir, *The Irish in Britain*).

As elsewhere in Britain, the Irish-born population of Birmingham continued to fall throughout the 1880s and onwards – although, if second and third generation people are included, then the Irish community was still a large one. Yet history books and contemporary accounts of Birmingham are silent on its Irish folk. Thankfully, Joe McKenna's dedicated research has found that the Irish themselves were not silent. In 1895, the first branch of the Gaelic League was formed in Albert Street. Called the Irish National Club, its first secretary was James Doherty, a businessman from Small Heath. Within a decade, the club had 200 members, was attracting hundreds to its weekly céilí night and was providing classes in the Irish language, history, music and dancing. (Joseph McKenna, *The Irish in Birmingham*).

A hurling team was also associated with the club. In 1962 'Sean' gave an account of the playing of Gaelic games in and around Birmingham in the early twentieth century.

It can definitely be stated that there was a strong and thriving Hurling Club – Erin's Hope- operating in Birmingham in 1907, and games were then being arranged with teams at Liverpool, Manchester, and London . . . Two more of its members – one a native of Birmingham – are known to have fought in the historic battle of the G.P.O. in 1916, and others gave their services for the struggle for Independence. Several of them were born – of Irish descent in Birmingham but were brought up in the solid Gaelic tradition. One such, who went over to Dublin in 1916, became a very successful businessman and was a Senator for many years. (Sean, 'Warwickshire County Board. A Brief History', *Trocadó*, vol. 1, no. 1, March 1962. Thanks to Charlie Clarke and Carmel Elmes).

Politically, there were two events that stood out in these years before the First World War. In 1881, the annual convention of the Irish League of Great Britain was held in Birmingham. This was done because the town was the bastion of Joseph Chamberlain, the leading politician who was so staunch in his opposition to Home Rule for Ireland. Then in 1913, strong support was shown for the General Strike in Dublin. Following the organisation of the Irish Transport and General Workers' Union by Jim Larkin and James Connolly, its members were locked out by the employers' federation. A bitter and

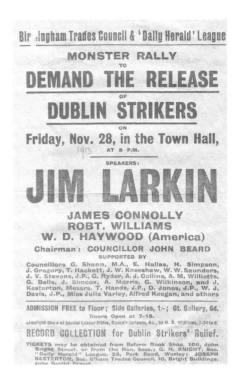
Poster about Jim Larkin's visit to Birmingham.

sometimes violent affair, it ended in a stalemate. A fund was set up for the workers of Dublin and great meetings were held in Birmingham's Town Hall. Jim Larkin himself spoke at two of them. That year the Town Hall was also the venue for a speech by John Redmond, the leader of the Home Rule Party. Afterwards, he was presented with an illuminated address by James Doherty, president of the United Irish League in Birmingham. (Joseph McKenna, *The Irish in Birmingham*).

Redmond's party was swept away by the Easter Rising of 1916. Larkin had formed a Citizen's Army to protect strikers in 1913, and this body joined with the Irish Republican Brotherhood (Fenians) and the Irish Volunteers to take control of the General Post Office and other vital points in Dublin. The Rising was put down by British force and many of its leaders were shot. Aroused by this, many people took part in or supported a War for Independence. This was partially successful for, in 1922, 26 counties of Ireland gained self-determination. The leaders shot in the Easter Rising had played a vital role in stirring so many of the Irish towards a sense of nationhood. Two of them had strong connections with Birmingham. One was Thomas Clarke. A signatory to the proclamation of the republic on 24 April 1916, he had been involved in the Ledsam Street affair. The other was Pádraig Pearse, President of the Provisional Republic.

Pádraig Pearse was the son of James Pearse and Margaret Brady. His mother's people had come to Dublin from Meath, whilst his father was born in London but raised in Birmingham from an early age. The son of a frame maker, James was apprenticed to a monumental stonemason and was employed by Hardman's, one of Britain's leading ecclesiastical outfitters, church furnishers and stained glass makers. The Hardman family was deeply involved in the building of Saint Chad's Cathedral and was one of the most important English Catholic families in Birmingham. James Pearse was working at Hardman's up to about 1872, after which he moved to Dublin. Through his marriage to Margaret Brady, he became a Catholic and took in Irish history via a family that had been involved in the 1798 rebellion and was steeped in the Gaelic language and culture. Pádraig Pearse emphasized that Ireland was to become his father's home and 'through his children, his name was to become an Irish name'. He also acknowledged the debt he had to both sides of his family.

"I have said enough to indicate that when my father and mother married there came together two very widely remote traditions - English and Gaelic, freedom loving both, and neither without its sting of poetry and its experience of spiritual and other adventures. And these two traditions worked in me, and, fused together by a certain fire proper to myself - but nurtured in that strange fostering of which I have spoken - made me the strange thing that I am." ('An

Autobiographical Fragment by Patrick Pearse', in, Mary-Brigid, *The Home Life of Pádraig Pearse*, 1945).

Raised in Great Brunswick Street, now Pearse Street, Pádraig Pearse does not mention his Birmingham relatives in his brief autobiography. It is known, however, that his father had two brothers, William and Henry. It would seem that James Pearse maintained links with Birmingham and his brothers, as about 1900 he bought a house in Bristol Street. Henry Pearse had a large family, the youngest of which was Thomas, who visited Dublin in 1916. (Michael J. Lennon, 'James Pearce', letter to *Birmingham Post*, 21 August 1947).

Years later, Ian Campbell, the famed Scottish Brummie folk singer, knew a man whose proudest boast was that he piped for Pádraig Pearse before his execution. Consequently, Ian Campbell wrote a song based on the line, 'Me father knew the man who played the pipes for Patrick Pearse on the night before the fateful day they took his life away'. At that time, Ian Campbell was an engraver in the jewellery trade in Birmingham's Jewellery Quarter. One day he was at work and an Irish subject came up. Working close by as a forewoman solderer was 'a very respectable working-class Birmingham lady'. She was drawn to the subject and stated that 'My dad's uncle was something very big in Irish politics, you know'. She added that the family did not talk about him because he was executed. Suddenly, Ian Campbell remembered the lady's name. It was May Pearse. The folk singer asked her if her uncle was Patrick Pearse. He was, 'and this was such a bizarre situation. I thought, Good heavens, if this woman were in Ireland this would be her proudest claim, "my Dad's uncle was Patrick Pearse".' Fittingly, the modern branch of the Gaelic League in Birmingham that was founded in 1974 is called Craobh Phádraig Mac Phearais Conradh Na Gaeilge. ('Singing the City', produced by Sarah Conkey, Radio 2, 23 June 1993).

CHAPTER FIVE
BROUGHT UP IRISH: THE INTER-WAR YEARS

Saint Michael's School Irish Dance Team, 1920s. Thanks to Beattie Eastment. Born a Volante, Beattie is the daughter of Italian immigrants and she stresses how all the children in Saint Michael's School were brought up Irish by their teachers and their priest. This photo shows the girls with Father Dan Daley, the parish priest and one of the main proponents of Irish culture in Birmingham during the inter-war years. These girls are of Italian, Irish and mixed Irish-English descent and were chosen for the team by the dance teacher, Miss Barber, and Miss O'Connor. Irish herself, Miss O'Connor was strict but fair. The dance team performed at the celebrations for Saint Patrick's Day at the Birmingham Town Hall. Father Daley also took boys from the school to holiday at his family's farm in Ireland.

By 1911, the numbers of Irish-born people in Birmingham had dropped substantially to 3,161. This number was less than it had been in 1841, and it made up just 0.6% of Birmingham's population of 525,000. A sense of Irishness declined amongst many second, third and fourth generation Irish Brummies, but for others their Irishness was maintained. In 1919, the Irish Institute was set up in Martineau Street, with Denis Lyons as its secretary, and an annual Irish ball was instituted. Its members were determined that the Birmingham Irish would live their lives in the open and 'remove the stigma which has marked their activities in the past'. The overriding aim was 'to preserve and develop the higher characteristics of race among the Irish people of

the city' through the study of the language, literature, music, history and drama of Ireland. There were strong discussions within its membership about the desirability of providing a bar in the premises, but these disappeared with the Institute itself in the 1920s. (*The Birmingham Catholic Magazine*, May 1919-March 1920).

Professor Bodkin was another Irishman who had a positive effect on Birmingham. Born in Dublin, he was Barber Professor of Fine Arts at the University of Birmingham. Interestingly, the emergence of the University in the early twentieth century had owed much to the inspiration and work of Sir Bertram Coghill Windle. The dean of the University of

Born in 1874 at Taverane, Cloonloo, County Sligo, Patrick Hannon was educated at university in Ireland. Deeply concerned about improving conditions for Irish workers, he became involved in schemes for the agricultural and economic regeneration of Ireland. After a time in South Africa, he came to England in 1910 where he gained influence in the British Commonwealth Union and the Comrades of the Great War. In 1921, he became the Unionist Member of Parliament for Moseley. He held his seat until he retired in 1950, even doing so in 1945 when Labour swept the board in Birmingham bar for Moseley. A deputy chairman of the BSA, Sir Patrick Hannon was involved with HP Sauce and a wide range of business and social activities in Birmingham. A devout Catholic, he was president of Aston Villa and was knighted in 1936. (Thanks to Tom Taylor).

Birmingham's Medical School, he regarded himself as an Irishman by education and adoption. Received into the Catholic Church at Saint Chad's Cathedral in 1881, Windle was an enthusiastic supporter of Home Rule, the Gaelic League and the Irish language. Indeed, he and his family were visited in Birmingham by Dr Douglas Hyde, who was to become the first President of Ireland. (Thanks to Leslie E. Blennerhassett).

Following the death of Sir Charles Haughton Rafter, his assistant was appointed as Chief Constable of Birmingham. He was Cecil C. H. Moriarty. A man of exceptional attainments, Moriarty served under Rafter for seventeen years and was praised as 'a professor of his profession' for his books *Police Law* and *Police Procedure and Administration*. The son of a rector in Dublin,

Cecil Moriarty was educated at Trinity College, Dublin, after which he joined the Royal Irish Constabulary. An outstanding rugby player, he was capped for Ireland. He retired from his post in 1941 and died seventeen years later. ('Mr C.C.H. Moriarty', *Birmingham Post*, 9 April 1958).

Patrick Downey: An Exciting Career

Michael Downey was one of a number of Irishmen who continued to be prominent in the Birmingham City Police Force. Born in 1908, he was one of six boys and one girl who lived with their parents in a little village in Galway. His father was a wheelwright and carpenter on the huge estate of Sir William Mahon and owned twenty acres of land. Michael takes up the story.

In 1922 when the great estates in Ireland were bought up by the then Irish Free State Government, my father was made redundant and left for Birmingham, taking his tool kit with him. My dad was lucky I suppose because his sister, my Aunt Kate, was by this time a Policewoman in the Birmingham City Police Force at Newton Street, and my oldest brother Andrew Downey was a Police Constable at Moseley Street Police Station. Dad soon found employment with Eadie Towers and Company builders of Wolverhampton, who at this time was building hundreds of houses in Birmingham, mostly in Witton, Perry Common and Monica Road, Small Heath.

I was 16 years old when Dad sent for me as he had a job for me along with him, working as a carpenter. I arrived in New Street at Whitsuntide, 1925. This was on a Saturday, and on the following Monday I was working with Dad at Witton for 7d per hour, later to be raised to 9d per hour.

The only time I was ever out of work was during the general strike of 1926. My father and I used

Sergeant Bill Doughty, standing front row, was an Irishman who served in the British Army and then became a police physical training instructor. He was one of the sergeants who led the police strike in Birmingham in 1919. He was sacked from his job and had many tough years as a result. (Thanks to Stan Doughty).

to go on holiday to Ireland twice a year and the full fare from New Street to my home in Ballinasloe was £2/7s 9d return each. Those were great days in old Brum and I was very happy.

When I reached 18, I applied to join the Birmingham City Police Force and attended the duty room in the Victoria Law Courts one day to be measured by the Recruiting Officer, Inspector Jimmy Spiers. The minimum height then was 5ft. 9ins, but sadly, I was just half an inch short of this at 5ft 8½ins, so I was told to go and join a gymnasium and put on the required half an inch.

My brother Andrew whose beat included the Moseley Road and Bordesley area, knew the secretary of the Dolobran Athletic Club at the Friends Institute, Moseley - a Cadbury institution then. I became a member of the Dolobran and stayed for two years, attending twice per week from my lodgings at Yardley. This was a very fine

athletic club with a splendid record and I was lucky to be a member of it.

At age 20 years, I again applied for the Force and this time when I was measured I was 5ft. 10½ins and 10½ stones in weight and was accepted and joined as a Probationary Constable on October 15th, 1929. You could say that the Dolobran did a good job on me.

My police career was very exciting and Police work in those far off days was almost completely devoid of danger. I had a wonderful time during the period I was a single man living in the old Bridge Street West Police Station in Summer Lane. It was here that I got the nick name 'Ginger the copper and Ginger Downey'. Summer Lane was supposed to be a tough area; suffice it to say that during the time I was there - four years - I was never assaulted or touched in anger. When they called me Ginger, it was with affection and respect and this I always returned. You could say I became one of them. They were indeed the salt of this earth.

Peter Harte: A Very Hard Working Man

John Harte's father, Peter, came from Ireland in the 1920s.

Dad was one of ten children, born in Claremorris, Co. Mayo in a village called Kilmaine. Some members of his family went to America; he was the only one who came to England. He arrived in Liverpool and made his way to Birmingham where he knew people who were living in Birmingham who also came from Mayo. He lived with a family called Stanton in Coventry Street, Digbeth. The Stantons later moved to Camp Hill and when I was young he would take me to a big house in Camp Hill.

Maggie and Charlie McKernan.

My father was a very hard working man, working seven days a week from 5 in the morning until 9 at night and only having every second Sunday off. When he first came he must have just done any work he could get, I know he worked in the building trade. Though he never said much, I know he was the first man to go on site at what is now Colmore Circus, then it was the top end of Steelhouse Lane.

He was the first man to start work on the Gaumont Cinema, and the last man to leave the site when the job was completed, he seemed quite proud of that, and rightly so, it was the finest cinema in Birmingham. My father met my mother, got married and set up home in Coventry Street, back to back houses, to get to our toilet, we had to go up the street into Allison Street and walk 75 yards across a big open yard full of washing lines and chewed dog bones. There was a big air raid shelter there too.

When I was born my father was working for Wathes, Cattel and Gurden, better known as Wacadens, that was a big dairy in Nova Scotia Street. My father was a labourer earning a pittance but he should have done better for himself because he was very clever with figures, a very good writing style and very good with his hands as we were later to find out.

I remember old Brum very well and I went with my father to the original Irish Centre in Bromsgrove Street next to the markets, it was just a small narrow building I think the bar was upstairs, I just sat there with my lemonade, too shy to speak to anyone unless they spoke first.

The Irish Centre was pulled down with everything else around it. I can't remember when the Irish Centre opened in Deritend. Before it became the Irish Centre, it was St John's restaurant.

I think his major concern in life was to make sure the family were fed and their backsides don't come through their trousers. Things are much the same today, the few have the big share and the majority have less. I am sure the managers at the dairy never lived in our circumstances or environment, but none of them could have worked half as hard as he did, maybe he had to keep his head down after the troubles he had left behind him in Ireland.

I heard at a very early age that Eamon De Valera stayed at our house for a few nights, he was moved out very quickly. So quickly that he left his razor blade behind, it was an open cut throat razor in an old brown case, my father used it every day, always sharpening it on an open razor sharpener. When my father went back to Ireland in 1968 he took it with him.

One Friday morning I received a telegram from Mayo saying my father was ill. I rang from a call box and it must have been the worst line ever, they could not understand me and I could not understand them.

On the Saturday I came home with my father-in-law to be from The Villa, only to be met by my mother-in-law to be, who told me my father had died. He was 76, I was 21. I made a phone call to Mayo only to be told they were going to bury him the next morning, Sunday. I had no chance of getting there and sadly I have to this day not seen his grave, but I will."

From Belfast to Birmingham to Find Work and Love by Natalie Dowds

My grandparents, Maggie and Charlie, came to Birmingham from Belfast to find work. They faced a lot of prejudice in Belfast at that time as they were Catholic. They didn't know each other in Belfast, came over separately, met here through mutual friends and eventually married.

My Nan, Margaret McKernan was born in Belfast in 1924. She came over in 1940 with a friend of her mother's - Mary Catherine Loney. Nan had been living with Mary Catherine in Belfast following the death of, first her mother and then her grandmother. She had no other family who would take her in.

On their arrival here they lived for some time in Ladywood. To begin with they still had difficulty in finding work as many places advertised

vacancies but also clearly stated 'No Irish'. Once the war really started to affect the home front though, companies were not as fussy. Nan had a number of jobs - working for canal shippers, making ship's lights, and working on the railway out of Curzon Street.

She moved at some point to a boarding house on AB Row run by a Mrs Kindall, who owned a shop and the women's boarding house was above and behind it. Nan lived here with her good friend Lizzie (also from Belfast). Mrs Kindall also owned a boarding house for men on Howe Street and it was here that Lizzie's boyfriend 'Smicker' lived. Also living there was my grandfather Charles Dowds.

Grandad was born in Belfast in 1916 and came over to Birmingham in the mid thirties. He also had a number of jobs mainly working on building sites and working shifts on the railway. Lizzie and Smicker introduced Nan and Grandad to each other and the two couples were eventually married and brought up families in Birmingham.

Nan and Grandad were married in 1944 at St Michael's Church and moved to Vauxhall (now Nechells). They lived at 17 Forster Street on the front of a back-to-back block of houses - right opposite the Co-op Garage. They had 4 children - Mary in 1945, James in 1946, Charles (My Dad) in 1949 and Christopher in 1954. They were forced to move to Millhouse Road in Yardley in 1963, when the houses in the area were being demolished. They have both passed on now, as have my Aunt Mary and Uncle Chris.

CHAPTER SIX
INTENDING TO STAY: BIRMINGHAM AT WAR

Delia's sister, Ellen McDonagh, at Little Bromwich Hospital, early 1940s.

A Small Cog in the Wheel of Irish Nursing Staff: Delia Lowndes nee McDonagh

Delia Lowndes was one of many young Irish women who came to England from the late 1930s to work as a nurse. Two sisters were nurses in Stoke and her older sister was already a night sister at Little Bromwich Fever Hospital, doing the rounds wearing a tin hat and a small low light torch to pick her way in the blackout to visit each ward three times during the night.

I arrived here in June 1940, having left the quiet peace of rural Ireland to arrive at West Bromwich District General Hospital into the hectic but disciplined way of life in this small hospital. All was fairly routine for the first few months, then the Germans decided to visit us each night. Nurses who were off duty went down to the shelters, staff on duty stayed in their wards and waited for the 'all clear'.

There was however, one night that none of us who were there will ever forget. It was November 19th 1940 and the bombs rained down for hours and hours. The incendiaries came through the roof and were promptly put out by the staff, thus saving the place being burned down. In the meantime it was decided to take the patients down to the shelter.

There was however, one patient who had a fractured leg and for some reason thought it would not be wise to undo the trappings he was attached to. He was in my ward and I was allocated the task to stay with him. I stood there – shivering I suppose, thinking that any minute those bombs could land on this poor chap's bed and put pay to both of us. We stayed there until the decision was made to evacuate all the patients to Hallam Military Hospital during the war. We stayed there in charge of wards for about three months, but were called back to West Bromwich to help with overflow of wounded into the General Hospitals.

These are just a few of my memories of the 40s in the Midlands. After that I went to train and qualify in Midwifery. I worked for several years in the Birmingham districts and met and married Roy who comes from Birmingham and was in the Navy during the war. I brought up my family and am now of course retired. I still go over to Galway to visit my family. My sisters continued to work in the hospitals here until retirement and we remained a very close family, but as I repeat, we were just a small cog in the wheel of Irish nursing staff in the hospital.

Mary Nolan: Birmingham Such a Bewildering Place

Mary came to Birmingham in 1936 from county Galway. She was just under seventeen. Her teacher had found her a job in the Eye Hospital in Birmingham, where Mary already had a relative living. She arrived at New Street Station at 5.30 in the morning with instructions to take a 36 tram out to Cotteridge where she would be met. Successfully finding the stop in Navigation Street, the conductor put her off at a stop too early. Eventually she found her relation's road, but did not know what number to go to. Mary continues:

Birmingham appeared such a bewildering place compared with my home village, Balyforan, we lived 3 miles outside the village which was made up of 3 shops, a pub and a church, we had no bus service, you walked everywhere, unless you were lucky enough to get a lift on a neighbour's ass and cart. I stood on the corner of Franklyn and Linden Road, 'what ever was I going to do' I asked myself when a woman approached me and asked me if I was Mary Fitzgerald. She had been waiting for me in Cotteridge and when she discovered I was not on the tram, had returned home for a cup of tea.

My relation took me into Birmingham city the next day to buy a nurse's uniform at Lewis's. I couldn't believe the size of the shop and the number of different things for sale, but the thing that really stunned me was the escalators – moving stairs – it was a real culture shock but never the less a great wonder to me.

I found the Birmingham accent very hard to understand so it was not long before I felt homesick; to be back home where people were always friendly and helpful. I was very unhappy, however, my relation told me to leave the eye

hospital and come to stay with her and she got me into the cottage hospital in Halesowen.

When I reached my eighteenth birthday I applied to Rubery Hill Hospital to do my training. The Matron wanted me to train at the Queens Hospital, but I managed to stay at Rubery which I was really glad about because the Queens only paid twelve shillings and six pence a month, but Rubery paid nineteen shillings and fourpence. I was really in the big money now!

I started at Rubery in early 1938, and in September 1939 the Second World War began. We had to work very hard at Rubery, we started at 7am in the morning until 8pm, we had to attend all our lectures after our ward duties, if we were off duty we had to come back to attend them. We had to be in the nurses home by 10pm every night, if we were late we had to wait until midnight when the ward sister would come and open up then it was a night worrying because first thing you had to report to Matron to explain why you were late. We were allowed one late pass per month but this could be taken off us as a form of punishment.

I passed my final exam in May 1941 and immediately applied to Dudley Road to do my general training to become an SRN. At this time a lot of nurses were going into the factories to earn more money and as a result a 'stand still' order came into effect. Matron refused to release me; she said I would have plenty of time to complete my general training when the war was over. But towards the end of the war I married my husband and eventually settled in the parish of St Bridget's in Northfield. I worked for over 35 years at Hollymoor Hospital as Ward Sister and had five sons.

Paddy Hogan: A Fitter on Lancaster Bombers

Gwen Hogan writes: My husband, Paddy, comes from Dublin; he came over in 1942 and joined the

In the 1950s Paddy Hogan played for Shamrock Rovers, a famed amateur footballing side made up mostly of Dubliners.

RAF. After training, he was posted to Mildenhall, Suffolk. His job was as a fitter on Lancaster Bombers. When planes came in after a mission he had, with other ground crew, to put the plane back into commission.

Many of the aircrews he worked with were shot down and he lost many pals. One of the pilots gave him a lift in a plane to visit his family in Dublin. He also went on a mission in a 'Lanc' to Holland when they were throwing food parcels out of the planes to the starving Dutch people. After the war he came to Birmingham in 1947 and had a few jobs, Lucas's, on the buses and at Rover."

J. P. McManus: Constructing Air Bases

At the outbreak of war 110 thousand Irish men joined the army and went to many places in defence of their adopted country, never has it been known during the troubled period any Irish person had been unfaithful to the uniform they wore. Many times getting great recognition for their bravery. The Irish men were responsible for having worked and put down most of the airdromes in England, especially in East Anglia, Suffolk, completing some of them in 5 – 6 months, wages £4 – 5 per working week, 64 hours each week. I am not so sure if they gave them full recognition for the services rendered. During 1940-42 saw English agents all over Ireland recruiting the labour force to work on Airdrome factories, farms etc. with expenses paid to their destination.

J P McManus from Co Longford, was one of them, working in various jobs connected with the construction of airdromes. During his time he worked on eight different air bases in Suffolk, Newmarket, Great Massington, Long Melford, Lakenheath, Debenham, Sudbury. It was a great experience for a young man of 24 years, not many English men worked on those jobs, as they were all away in the forces, although some were senior citizens with whom I had a good working relationship.

Barry Rogers: The floor was shaking

I am an Irish man, born at Castlereagh, Killala Co. Mayo, in the west of Ireland. Arrived in Birmingham May 1935. On Sunday night 26 August 1940 I was at an Irish Club in Moor St, as far as I can remember. I was with my friend Tom Bell from Northern Ireland. When the air raid warning sounded, the building was cleared. I remember going down a shelter opposite the market main centre steps, we were not in there long when the bombs arrived. The floor was shaking under your feet, then the smoke started seeping into the underground shelter.

When the all clear came, I got out from the shelter, with several hundred people and got a tram car going to Washwood Depot. Everyone was thanking God that we escaped a direct hit. The hot air pressure kept a lot of smoke out, saving all of us. I got married when the war ended. So far so good after all these years in Brum.

John O'Neill: The Irish have a lot to thank Birmingham for just as Birmingham has a lot to thank the Irish for.

In 1938, Jack O'Neill left his wife Kathleen and six children in Dublin. He came to Birmingham for work and his wife waited anxiously for the money that he sent home. Jack sent the fare for his family to join him in Birmingham at 1 back of 131 Gooch Street. Soon after, war broke out and the older children were evacuated with Saint Catherine's School. They came back in time for the bombing. John O'Neill explains what happened.

During our absence Mam and Dad had moved to a larger house in 22 Belgrave Road, between Hanover Street and the junction of Sherlock Street and Pershore Road. Mam was able to take in lodgers and they were all Irish and a big ledger was kept in which their names were recorded and

where they came from and where they worked. This was inspected regularly by the police. Some Irish lads would object to their names being recorded but my Dad insisted that was the law and nothing would make him bow to their wishes.

One particular night in late November 1940 the shrapnel was extremely heavy and the bombs were falling thick and fast. We had been in the entry but Dad said we were all to go down the cellar because that was the safest place. Mam and Dad had put beds down there for us to sleep so that we would not be too tired for school. The cellar was large and we were down there for a few hours and we could hear the screeching of bombs falling around the area. There were other families there as well as the lodgers and I heard one person say that if you could hear the bombs screeching you were safe. That was little comfort to a scared kid, believe me.

Dad decided he would go up to the kitchen to make a cup of tea and while he was up there the house caved in on top of us. The roof of the cellar held except for one brick which fell on my mother's head while she was holding Annie. It didn't have far to fall so it did no more than break the skin on her head but she used to say ever afterwards that her head always itched on that exact spot. We had a lighted candle which was blown out and we were in total darkness.

Somebody lit a match and I heard my Dad, who was covered in rubble at the top of the steps, roar at them to put the light out otherwise they would blow us up as gas was escaping. I don't remember how long we were buried but Mam kept calling Jack, my Dad, to make sure he was all right and eventually the ARP and the Police came and we could hear them above us at the grating. They got us out and Christie and I were the last out holding hands.

We heard that all the houses were down and many

Irish lads next door, who hadn't gone to the shelter and had remained in bed, were killed. We were taken across the road to an air-raid shelter and the conditions inside were appalling. Condensation was running down the walls, and I mean running. The place was packed and there was no room to move. An old lady was there who was covered in bandages with blood seeping through, she had been caught in a blast and was badly injured. I heard a doctor pleading with her to go to hospital but she refused. Eventually I saw them taking her out of the shelter.

The O'Neills outside their home in Belgrave Road before it was bombed. Looking through the railings is John. Then comes his father, John, Jackie Byrne (a cousin), Auntie Margaret, an unknown couple and Terry O'Donnell. At the back is John's mom and his brother Tom is in the doorway.

The next day we had no clothes only those we were wearing. Everything was gone. A few weeks previously Tommie and Marie had been confirmed and all their new clothes were destroyed. I myself had made my First Holy Communion earlier and my new clothes were also gone. I believe somebody later found my short trousers. Worse than that Dad was missing.

Mam had tried everywhere to find out what happened to him but it took three days before she found him unshaven with a red beard in Dudley Road hospital with a broken collar bone. Everything was in chaos and there were no records being properly kept because nobody knew half what was happening. We had found that a mine had hit our house and the houses from Hanover Street down to the last two houses from the corner had been demolished and the

front of the houses opposite had fallen down revealing complete bedrooms and living rooms open to view. The devastation was horrific and there were many people killed as I said earlier.

The O'Neills moved to lodgings in Varna Road and when a bomb went off nearby, John's family was listed for dead and their parish priest, Father Bernard Cusworth, said a Mass for the repose of all their souls. John and his sisters were sent Dublin and after they returned he contracted TB and was sent to Mayo to the family of their lodger, Terry O'Donnell. After three years John came back and, aged nearly fifteen, he got a job as a telegram boy in the Post Office. He was perplexed at the anti-Irish feeling that was mounting. His father had been decorated in the First World War and he had relatives killed in the British Army in the Second World War. On one occasion some people came to the door at their house in Gough Road with a petition to get rid of the Irish from England. They were sent on their way politely. John himself has never felt any bigotry, other than minor, and feels at home in Birmingham. He stresses the importance of St. Catherine's Church in the Horse Fair as a great centre for many Birmingham Irish.

On the right are Bridget and Frank McGilly, who ran the dances at Saint Catherine's and also at the Holy Family. Next to them is John's mother Kathleen O'Neill, who looked after the cloakroom. Saint Patrick's Night, 1945.

The first Parish Priest we knew was Father Cusworth who initiated dances in the school behind the church. Initially these dances were on a Saturday night. Later they were on Fridays,

John O'Neill (left) and John Kerrigan are joined by (left to right) Veronica Campion, Annie O'Neill and Rosalin McLacklin. They believed that they were the first Irish dancing group at the Town Hall, although it is likely that they were preceded by girls from Saint Michael's. The Saint Catherine's School Dance Group was taught by Francis Vaughan whose mother and father were Irish. Her Dad had been in the Royal Irish Constabulary and, as with many of his fellows after Irish independence, was transferred to England, in his case to the Birmingham City Police. His daughter was born here.

Saturdays and Sundays. Fridays were a mixture of ceilidh, old-time and modern, Saturdays were modern and Sundays were ceilidh and old-time. They were organised by Frank and Bridget McGillie who lived in Muntz Street, Small Heath, and they worked tirelessly to make them successful. Many marriages came out of those dances including my sister Annie who met her husband Pat, a Westmeath man, there. My sister Agnes also married an Irish man from Piltown in Co. Kilkenny, Joseph.

Father John McGovern used to sing at the dances, particularly on Sunday nights and he brought a tear to many an eye with his rendering of Irish songs which he, too, must have learned at his mother's knee. The clergy at the church were excellent and took a great interest in all that was taking place.

None of my family has a bad word to say for Birmingham where we have had our home for nearly all our lives. Indeed my mother was royalist and would not condone any criticism of the Royal Family, particularly the Queen Mother whom she held in very high esteem because she had been forced into the role she played and later lost her husband at an early age. She maintained that they were brought up the way they were because that was what had to be done whether they liked it or not, and, of course, she was right.

The Irish have a lot to thank Birmingham for just as Birmingham has a lot to thank the Irish for."

Mag Hughes (Byrne): He was only Fifteen

Mag Hughes's dad, Thomas Byrne, was a regular in the British Army in the inter-war years. After leaving, he could not find work in Dublin and so, just before the war, he came to join his oldest daughter, Frances in Birmingham, 'cus her husband John Devine was in the army. With the letters she used to write to me mammy and daddy and with no work back home, me daddy come over. Me daddy was over before mammy with one of the triplets. He was supposed to be looking for a place, but when me mammy came over he had nothing. We came over in 1939.' With help from an English Brummie family, Clifts the bookies, the Byrnes settled in Sparkhill. A veteran of the First World War, Thomas Byrne joined the local Home Guard when it was formed after war broke out. In a tragic case, Thomas was called to the Carlton picture house in Sparkbrook when it was bombed. His one son, Ted, was amongst those who died.

He says to me that Friday night, he says, 'Mag, will you take them beer bottles over to the Antelope?' So I says, 'What for?' He says, 'I want to go to the pictures.' So I took them over to the Antelope, the beer bottles, got the money back and he says, 'When you get the money buy me five Woodbines.'

Anyway I bought him the five Woodbines in Dunne's next door to the Antelope, came over and they were looking in the papers which pictures to go to and of course Ted, my brother, says, 'Oh, I've seen that one at the Carlton', he says, 'Typhoon', he says, 'I don't want to sit through a picture again.' So anyway, they looked all at the Olympia and the Warwick and all the other, 'Ah, there's nothing any good.' So this Richard Hannon and Nipper Bourke as they called him, Jimmy Bourke, they says, 'Ah come on, go down the Carlton, it doesn't matter whether you've seen it again or not.'

The wedding of Maureen Devine and Christopher Duffy, young Dubliners in Birmingham. Mag Hughes, née Byrne, is standing behind the bride and her husband, Billy, is on her right. Her brother John Byrne is just in front of Billy and to the left.

So anyway, they went and that was the night that the Carlton got hit. And me daddy was in the Home Guard then and they came up for him to go and help take the bodies out. While me daddy was down at the Carlton a copper comes to the door and he says, 'Mrs Byrne?' So she says, 'Yeah?' He says, 'Well would you go to Selly Oak. As Edward has been brought there.' So when me daddy came back with my brother-in-law John Devine, me mammy says, 'You better go to Selly Oak. Ted. Ted's in there.' So he went in to Selly Oak. The nurse brought him to the ward and he went in and, he just seen Ted there and he says, 'Y'alright Ted?' He opened up his eyes and he says, 'Yes dad' and then he died. He was only fifteen. (Interview, 'Brummies', BBC WM, 26 December 1995, *BirminghamLives Archive*).

Not the Same after the War by Barbara Gartside

Barbara Gartside recalls her father, Columba Ferguson who was born in Ballinamore co. Leitrim.

Dad was the youngest of twelve and born on St Patrick's Day 1918. He came to England at the age of 15; he ran away from home and never lived in Ireland again.

When he came to England, he lived down in London for a number of years then he came to the Midlands, during the war he joined the army and was later transferred to the SAS Para Regiment, the 1st SAS. This was one of the first groups of Paras formed and trained on Salisbury Plain and one of the islands off Scotland. He did service in the Middle East, France, and parts of Germany, Norway and Africa. I think he was also at Farnham.

He met my mother at a dance at St Thomas More's Sheldon. They married in 1944 they had the wedding all booked up for 1942 but he was sent abroad the day before the wedding, so mom put the cake away and everyone shared the food out. Dad was missing presumed dead about three times and was also taken prisoner for a short time.

After the war he had quite a few jobs – plastering, road works, bar man, coal man, grass laying, but didn't work indoors much – he always liked the outdoors. He had many Irish friends and contacts. He also loved the beer and would give mom her wages on a Friday and have most of it back on a Saturday. He never seemed quite the same after the war, mom said, and was either at work or in the pub. My father was one of the few who never took a driving test – because he had driven in the army, that was how he got his driving licence.

Dad only returned to Ireland six times after leaving at 15 years of age.

Making 20,000 Little Components by Norah Cadden

I came to Birmingham in 1943. Never been out of Cork. I was aged 23. My first train trip to Dublin. How anxious and strange I felt met by agents from 'Cooks' and taken to the Fitzwilliam Hotel by pony and car. Had strict medical examination. Given passport. The boat trip was very rough on The Princess Maud.

At Birmingham I was given digs with Mr and Mrs X. They had three children. That night Mr asked me did I know anything of love. I said yes and immediately he asked me to sit on his knee. Quickly I got out and left. Then I got digs in Thornbridge Avenue with Mrs Allen and shared a small room with two other girls, strangers in one bed. I worked at ICI and in the first week got free digs and 10/- pocket money and then 25/- a week. We worked 10 hours a day or night shifts or Sundays with only time off to get to and from Mass. We stood and worked in soapy suds and had to make 20,000 little components on the shift irrespective of machines constantly breaking down, our fingers were often cut and bruised from copper and brass.

Some local workers used to say we kept pigs in our kitchens in Ireland and many other slurs. When we exchanged digs we had to go to the police station and tell them why and give them details and they quizzed us and kept a strict call on all Irish once they got us here.

The Campbells and Yourells: Joining the Services

Dave and Eileen Henderson recall the life of William and Elizabeth Yourell, née Campbell.

William came to England in 1939 with a friend,

Jimmy McGarry, and found digs at 223 Park Road, Aston, Birmingham. This was the home of the Freers, 'who were later to become the best friends anyone could wish for. By November, William had saved enough money to send for his sweetheart Elizabeth to join him. Soon after, they were married at Saint Joseph's and moved to 198, Phillips Street, Aston'.

William was a driver and went around to the different farms collecting the milk and was also a firewatcher. Elizabeth worked at Hercules, the bike factory. Elizabeth's mother was dead and her father was a violent man and Elizabeth's brother, Frank, joined them and their baby. After their father died, Elizabeth 'wrote to all her extended family to ask for financial help and it was her Aunt Maggie Eccles who let her borrow money so that she could bring the younger children to live with her in Birmingham'.

The house in Phillips Street had one living room downstairs with a small pantry, which had a sink in it and steps leading down to the cellar. The living room had four doors in it, one was the front door, one was a back door into an entry, and one was a door into the pantry and the last door led to the stairs. Upstairs there was one bedroom, then the next flight of stairs led up to the attic.

The house had open fires in each room, the toilet and brewhouse were across the yard and had to be shared with four other families. In the attic were two double beds, boys in one and girls in the other. The lower bedroom had a double bed, single bed and a cot.

While at Hercules Frank was called up by the army and went into the Paras. Jack also went into the army joining the Paras, and Chris joined the Royal Artillery. Pat also joined the services and went into the land army. Always, on return home for leave, they stayed at Lil and Bill's.

I intend to stay in this country so I will fight for it by Richard Scott

Both my parents moved to Birmingham. My father was a Dublin man, who like many others came to this country in the late 30s to seek work. I believe that at that time he worked as a builder. My mother was later to tell me that one of the buildings he helped build was Father Hudson's Homes in Coleshill.

He did say that on one of the bricks on the main tower, he inscribed his name before laying it. Needless to say I do not know if this is true and there is no way I am climbing up to find out. I understand that he also worked on either a police station or the fire station in the same area. After the start of the war my mother travelled down to Birmingham from Hartlepool, to work in what was then an ammunition plant in Common Lane Washwood Heath.

On the war breaking out my father also started work at the same works as my mother as a stacker truck driver. They of course met and married in 1940. He can't have liked married life because whilst being a Free State man who could have returned to Dublin, he enlisted. I remember my mother saying that he said, 'I intend to stay in this country so I will fight for it '.

He joined the Royal Artillery in 1940. His passbook shows his condition as A1. When he eventually left in 1945 it was shown as C3. Considerable deterioration you may feel. Still many others didn't come back at all. I was born in 1942 . . . Having left the army in 45 my father spent considerable time in and out of Hospital before dying the year I started school in 1947, at The Rosary, which I think you will know well.

CHAPTER SEVEN
LEAVING IRELAND: REACHING BRUM

John Henry was the driving force behind the Birmingham Armagh Association and the Birmingham 32 Counties Association. In 2001 he played a leading role in saving Birmingham's Irish Club when it was faced with closure. A passionate Irishman, he was as passionate about being an Irish Brummie, and his powerful marriage to his wife, Peggy, epitomized the coming together of Irish and English in our city. John died last year. May he rest in peace. In this photo John is with his beloved wife Peggy and their family holding a painting of the whitewashed house.

The Little White House by John Henry

As far back as I can remember, there was my whitewashed house on the side of Slieve Gullion in County Armagh. There was a family of seven of us and the nearest house was half a mile away. We went to the local Ballinlas School where we mixed with children for the first time.

My father had a mixed farm on which we had to survive. There were always a couple of cows to provide milk and butter and we harvested plenty of spuds. We never went hungry. The crops were rotated and provided feed for the animals and

hens. The main income came from the mountain sheep on the side of Slieve Gullion.

During the 1940s onwards our main form of entertainment was the ballroom of romance. These country dance halls were very popular with the young and old. Our local ballroom was Ballinlas AOH Hall.

I was a teenager in those days, however, I can still remember vividly those dancing nights. Us young lads would go as a gang and most of the time we never had the 6d entrance fee, and would sneak in later.

Supper was served during the evening, usually spam or cheese sandwiches with tea and red lemonade. There were no alcoholic drinks. A few of the hard cases would have a bottle in their pocket as they always paid a visit to the local bar first.

I think my greatest memory was the men lined up on the left hand side and the women on the right hand side of the ballroom. The parish priest would often drop in with his blackthorn stick, and pity any couple found in close proximity. Of course these strict rules also applied in church on Sunday where the men were kept to the left and the ladies in hats on the right.

If they were well off the men usually arrived to the dance on their bicycles, many with no lights or brakes. If you had a bicycle your chances were good with the ladies.

You would ask the girl that you fancied to save you the last dance and if she picked you for the ladies' choice you knew you were doing well. So you took her home on the crossbar of the bicycle.

Of course not everyone went straight home and would look around for the best haystack or field. By now the parish priest would be sound asleep. Of course matches had to be made somewhere. Most of these young couples and thousands of single boys and girls emigrated to England in that period and I myself was one of them.

THE COUNTRY BOY

Frank Moloney of Killarney

Where has the country boy gone?
I knew so long ago.
A lad as free as the lark on high
He's gone that's all I know.

In concrete city jungle,
He could never survive.
Where has the country boy gone?
Perhaps the lad had died.

Through fields of Ox-eyed daisies,
O'er cornfields green then gold.
Down in the shadowed woodland,
Or to watch the dawn unfold.

To hear a cuckoo call in May,
Or the reaping of the corn.
This was the country boy's way,
Please tell me where his gone?

He came into the city,
His fortune for to seek.
Within the factory walls,
He used to work each week.

But like a songbird in a cage,
His heart could never sing.
He missed the swaying flowers,
And the budding in the spring.

When darkness falls around me,
In my bed I lie awake,
Where is the fortune I once sought?
The one I never made.

I close my eyes and drift away,
O'er rolling pastures green.
The country boy's come again,
Where ever has he been?

He walks the meadow by the brook,

Through shady country lanes.
The scent of blackthorn blossom,
Greets him once again.

He can hear cattle lowing,
From the farmyard on the hill.
The rising of the harvest moon,
That brings an evening chill.

Then the clatter of the milkman
Loudly greets the winter dawn.
Another day in city life,
But the country boy has gone.

Terrible Cattle Boats by Delia Healy

I came to England in August 1935, nursing at the Fever Hospital in Rotherham, Yorkshire for two years. I then came to a hospital in Birmingham in August 1937. I will never forget my first journey from Ballygar, Co. Galway by train and those terrible cattle boats to England. I was sick most of the way. Things have got better over the years. I was here in Birmingham all during the last war. It was a busy time at the hospital. We nurses could not go to a shelter as our patients came first. Some nights were bad, but we did have some good times. A few of us would go to the dance in St Michael's in Moor Street before it was bombed and to St Catherine's in Bristol Street.

I met my late husband Joe Healy who came from Castlebar, Co. Mayo. He was a bricklayer. We were married at St Catherine's and we had forty-two happy years together. Those I shall always treasure. My parents had ten children, so it was hard work to feed and clothe us. We had a farm, so we had fresh vegetables, eggs, milk, butter and bacon when a pig was killed and chickens.

Heavy at Heart at Leaving My Homeland by Frederick Corduff

Frederick was the son of a member of the Royal Irish Constabulary. Born in county Clare, he was reared in Rossport, county Mayo, an area that was called the fir gaeltacht for 'it is the true Irish. The men over the age 30-35 did not speak any English'. Frederick has lived in Birmingham since his arrival during the Blitz. His son, Father Eamonn Corduff, is well respected for his work in helping young people.

I cannot recall the actual scene of leaving home or of my journey to Kingstown (now Dun Laoghaire). I remember the boat S.S. 'Princess Maud' lying at anchor in the harbour, with an ugly looking anti-aircraft gun pointing to the skies – a grim reminder of the times we were going through. We left harbour early in the afternoon with a huge crowd of passengers, no doubt emigrants fuelled with an ambition of returning one day with bags of gold. There was a mixed cargo of livestock on board, and the travelling condition left a lot to be desired. – the aroma and the euphony which belched forth from the hold was not exactly like an evening in Paris; but I did not feel in the mood to be bothered as I still felt heavy at heart at leaving my homeland and parting with friends whom I accumulated over the many years, and tried to console myself with the thought that parting is the lot of all mankind, and this life is a constant scene of leave taking, and how often do we part from loved ones with a light goodbye and whom we never meet again . . . I can still hear some lonely emigrant at the bar singing with feeling and emotion, 'I'll Take You Home Again Kathleen' with the aid of a couple of jars under his belt. We had a safe crossing and landed at Holyhead sometime in the late afternoon and then on by train to Birmingham. It was a slow journey and to make matters worse there was a long delay at Crewe due to enemy action, whatever that implied. Eventually we arrived in Birmingham in complete darkness late at night. Outside lights were strictly forbidden after 'lighting up time' . . . For a long time I wondered how all those passengers off the train dispersed so quickly and just disappeared into the night. What it was: all these people were prospective employees for various factories in the West Midlands and arrangements had been made for agents to meet their respective groups and transport them to hostels and other institutions for the night and then on the following morning to the places of their future employment; but since I was a lone passenger there was not this facility for me, hence I found myself stranded in a city, the second largest in England. Here I was a lost sheep, tired and weary without having eaten all day, but I just didn't feel like eating. There was nothing I could do now only lie down in some shop doorway and await the dawn. (Frederick Corduff, My Early Childhood, 2000, *BirminghamLives Archive*).

A Day Out by Ann Cullen

The boat swayed and rocked as I ran up and down the deck, playing with my brothers and sister, unaware of people getting sick over the sides of the ship from the torrents of the tide. We'd embarked on the 'Princess Maud' from the North Wall heading for Liverpool, that was the most popular and cheapest form of travelling to England in those days. We were on board the cattle boat. I glanced over at my mother who'd been lucky enough to find a bench to sit on, she was bottle feeding my youngest sister, who was about 6 months old. There were five of us children, Bill, Tom, Marie, Jean and myself (I was the eldest). My older brother George had been left in Dublin to be granny reared, which was an acceptable situation in those time.

In the late 1940s Ireland was suffering unemployment, poor housing and poverty, the people of Dublin City were eking out a living wherever and however they could. It was a penny-pinching survival for most families and the

grim grey walls of Mountjoy Prison were beckoning to many a good man who, out of desperation turned to crime to feed his family.

Bill rolled around the deck, with Tom copying him as he always did, not a care in the world of his clothes becoming dirty and dishevelled and Tom, he just liked doing the things his big brother Bill did. Marie and I clapped hands and jigged, we weren't going to get our dresses soiled, after all Mom wouldn't be very pleased. We were excited at being on a boat and getting so much attention from other passengers, we were having a good day out and were happy kids.

I recall suddenly feeling very cold, I do believe that it was at that moment that I felt for the first time a sense of responsibility for my siblings and an awareness of our situation was seeping into me. The year was 1949 and we were leaving our roots behind as we headed for Birmingham where we became the Irish immigrants of the 50s, my parents were in search of a better way of life.

My Visit to Rowton House by David Chambers

I was born in Baubridge, Co. Down, Northern Ireland and qualified as an Industrial Chemist at Queens University, Belfast in 1942. From 1942 to 1945 I worked for ICI at their Nobels Arden Explosives Factory in Ayrshire, engaged in the manufacture of cordite and nitro-glycerine. In 1945 a good school friend, also a chemist, got a job with Bakelite and he suggested I seek a position with them.

On 19th July 1945, I came to Birmingham for my interview. I thought that most people would be away on holiday and I would have no trouble getting fixed up with accommodation.

Sadly this was not the case and after trying to get accommodation in the City and around Tyseley, I asked the police for help, at the police station on the Birmingham side of the Swan junction on the

Coventry Road. They said OK, and took me to Rowton House.

I recall going into this place and the steel shutter door closing, paying my 1/6p and being shown to a small cubicle with a single bed but little else. I did not get much sleep that night, worrying about possible lice and other creatures and as you can imagine, I was up at about 5am, taking myself to Snow Hill station for a wash and brush up.

My interview went well but the position offered was in Research and Development. I wanted a job in production, so I did not accept. About three weeks later I had a letter from Mr Hoyle, offering a job in a new Department known as PPI (product and process improvement). This one I did accept and came to work for Bakelite on 1st October 1945. I stayed with Bakelite in various capacities, initially on technical work on laminates and from 1971 in production management at Tyseley and Aycliffe – retiring on 30th June 1984.

Exile. By Des Connaire

I left Dublin for Birmingham just for the crack, and I never thought that I'd never go back.
I'd never go back.

My family and friends they were all left behind, I just hopped on the ferry, my fortune to find.

I landed in Brum on a cold frosty morn, and soon I was wishing I'd never been born.

I knocked many doors in this dirty old town before I found some-where to lay my head down.

"No Irish, No Blacks", no bloody dogs, the Irish were "Paddies", the blacks they were "wogs".

Well, I paid her a pound and she showed me my bed, there were five other beds there, but she hadn't said.

Des Conaire and Terry Ward on the buses, 1959.

Then I worked on the buses, I worked on the roads, I worked in the factories, giving it loads.

Then I married a "Brummie", a nice little thing, I took here to "Samuels" to buy her the ring.

She gave me four children, three girls and a boy, for many long years they were my pride and joy.

I had to work hard then with four children to raise, and soon put behind me my Teddy Boy ways.

I delivered the milk, I delivered the bread, then in the evening sold ice-cream instead.

Got a job on a jack-hammer up in the town, the hammer stayed put, I went up and down, the foreman said hey son!

You better go home, come back again when you've gained a few stone.

Now a night shift in Lucas,
Should have stayed in my bed,
Turned out two thousand screws without any thread!

Pat McGrath.

The kids have grown up and gone,
Now, the wife has gone too,
And I am retired now with nothing to do.

It's sad when you think your life is gone in a
flash, it wouldn't be bad if I'd made loads of cash.

There is no-one back home now, they have all
passed away,
I can't pay a visit, there is nowhere to stay.

Sometimes I feel just a little bit sad when I think
of my life back home as a lad,

With Prince by my side the green hills we would
roam,
on hot summer days we were never at home, a
swim in the "Dodder" below "Hell Fire" club,
then out with the pan and scoff all your grub,
a day at "Portmarnock", a climb up "Howth
Head", then home for your cocoa and fall into
bed.

I believe back at home now they are all rolling in
dough,
And ex-pats from England, they don't want to
know,
I just hope they know how lucky they are, for the
standard of living is now better by far,
For the wages and life style went up like a
balloon, it's just my bad luck I was born too
bloody soon.

Well there is no going back now, it's over and
done,
Though I've shed a few tears, I've had lots of fun,
I've had a full life and things can't be bad,

When Callum and Lauren say "Hello Grandad".

Well, they will plant me in Witton when I pass
away,
And here in this city forever I'll stay.

**Pat McGrath: An Extract from the Memoirs of
Pat McGrath The Way We Were.**

It was midday on a Sunday when we arrived at
the wondrous Snow Hill Station after a dreadful
12-hour journey from Fishguard. We had left
Waterford City at 6 o'clock on a hot Saturday
evening - now here we were in BRUM. Smoke
dried and bleary eyed we stumbled up the long
steep steps, into the blaring sunlight.

We had been duly told that Sparkbrook/Sparkhill
was the Irish quarter. Is that North, South, East
or West? I enquired at the bus stop.

'The 13 or 24 bus will take you there mate',
quipped the cocky chap. 'Ask to be dropped at
the Mermaid Pub or Lion and Lamb or the Ship.'

'They call that the Irish Labour exchange', said
his mate. We thanked them and boarded the bus
20 yards further down.

Fortunately, before we had left Waterford, my
mother gave me the address of an old adopted
Aunt, who my Grandmother reared. She had
spent all the war years working in Brum, now old

and retired she lived in a small flat in a big house off the Stratford Road. She made us a welcome cup of tea and sandwich and allowed us to leave our suitcases in the hallway while we searched for accommodation.

'Try the Mermaid Pub', someone said. 'Try the Antelope', another said. 'Try the notice boards', another said. The notice boards were on the pavement along the Stratford Road - other notices were in shop windows. Some of the notices said 'NO DOGS, NO BLACKS, NO IRISH, need apply'.

We sat and rested awhile on the pub seats outside the Mermaid, as we watched the pub customers slowly leave for their homes and Sunday dinner. An hour later the Stratford Road was much quieter as we vainly continued our search for digs in the various side roads, without success.

It was coming up for 6pm, the day still warm, a man suggested 'try the Bear Pub, near the Park, plenty of Irish get in there, maybe they can help you', and so to the Bear we went. Our finances were low, we had just £12 between us, our drinking had to be curtailed - it was to be sip rather than drink! The regulars started to come in about 8 o'clock, everyone was wanting to help, but unable and so that was the situation until the pub closed and once again we watched the drinkers drift away.

"What now?" said my friend Smithy. "I'm knackered," I replied. "Me too," he said. We both looked over at the Park. "Let's have a look," I said, as we made our way into the Park for our first night in Brum: and indeed - a rude awakening…..

I love Birmingham by James McTeigue

My story began way back one bright, early summer morning in April 1954. Arriving on the overnight train from Holyhead, I was a shy young 17 year old from rural Co. Cavan. I was met at New Street station by some friends who themselves had only recently come over. I found lodgings in Long Street, Sparkbrook with the late Johnny Burke. From there I found my way out to Cadbury's. Twelve months later, owing to my health I got a job at the Austin Motor Co. I loved the work there, and I got lodgings in Trafalgar Road, Moseley. Some time later, I met a Co. Cork Bus Conductress, Mary, on a blind date and as they say, the rest is history.

I love Birmingham and it is my home, we had good times and not so good. I will always be grateful to Birmingham and the English people, which I have many friends. I still have fond memories of my early days in Brum, many spent in St Catherine's old hall in the Horse Fair and all the other dance halls with thousands of young men and women mostly Irish. They were lovely days. I still go back to Co. Cavan fairly often now we are retired.

Spreading My Wings by Maura Bye

Hailing from Mullingar in Westmeath, Maura is happily settled in Brum and has no regrets about the course of her life. She is married to a Brummie and has five children and seven - nearly eight - grandchildren, all of whom live in the city. However, Maura still recalls powerfully the homesickness which at times nearly overcame her when, as a nineteen-year-old, she tried to make a life for herself in a different land. With a good job at the GEC in Witton, she was able to send money back home but her unhappiness at being away from her people led her to lose weight significantly. When, after many months, Maura did return to Ireland, her mother knew she had to build her up and did so by feeding her daughter with a mixture of Guinness and milk.

SPREADING MY WINGS

Maura T Bye, Co Westmeath

Way back in the sixties great notions filled my
head
I thought I knew it all, and my wings I would
spread.
My maiden flight landed me, this side of the pond
And I grieved for long months, for my family
beyond
I climbed the stone steps, to the bed-sit I found
With my old cardboard case, and the sum of six
pound
I look through the window, to survey the scene
Just back yards and dust-bins, the sun never seen
For my Mother's front parlour I thought I would
die
My tear ducts dried up, I could no longer cry
Where are the green fields? No sigh of the birds
Just a visiting landlord, a man of few words
In dreams I was failing, I could never compete
'Stop whining,' a voice called, 'Stand up on your
feet'
Cause the things that you pine for, you'll find
any-where
And it's seldom a broken heart's, beyond repair
Well I stood up, and clung on to every moon
beam
And I searched every-where, for the voice in my
dream
The years quickly passed, and my confidence
grew
Twas the voice of my Mother, directing me
through
Ah yes! I've been so lucky, fate dealt me a mighty
hand
Love, good health, children, the strength to make
my stand
Now I've got my own stone steps, they boast an
inner glow
My brood won't rush to spread their wings, like
me, long
Ago...

Kate Byrne, She Had a Big Heart, by George Byrne

I came over from Ireland when I was 7, with my mother, 1 sister and 4 brothers; my other sister was left with my Nan in Ireland. We came over in 1947, the year of the big snow. My dad was in the English army and wasn't very good at sending money to my mother. If it hadn't have been for my oldest brother Mick, we wouldn't have been able to survive. He worked in a store in Dublin, and used to go after the coal man picking up the coal so mom could have a fire.

Times were very hard for us then, so mom decided to sell every little thing she had, which wasn't a lot, and decided to come over to England. My Uncle Tom who was my mom's brother came to put us on the boat at the 'North Wall', if you could call it a boat – it was more of a tugboat.

We came to Snow Hill station; my dad wasn't even there to meet us. We met dad coming up Snow Hill. He told us he had a room for us in Ledsam Street. When we got there we had to sleep on the floor. Then after a time, mom heard from another Irish person that there was a room with a bedroom and attic over Green's, the jewellery shop, facing the cemetery in Key Hill Drive. We grew up there, and times were very hard until we grew up and all go jobs.

Dad had only got one leg. He got knocked down at the crossing in Great Hampton Street when he was coming from the pub, which was called the Trees. He only lived a few days after.

Then mom got a house in Great King Street. When we lived in The Drive, it was nothing to get up in the morning and step over someone sleeping on the floor. When the Irish came over and had nowhere to go, mom used to let them kip on the floor. A lot of people loved Kate Byrne and she always said she loved England.

Sadly she is not with us any more. As you know I am happily married to an English girl, Pat, and I have a lovely family. I thank God for that.

A Wide Eyed Irish Lass Waved Goodbye to Her Parents by Delia Keogh

My name was then Delia Higgins (Bab for short) now Delia Keogh. I was born in Rathra Frenchpark, Co Roscommon. I always wanted to

A Celtic Wedding. The wedding of Delia's son David, of the dynamic band Wylde Green, to Abi Fewtrell, 2002. Delia is in the middle. (Photo: Kay Chinn.)

travel as most young people did in those days. I asked my Dad many times to let me go to England and join my friends who had left before me. I managed to get my fare together and with a mixture of sadness and excitement I head for Dublin to catch the boat. It was a very rough crossing. The boat was called Princess Maud. They called it the 'cattle boat' as it was used to ferry cattle to and from England. It was an experience I can tell you. With my rosary beads in my hand I prayed for a safe and speedy crossing.

I had arranged a job as a trainee nurse in a fever hospital with my friends in Congelton, Cheshire. The discipline was very strict, uniforms had to be immaculate, starched collars and hats. You were not allowed to have a hair out of place. Patients had first class treatment, good food, and even warm bed pans. I was very happy there but the wages were very poor.

My next job was in Broadstairs, Kent as a nurse in a convalescent home for children. I stayed there for a few years. My sister Ann had come to Birmingham from Ireland so I joined her. We shared digs in Bowyer Road Alum Rock ('The Rock', as they called it). A big change from nursing. I got a job as a conductor on the buses. Half the time I didn't know if I was at the terminus or in town.

The money was much better, life there was great and I soon made new friends. The dance halls were always packed with young Irish people. The Harp, The Shamrock, The Rosary and many more. I met my husband Paddy and we were married in the Rosary Church Alum Rock. We had three wonderful children, and like most people we had our ups and downs, but thank God more ups than downs. I made many friends both English and Irish and we still are enjoying a good life in England.

It seems a long time ago now since that wide eyed Irish lass waved goodbye to her parents, in Co. Roscommon, Eire.

CHAPTER EIGHT
THEY WERE CRYING OUT FOR US: THE 50s AND 60s

This classic photo of workers at Spaghetti Junction, Birmingham, in 1972 was taken by Brendan Farrell of the Irish Post. The priest in the centre with the hard hat is Father Daniel Cummins. From Derry, he was based at the Abbey in Erdington and he looked after the spiritual needs of the, mostly, Irish workers. Thanks to the *Irish Post*.

Irish workers played a major part in the rebuilding of Birmingham after the Second World War – and not just in the construction industry. They were prominent in factories, on the buses, in the hospitals and in many other crucial fields of economic activity. The active recruitment of Irish people to work in Birmingham began in 1941. So short was labour in Birmingham and so great was the need for workers for the war effort that ICI and Austin sent agents to the Republic of Ireland to sign up employees. So too did the Birmingham Transport Department. Mr T. Hayes was the personnel manager for the traffic division of the department and he went to Dublin in 1942 to set up an office, especially for the recruitment of conductresses. At this time, Irish workers

could not just enter the country. They had to have jobs to go to. Those taken on by the Birmingham Transport Department had a third class fare paid and were reimbursed their costs for photographs and travel permits. The training period varied from three to four weeks. So important were Irish workers that the chairman of the city's Transport Committee declared that, without them, the Birmingham transport system would collapse. (Letter to Joe McKenna, 7 March 1991).

With Ireland experiencing difficult economic conditions, the numbers of Irish people continued to grow after the war and by 1951 there were 36,000 of them in the city. Ten years later, this figure had expanded to 58,000. From 1943, the Irish Citizens' League and Advisory Bureau gave support for new members of the Birmingham Irish community. This was replaced in the 1950s by the Irish Information Centre in Moat Row in the Bull Ring.

Always in a Factory by Pearl Brophy

Pearl Brophy was one of the many Irish workers who came to Birmingham from the late 1930s as the pace of immigration to the city picked up. She came over to join her father as 'jobs at home were terrible'. From rural Cork, she brings to mind that 'didn't some people say that De Valera sold us? De Valera got 30 bob for every Irish person that came over. 'Cus they needed all the roads for building. The government here was crying out for Irish workers, especially on the roads.' Pearl's first job was in a factory and she was 'always in a factory since'. (Interview, *BirminghamLives Archive*, 1991-3).

Pearl Brophy.

Birmingham Always Lured Me Back By Breeda Harrison, nee O'Driscoll.

I left my home in Bantry, Co. Cork in March 1944 and lived ever since in Birmingham. Recruitment was on for workers and as my older sister was already here, I, though under the required age of 18 years, was allowed to travel by special permit. Luckily I knew my destination, normally it wasn't revealed until reaching a special centre in Dublin, when you had a medical and overnight stay, and in the early hours of the following morning, escorted to the ship sailing to unknown territory. It was all very daunting, but exciting. Someone in authority met the groups at the end of each leg of the journey, directing each one to the right train etc. and answering queries.

It was evening when I arrived at Snow Hill Station where I was met by my sister and friend. We boarded the No.2 tram to Erdington, where all three of us were billeted with a family. It was 'love at first sight' for me with the trams. I really enjoyed the rides and the sound of them. Too bad they were axed.

Next day I checked in at Aeroplane, Motor, Aluminium Castings factory in Wood Lane Erdington, AMAC for short, where my sister and friend worked in a stifling hot foundry, die-casting pistons for planes, dangerous work and terrible conditions. Imagine being thrown in at the 'deep end', when none of us had seen a factory, let alone worked in one. Luckily for me I was given a cleaner and cooler job in the Inspection Department. Despite the conditions, I enjoyed my time there, and everyone was friendly and most helpful, very much appreciated by an inexperienced lass far from home and missing family and friends, the sound and sight of the sea and mountains which to this day I still miss so much.

My first introduction to chips was in the AMAC canteen, I thought they were wonderful. The

Ned Grogan and pal helping to place the largest plate glass window in Birmingham at Marshall and Snelgrove, New Street. It was a huge window. Ned was from county Dublin and managed Shamrock Rovers Football Club. (Thanks to Ned's daughter, Carol.)

buildings and surroundings were all strange, as were the accents, sayings and customs and it took a little time to get used to them. Very shortly after my arrival the air-raid sirens went off. We were rushed out in the garden in the dark and urged into the shelter, assured steps were installed. To my horror they were missing and I fell into this black hole, ripping my leg badly on the sharp iron of the door. That was my first and, thank God, my only experience of air raid shelters. The end of the war was in sight and the raids eased off.

Our wages, after expenses were paid, didn't allow for much saving for fares home, but we were very fortunate to be issued with two travel vouchers per year, costing just 7s/6d each, enabling us to visit our families and reassure them that all was well with us. We had some good fun on very little money.

I spent a few years at AMAC until the restrictions on job changes were lifted. Dunlop was close by so my friend and I fancied a change and spent some happy years there in a much cleaner environment and our welfare was very important to the company. Food of course was still rationed but the works canteen served us well. At weekends and off-time we frequented the Queen Anne Café in High Street, Erdington, right opposite the Palace Cinema, where we parted with our limited funds on food and entertainment.

Breeda met her husband in that café. He was a Welsh lad named Phil, who had also come to Birmingham for work. They married in 1952 at the Abbey Church Erdington. In the early years, Breeda was 'very reluctant after holidaying, having to leave behind my beloved seaside and return to the "Big Smoke", but somehow Birmingham always lured me back, and it's been good to me. I've made some wonderful lasting friendships and despite the disasters attributed to the Irish, I've never experienced prejudice at any time.'

Tales of an Irish Nurse by Terry Tracey, nee Higgins

Terry left Ballindine, Mayo in 1952 to train as a nurse in Barnsley, after which she moved on.

In October 1953, after a holiday in Ballindine, I arrived at New Street Station, Birmingham (how many hundreds of Ballindine immigrants must have done the same?). I remember Michael Ruane meeting me at around 6 am – Matt (my brother) and the other Ballindine boys were on nights at Cadbury's. Thus started four very happy years at Selly Oak Hospital, and it is worth noting that out of nineteen members of my Preliminary Training School at least ten girls were Irish.

Though nursing has changed and advanced –

sometimes almost beyond recognition – one thing has remained constant, the companionship and friendship – some of my PTS colleagues became my life-long friends and several of them attended my retirement part in 1995. But I also remember how most of the English staff members showed us much kindness – in my forty plus years nursing I have never encountered any anti-Irish sentiments – in fact at the time of the Birmingham bombing tragedy I was asked to go on a stand-by rota to work at Birmingham Accident Hospital if needed. We worked extremely hard for little monetary reward (£7 a month as I remember), but we also played hard. Below is a typical Sunday duty.

On at 7.30 am, Mass at 9.30 during our half-hour coffee break, off at 2 pm in time to attend the afternoon dance at the Shamrock Club, Hurst Street, back on duty at 5 pm to 8.30 pm, then off to the Shamrock Club again, or one of the other Irish dance venues in the city. (I am sure some of the readers will recall catching the all-night service bus at Colmore Row). We then went back on duty at 7.30 am the following morning. Our official working week was 48 hours with much unpaid overtime in addition, and one day off per week.

Our local church was St. Edward's, Selly Park, and the parish priest, Father Corcoran from Tipperary, was very keen to get the Irish nurses and their friends to attend the Sunday hops. Several romances flowered during the singing of 'Faith of our Fathers', my own being one. I met my future husband Bernard at one of these dances.

But what is it like for the present day diaspora? Are they received with the kindness and courtesy with which we were, and do they integrate as we did? But no matter how settled and happy a life we emigrants carve out for ourselves we still feel love and affection for the land of our birth. I will never forget the time my father said to me on one

Terry Tracy (Higgins) during her 'training days' at Selly Oak Hospital, Birmingham, at Christmas 1955.

of my visits home, 'Terry, you will always feel the pull of the ould sod", and I do.

An Irish Man or an Irish Emigrant by James (Seamus) Reilly

Jim Reilly was born in Killeen, Dunsany, county Meath. A keen sportsman, he used to run about three miles into Dunshaughlin for boxing training under the guidance of a Garda sergeant.

Sunday mornings we used to play pitch and toss, then in the afternoons it was off to play or watch Gaelic games, i. e. football or hurling. We used to walk to school over fields sometimes in bare feet as our parents couldn't afford shoes or clogs. For our lunch we used to have bread dipped in milk and sugar. Dinner was spuds and butter, we used to churn our own milk to make butter and buttermilk. Times were hard then, but we used to enjoy ourselves for we did plenty of bicycle riding in the latter years. We used to pick the potatoes, weed the turnips, and snig them in the winter and oh it was cold on the hands.' Jim wanted to become a jockey but was too heavy and so, from the age of fourteen, he worked on a farm doing all sorts of work.

In 1953, I decided to come to England. My parents were not very pleased at the time, as I was the first of the family to leave home. I have five sisters and two brothers (who have both died).

James Reilly as a bus conductor in 1953 with his driver and pal Ray Cox.

On the 16th of June 1953 I caught the bus to Dublin got my train and boat ticket to Birmingham. Arrived at New Street early next morning. My uncle met me at the station got a Midland Red bus (169) to Shard End where I lodged in Longmeadow Crescent.

I started work with the Birmingham City Transport in July 1953 as a bus conductor at Washwood Heath Bus Depot as I was too young to drive. I enjoyed my time on the buses I met my wife on the buses (she was a passenger). I went to a dance at St Vincent's in Duddeston she was there and I had quite a drop of Guinness in me. Asked her for a dance and I told her my name was Paddy Magee and she didn't find out my real name until one of her friends asked her if she was still going out with Jimmy Reilly. (Oh did I cop out).

In 1955 Lea Hall Garage opened I worked there from day one for about 3 months until I went in the Army to do my national service, I joined for 3 years I was drunk when I signed for the extra year, but I enjoyed my spell in the army. Got demobbed in 1958 . . . and went to work for SPD (speedy prompt delivery) delivering Birds Eye Frozen food all over the Midlands. In 1959 I got married we have two sons, two daughters and four grandchildren.

In 1964, I went back to Lea Hall on the buses until I took voluntarily redundancy in April 1986 . . . It was a very good life on the buses for sport (social life was bostin).

I was joined in Birmingham by my eldest sister Nancy, then Peggy, Aggy and my brother Val. Didn't I cop out when they came over to Brum because I told them how good it was in England. I do look forward to going back to Ireland at least once a year to the house we were all brought up in and I still love mucking out the horses (even if its in my best suit).

Looking back over his life Jim knows that 'Ireland has great memories for me but what am I, an Irish man or an Irish emigrant? I owe a lot to Ireland but I think my home is now in England. With all my family brought up here in Brum, I think the answer lies there. I met and married a very good Brummie, have a nice family and of course the grandchildren are my pride and joy. I still keep in contact with old Ireland by reading the Meath Chronicle (which my sister gets weekly) and the odd telephone call to my sister in Ireland. There will always be Ireland in me.'

We Didn't Do Too Bad by Betty Campbell

Betty is from Athlone. She had a magical time there as a teenager, but was pulled by stories of Birmingham into emigrating.

Peggy Roper is one of James Reilly's sisters. For many years, Peggy was the well-loved gaffer of the 'Albion Vaults' in Nechells. So strong was her association with that pub that it was known as Roper's. On the weekend before she retired, hundreds of Irish and English Brummies poured into the pub to give her their best wishes for the future. Here Peggy is third from the right with her daughters, sister-in-law, and her close friends outside the 'Albion Vaults' on the last day.

My best friend, also called Betty, left the factory in 1960 and moved to Birmingham. I was devastated when she went. A year later she came home on holiday, and sitting by the banks of the Shannon, she enthralled me with stories of her 'lovely flat in Birmingham' and her job as a conductress on the buses. Needless to say, a week later I packed my job up, and arrived in Handsworth in June 1961. I can still feel the devastation when I looked around this dark, big room, cold even in June, I cried bitter tears, and wondered what had possessed me to come here!

I had to pick myself up, and within a week, I was working on the 15 & 17 buses from Liverpool Street garage a fully-fledged bus conductress. The passengers were asking me to tell them when we got to C&A. I did not have a clue, what C&A was, or were, in fact I did not have a clue whether we were going into town or out of it; when we missed our duty, which was quite often, we would be sent on the No 8, Inner Circle. What a crack that was, all the Paddies going to work, and asking 'me' to put them off at 'Stoney Lane'. It was 'no man's land' for me going around the Circle, so they could still be going around on it now: no use asking me.

How we survived in our Handsworth flat, I do not know. We were useless at managing our money, and we lived on spam and beetroot sandwiches! No wonder we all had figures like Kate Moss! My vivid memory is of the cold in this flat. Of course we never had enough money to feed into the gas meter. We would be searching in old bags and pockets for a shilling for the fire. Running up to the Hamstead Road at 3.30 am for the bus into work, a lot of fear was there as well. It's strange, but I still dream about that first flat we lived in – it usually ends in a nightmare.

I met my husband Colin, in St Francis Hall in 1963 and we married in 1965. We have two good sons, and we moved into Great Barr in 1967. The buses, the craic, the many, many friends I have made here, are very vivid in my mind. It's hard to believe, that I will have lived here now for more than 40 years. We lived to tell the tale, good and bad times. I look around my little garden, count my blessings and think 'we didn't do too bad'.

Very Grateful to Birmingham by John Kiely

John Kiely grew up in Pallaskenry, co. Limerick, where life was not too bad because the land was very fertile, but when he was eighteen he had some savings and decided to try his luck in England.

I arrived in Birmingham at about 6.30 am on a Sunday morning, 23rd January 1956, a cold and frosty start, but a kind couple (Brummie) saw my situation and invited me to their home at Six Ways, Aston. I had breakfast with them, and they showed me around the area, I found digs, a nice room fully furnished, and breakfast and evening meal for £2-12s-6d a week, by Six Ways, Aston.

Next morning I found out that ICI Ltd, Holford Drive, Perry Barr, were looking for workers, so I filled in the appropriate forms, passed the medical etc., and started work next morning at 7.30am as trainee caster and crane driver (overhead) at £16-10s a week, a 'small fortune' in that era! After a month's training, I passed the full safety tests of being efficient at casting brass, pouring the metal in to ingots (moulds), and a safe and responsible overhead Crane Driver!

My wages now went up to £23 per week, plus shift allowance, what a country!

I have great memories of ICI Ltd, but after 8 years, I had to change my job (on Doctors orders), as the heat and smoke was making my skin too dry, So I got a job at Rover Cars Ltd, Solihull as a Track Storeman, at another good wage (all days), so I took on a part-time job as well in the evenings in the theatres, props and fly's etc. I also got myself an Equity Card and worked as a 'walk on' actor in series such as 'Crossroads' (ITV) and 'The Newcomers' (BBC) at the Gosta Green Studios, by Aston College, now Aston University. I made great friends in 'The Newcomers' especially Wendy Richard.

I am retired now, but I shall always be very grateful to Birmingham and its friendly people. I am also a proud member of the RAOB, (Royal Antideluvian Order of Buffaloes), a Royal order!

I Worked with Some of the Best Mates Possible by Patrick Rowan

Patrick recalls hard times in his childhood in county Kildare where his father was a labourer finding a day's work with local farmers here and there. One of nine children, born in 1934, by the time he was five years old Patrick could set snares and traps to catch wild rabbits, which his mother would cook, mostly in stews. The family grew its own vegetables on the half acre of land that was part of their cottage and, when he was seven, Patrick was away from school for the summer months to work on the peat bogs.

In 1952 when I was 18 years old, my father and I were working for a company called Bord Na Mona, they saved and bagged dried peat moss which was and still is, sent all over the world for gardens and potting compost. In the September of that year, there was a cut back in production and I was made redundant . . . my sister was home on holiday from Brum, so I came back here with her. Two of my older brothers were bus drivers in Washwood Heath Garage, then I too wanted to be a bus driver. However you had to be 21 years old to take tuition.

I took a job in Aston, training as a brass finisher, 18 months later I was told I would have to do National Service in the army (Once an Irishman was resident in England for a certain time he was liable for national service). On completion of 2 years in this country, on 5th March 1955, I was sent to Omagh, Co. Tyrone for training, 4 months later, I was on my way to Cyprus for 18 months, which I enjoyed very much, scary but good. I was demobbed on 5th March 1957. I did not go back to brass finishing, I joined British Leyland as a sheet metal worker. I worked on the Morris Minor car for 18 years. Then I worked for the Jenson Motor Company for 3 years. I then joined Fisher and Ludlow for 3 years working as a sheet metal worker, working on Jaguar Cars and then I was made redundant in 1981.

I returned to Ireland in 1981 with my Birmingham wife and two daughters and built a lovely bungalow, learned to drive heavy machinery, bulldozers etc., work was very hard to find, so we returned to Birmingham in 1984. I worked for Jaguar Cars in Castle Bromwich until 1989 when I had to have major cancer surgery. It ended my working life; I am 67 now and keeping quite well.

When I look back at my humble beginnings in Ireland, hard work, poor education, then to Brum, rated 1st class soldier, 1st class sheet metal worker. I worked with some of the best mates possible and I keep in touch with lots of them still. The children in Ireland today know no hardship, as it is a very prosperous country. At Christmas I used to search the hedgerows for Guinness bottles, wash them to get one old penny back.

Committed to Her Work by Michael Talbot

Margaret Mary Talbot was born in 1931 in the village of Annagh, overlooking Tralee Bay, in Kerry. She and her boyfriend, John Joe, moved to Birmingham, where they were married at Corpus Christi Church, Stechford in 1953. John Joe was a lorry driver with the Salvage Department at the Castle Bromwich depot, whilst after a brief spell at the old Woolworth store in the Bull Ring, Margaret became an usherette at the Ritz ABC picture house in Bordesley Green. With the decline of cinema-going, this became a bingo hall.

Margaret Talbot with Norman Vaughan at the Ritz, Bordesley Green, late 1960s.

Margaret gained more responsibility and became assistant manager. In 1965 the bingo club was taken over by 'Mecca', a major entertainment company fronted by husband and wife team Eric and Julia Morley. The new owners refurbished the building with luxurious surroundings to attract customers with bingo, prize bingo, musical groups, light refreshments and, to attract crowds, celebrity appearances. Famous names that visited the Ritz included Norman Vaughan, the late comedian Arthur Hanes and Coronation Street's Elsie Tanner (Pat Phoenix). In 1976, Miss Jamaica (Cindy Breakspeare), who won the Miss World title, came to the Ritz to meet the patrons, sign autographs and call the numbers for a bingo game.

Totally committed to her work, Margaret played a major part in the success of the business. Regularly she would work from nine o'clock in the morning until the club closed at eleven o'clock at night. She and her family lived across the road from the building and when she was not at work she acted as key holder in case of burglary or flooding after the night-watchman was not replaced. A key figure in the local community, Margaret helped to organise Christmas dinners for up to 700 patrons who included senior citizens and other members of the community. There were trips to Blackpool to see the lights and to London to see the Miss World competition.

Margaret later moved to a new bingo hall at the Fox and Goose, Ward End, where she stepped back from management and became chief cashier. By now she was caring for her terminally ill husband. Margaret retired in 1996 and was featured in the *Birmingham Evening Mail*.

Same As At Home in Ireland by Betty Rose

Betty worked at the Birmingham branch of the National Bank on the corner of Colmore Row and Bennetts Hill Birmingham. It was opened on 1 June 1958 by the chairman of the bank, Lord Longford – who was then Lord Pakenham.

The Bank served to assist the Irish population in the City, the Irish businesses like Aer Lingus and Bord Failte who had offices in Birmingham and our Sisters and Fathers in the Catholic Church. We helped many Irish people with savings accounts in Ireland who came in with their little green books and wanted cash withdrawals – before the days of plastic and current accounts – and we would ring up the Irish branch perhaps in Sligo or Cork or Dublin and obtain permission to pay. Sometimes when we rang Ireland the Manager would be out fishing and the Clerk would have to go and find him!

The National Bank, Colmore Row and Bennetts Hill, c1958.

They were wonderful days in the Bank – my colleagues were all Irish – Eugene came from Dublin, Mac from Sligo and the Branch Manager – John Ansbro from Mayo. I still keep in touch with Eugene who has been back in Ireland for many years but he and his now wife – lodged in Birmingham and my Mother would not let Monica be married from lodgings and she was married from my home, looked after by my Mother a Brummy. As a Brummy and proud of it – we had a wonderful time working in those days – I stayed with the Bank for the whole of my working life – starting out with The National, an Irish Bank, and finishing after 33 years with The

Royal Bank of Scotland, a Scottish Bank – through various mergers in the 1970s etc. . . . The Irish people who came into our Branch were wonderful – we got to know them and their families and they trusted the Bank because it was the "same as at home in Ireland".

A Very Proud Man By Laura Grigg

John and Rose Connelly.

John Francis Connolly was the eldest of six children, growing up in Nahil, a homeland of Threemile House, co. Monaghan. His father expected him to work on the farm, a task he hated, so approaching sixteen in 1957 he replied to an advertisement in a local paper for trainee nurses at Highcroft Hospital in Erdington. John borrowed £5 from Granny McCaul and took the train to Larne to catch the boat to Stranraer. He found lodgings on the Witton Road, not far from the Sacred Heart Church.

He left Highcroft and worked for a while as a crane driver and was then employed on the buses, which is where he met mom, she was a clippie and he trained to be a driver. They married in September 1965 at St Mary and John's Church. Mom and dad left the buses and set up a business selling ice-cream, we had 4 ice-cream vans at one stage including one of the great big Superman vans.

As well as the ice-cream vans they had a small

shop in Mere Road in Erdington, it was not much more than a front room converted with a counter but it was the meeting place for most of the local residents and many a story can be told about the goings and comings of the customers.

They sold the shop to concentrate on the ice-cream business. Dad drifted into the fencing trade which he has continued for the last 20 + years. He has completed urban renewal, put up fences for the grand prix, security fencing at Winson Green, the list goes on.

My father is a very proud man and he always reminds us that he came to this country with a borrowed £5, which he repaid 5 months after he came. He owns his own house/hotel and industrial property and owes nobody a penny.

Although he never had the opportunity to gain qualifications he is a very intelligent man. So Carl not everyone came on the boat to Holyhead to seek employment on the building site with no firm job. Not much has changed on the labour market, we still recruit hospital staff from Ireland.

An Irish Doctor by Helen Price

Helen Price, a teacher at St Thomas Aquinas Catholic School, recalls many Irish doctors in Birmingham, one of whom was her father.

Dr Dermot Grogan was known as Dr J C Grogan (Jeremiah Christopher). He came to Birmingham from Dublin in 1953 and began his career in Yardley Wood with Dr Dennis Cadigan from Kilkenny. Dad got his own practice in 1956 at 149 Golden Hillock Road, Small Heath. This house/surgery no longer exists, having been demolished to make way for what is now 'Poet's Corner'! Dr Grogan was successor to Dr Foster-Sinclair who was retiring at that time.

In 1962 Dr Grogan and his family moved from

149 Golden Hillock Road to Arden Road, Acocks Green and Dr Grogan's practice was then further along Golden Hillock Road at numbers 67 and 69. This was two front rooms of an ex-patient of Dr Grogan's called William Barker. In 1972, Dr Grogan finally moved into practice with three other doctors in the Coventry Road Health Centre, Small Heath. ('Dad used to refer to this building as "Colditz"). It used to be an old dispensary. Here, he was in practice with Drs Brown, Coles and Ince until he retired in 1989.

Dad is disabled – lost his left leg in 1961 – so people may remember him walking with an artificial leg. When he retired, he had a hip replacement operation which went well. Although he has slowed down, because he still gets quite a bit of pain and discomfort, he's doing great for his age, watching all the sport, watching Tara TV and enjoying life still with Mom – Anna – and his six kids, sons and daughters-in-law and 10 grandchildren! Much to keep him busy.

A Legend. J. J. Gallagher

John Joseph Gallagher was the founder of the Bordesley Green development and construction company. Born in Mayo in 1911, he came to England when he was seventeen. Like so many of his fellows from the west of Ireland, he worked as a seasonal labourer. Then in the 1930s, he started as a driver for the construction company of R. M. Douglas. Hard-working and astute, Jack Gallagher bought his own lorry and transformed himself in to a major businessman. At first he operated in the hard core sector and acted as a subbie, but after the war he moved into demolition work and became involved in the massive redevelopment of Birmingham. His company became limited in 1955 and in the following years, Jack Gallagher bought land, became a house builder and engaged in civil engineering. Regarded as a legend, he died in 1994. His firm continues to thrive under the leadership of his five sons.

J. J. Gallagher was one of the main contractors clearing the old Bull Ring and the land for the inner ring road. The old Market Hall is on the right. (The late Michael F. Cann.)

'Cherish your family and be proud of your roots' By Joan Cunningham, *The Harp*

A much-valued councillor in Birmingham and honoured for his work for the community with an MBE, Matt grew up knowing very hard times in the Monto area of Dublin.

He's achieved so much down the years but he's the kind of man who doesn't let such accomplishments change his endearing and charming personality. He starts by speaking of his family, particularly of his love for his mom, Bridget.

'My mom was a wonderful woman. I feel so grateful to her for bringing us into this world and looking after us so well.' Sadly, she died in 1950 and I still miss her dearly today.

'Myself and my two brothers, Patrick and Brendan, were brought up solely by my ma and her close family, as dad decided to up and leave when we were just lads, leaving mom a single mother with three young mouths to feed.

'I wouldn't say we were well off but she did everything in her power to feed us, keep us clothed and try her hardest to give us a good upbringing.'

Upon reflection, the life and times of Matt Redmond would be an entertaining read for one and all – something for the future perhaps for this busy man? I reckon so. He surely is a busy lad. He spoke of the numerous committees he's been part of during his lifetime. One thing's for sure, he's made an enormous difference to the people of Birmingham in more ways than one. This was duly recognised when Matt was awarded an MBE. Even receiving such a decorative honour, he still plays it down.

'It's probably the most used MBE ever. Everyone I know has had their picture taken with it. I think of it for the people of Birmingham, not just for me. I enjoy sharing such a gratifying award with the community. It's as much theirs as it is mine.'

I think the most beneficial work Matt became involved with was heading the Road Safety Unit, which subsequently introduced the Drink Driving Campaign. No doubt this idea has helped save many lives down the years. Another string to his bow included Chair of Urban Renewal. During his chairmanship, Matt helped set up 'Warm, Safe and Secure'. The campaign was introduced to ensure the safety and wellbeing of the elderly by providing grants, free gas fires, gas checks and drafting in British Gas to help carry out the work Matt was also Chairman of the Cycling Advisory Route, chaired the committee for Housing Repairs and Maintenance - responsible for introducing Upvc to the majority of council houses in Birmingham and was the longest serving chairman of the Road Highways Transport committee.

His list of achievements is endless. It makes you wonder where this man gets his enthusiasm, drive and commitment in making a difference to people. He tells me: 'I must admit, I owe a lot of my success to my wonderful wife, Carol. She's been so supportive during our past 44 years together. Mine would have been a different story if it wasn't for her.

"I adore my children and ten grandchildren. Always cherish your family and be proud of your roots, Joan. I've lived by these two rules during my years and I haven't been let down yet.'

This is a deeply touching photo. It was taken, as were so many potraits in Birmingham, at Jerome's studio in Corporation Street. It is dated 1954, shortly after Matt had arrived in Birmingham. On the back is written 'To Aunt Molly and all the family with best wishes from Matt x x x x x.' Aunt Molly reared Matt after his beloved mother died.

CHAPTER NINE
MAKING BIRMINGHAM HOME

Eileen, Margaret, Peter, Ann, Frances and Michael Murray. (Thanks to the late Margaret Murphy, a true Irish Brummie.) The Murrays were an Irish family of four girls and two boys who all lived at 106 Ryland Street, Ladywood, from late 1943 until 1958. Their home was down the factory yard between Ryland Street Motors and the Hermetic Rubber Co. and they lived in a flat at the top of a block of offices which meant a climb of 40 stone steps to get in. The landlords were two brothers, Mr Peter Danks and Mr Robert Danks. The rent was 10s 6d per week.

My Life in Birmingham Has Been Good by Ann Coughlan

Ann Coughlan was born in 1930 in Limerick to a working-class family of seven boys and four girls. Sadly, four of the boys died - two at birth, one as a baby and the other as a toddler. Ann herself was only 3lbs when she was born and was not expected to live more than a year but 'I'm still here to tell the tale'. Unhappily, her mother died when she was 13. Her older sisters were in England and her brother was in the Army.

In 1947 my sister sent me the fare to come to Birmingham, which was £2/10s. As I had no work, my eldest sister was glad to get rid of us. So here I came. On a freezing cold morning in March 1947, I arrived at New Street Station, and was met by Mary, my sister. We got on a tram in Martineau Street, No. 8 to Alum Rock. I thought I was in a ghost town. Every building was bombed. They had just started cleaning up after the war. I couldn't believe my eyes at what I saw.

At midday on the day I arrived I was taken into town to the food office, got my ration book and identity card. On Monday, I started work at the GEC in Landor Street. It was my first job in a factory. I was so green I couldn't do the job properly. I had more scrap than good ones. My wages were 18s/6d. I stayed there for 3 months, and then I went to Hercules Bicycles. There were lots of Irish there so soon I made friends. We would go to the Irish dances at St Anne's and St Catherine's, The Abbey, Witton Drill Hall and The Rosary. Our Saturdays were spent in the Bull Ring and Town. On Sunday after Mass, we would go and watch the Gaelic matches. The Lickey Hills was very attractive. We really enjoyed our teenage years. One night at The Rosary dance I met a very nice lad, later to be my husband. We went out together for 5 years and then got married. We were very happy and had ups and downs.

Tragically, Gerry was killed whilst working on the scaffolding. Left on her own to raise five young children, Ann was fortunate to have the love of a wonderful next door neighbour who was 'just like a mom. She was always there for me'. After 21 years of widowhood, Ann remarried to Mick, whom her children really respect and get on with. With a good man and caring children, Ann is happy. She feels strongly that 'my life in Birmingham has been good. I am sure had I stayed in Limerick I wouldn't have had better'.

Her Heart was in Ireland Her Home was in Birmingham by Catherine Downes A True Irish Brummie

My dad came to England from Ireland with my grandfather in 1943. They both worked mending barrage balloons in Coventry. My mom arrived two years later. They got digs and married in February 1946 at St Mary & St John, Gravelly Hill. Their first home together was a bed-sit on Kingsbury Road. Then they moved into 2 rooms in the railway cottages at Station Road, Stechford, where he worked. My two elder sisters were born there in 1946 and 1951, shortly after that they moved to Rupert Street, Nechells.

During 1952 they moved yet again, this time to Alexandra Street, Ladywood, where I was born some 4 years later. They were back-to-back houses with a courtyard and shared toilets. The living room was directly through the front door with a tiny kitchen off that. Upstairs on the first floor was mom and dad's bedroom, and upstairs again to the attic where us three girls slept.

Our parish church was St Peter's RC off Broad Street, and we went to that school. Often the priest came round and we would have to be on our best behaviour. On Sunday mornings dad would red the step and whiten our shoes and off we would go to mass, complete with straw hat and ribbons in our hair. When we got back we would change our clothes and have breakfast. Dad usually went for a few pints at the Bell or the Shakespeare. After dinner we sometimes went to the fountain in Victoria Square, Summerfield Park or the Rezza (Edgbaston Reservoir), weather permitting, or just down the rec.

I remember everybody mucked in together and helped each other in the yard. I especially remember bonfire night. All the moms supplied something baked, spuds, toffee apples, periwinkles or just bread and dripping. My mom made the toffee apples and they were the best you ever tasted. St Patrick's Day was another cause for celebration. Shamrock used to arrive from Ireland days before, and we wore it to school pinned to a ribbon. It was all shrivelled up but so was everybody else's.

We moved to Washwood Heath into a maisonette in 1961 just after my brother was born. What luxury, a bath with taps and an inside toilet. Dad was working at Saltley Railway sidings by then, and although the pay wasn't much good, it was regular work and supplied a uniform (long coats for our bedspreads) and a few free passes a year for the trains and boat. Mom took us to Ireland for two weeks in the summer and dad went in September for a week. We only went altogether a couple of times.

A Little Back House with One Attic by Mary Whitaker

I came over from Ireland when I was eight years old and my mom and dad and my brother and sister had nowhere to live so we all went to St Patrick's Church on the Dudley Road and they put my mom and dad and three children in the big house on the reservoir where the Tower Ballroom is now. There was a man and his wife with their daughter. They took us in, their daughter was a nun. Then from there the man of the house gave us a little back house with one attic, one bedroom and one room downstairs on the cut in Ludgate Hill. There were two little houses on the front of Ludgate Hill and three houses on the back down an entry. We all played in a park in St Paul's Square.

My mom had three more kids which made six children living in that little house. We went to St

Peter's School off Broad Street, then to St Chad's Girls' School in Brearley Street. My brothers went to the boys' school in Shadwell Street behind St Chad's Church in Snow Hill. We were well known all over The Parade, Winson Green, Ladywood and Summer Lane.

My name was Molly Sharpe and there was Leo Sharpe, Jack Sharpe, Emma, Philomena and Patsy Sharpe. My brother's name is Les Sharpe and his son's name is Lee Sharpe and played for Man United. We all grew up poor. We had shoes from the Mail office.

The Kind of Mates You Don't Meet at This Present Time by L Trimble

I arrived in Birmingham in the fifties from Dublin like many of my mates. We would all meet at the Circle Cafe facing Stoney Lane, Stratford Road Sparkbrook. We had many happy times, on Sunday as you know the pubs did not open until twelve o'clock, but we used to have a drink at 10.30am in the territorial barracks in Golden Hillock Road, just up the road from the BSA.

My first job was at United Wire Works, Adderley Road, Digbeth at the beginning of 1951. I left my employment to take up work on laying gas mains for Whittaker's and Ellis. After two months we arrived at Henley in Arden, that is where I had a very lucky encounter.

I met this young girl who was just turned sixteen years of age. I was 27 years old at that time. Most of my mates and friends of this girl said it would not last because of the age difference. We are still together 49 years now. We had a large family, 5 boys and 4 girls, 18 grandchildren and 2 great-grandchildren, all born in Birmingham. I have not seen most of my mates for some years now, some of them have passed away.

I lived in digs with some great blokes. One was

Alec Farquharson, Alec and myself and some more of my mates lived in digs at 236 Stratford Road, Sparkbrook. We all used the Angel pub and had some great sing songs there as well as many scraps. We always stood by each other, when any one of our mates was arrested and brought to court, we all made a collection to pay their fine. They were the kind of mates you don't meet at this present time.

The thing that I remember most is how the Scots and us always stood together. We always stood by each other. I was glad I came to Birmingham to seek work and I have made many great friends who were born in Birmingham. It is a great city, which is why I have lived here for close on 50 years, and I would not choose to live anywhere else.

Settled into Life in the Big City by Frank Griffin

Frank was born in Mullingar, Co. Westmeath and moved to Kells, Co. Meath when he was about three years old. He served an apprenticeship as a carpenter and joiner with the local building contractor. When the firm could no longer keep him on he joined thousands of other young men on the dole. Unhappy with unemployment he emigrated to England, where 'they were crying out for skilled workers, especially in the building trade'.

So on 8th August 1955, I set sail for England on the 'Princess Maud' (God help us!) from Dun Laoghaire to Holyhead, and then on to my destination, Birmingham. I was lucky because I was able to stay in lodgings with lads I went to school with in Kells who already had jobs here and looked after me for those first few months when I felt so lonely after leaving home. I was aged 20 at this time.

I settled in the lodging house in Hatfield Road, off the Birchfield Road in Aston. After a few hours rest, one of the lads showed me to the nearest labour exchange at Six Ways, Aston where I applied for work and was issued with National Insurance cards, etc. and the address of a building firm named J Emlyn Williams in Victoria Road. I got a job straight away starting on 9th August and I was never out of work until the day I retired 43 years later, on 30th October, 1998.

I changed jobs only once from J Emlyn Williams to B Whitehouse and Sons Building Contractors of Monument Road, Edgbaston. They were eventually taken over by Tarmac Construction of Wolverhampton.

When I settled into life in the big city, I used to go dancing in the old Irish clubs: St Francis' in Handsworth, St Mary's in Whitehouse Street, The Shamrock in town and the Sacred Heart in Witton Road, where I met my wife Edna, a Birmingham girl. We had great enjoyment at these dances, where the strongest drink was a glass of pop or a cup of tea in the interval. When I had been in England for a couple of years, I was called up to do national service for two years in the army . . .

After demob I settled back into 'civvie' street and lived through, and felt part of, so many dramatic changes in Birmingham, especially during the building boom of the sixties . . . I watched the old 'Bull Ring' being demolished and the 'new and exciting' markets area springing up of which everyone was so proud, especially when Prince Phillip came to declare the project open. Alas time has exposed the mistakes again and now I'm witnessing the pulling down, once more of the Bull Ring area. Let's hope the planners and designers get it right this time and regenerate the market spirit that will always thrive in the people of Birmingham and the surrounding districts.

As the years went by, I began to realise how tolerant and kind hearted the Birmingham people were to the Irish and other immigrants who came to the city in great numbers. We became part of the city life and up to the present day, if you see three people standing talking, at least one will be Irish or be of Irish descent. The only time I felt ashamed to be Irish was the day after the Birmingham Pub bombings in 1974. I was not made to feel this way by my neighbours or the people in the road where I live or by my workmates. But I could not help feeling so guilty, if that is the right word to use, after such a terrible outrage against ordinary people having a night out in the city centre. This was a test of tolerance and kindness, which the Birmingham people continued to extend to the Irish community at this time and of which they can be justifiably proud.

Edna and I were married twenty years and just when we thought that we would never have a family, our son Kieran was born (our only child). His hard work at Handsworth Grammar School gained him a place at the University of Birmingham graduating with a 2.1 masters degree in Mechanical Engineering. We are so proud of him.

The pinnacle of my years at work was when I met the Queen at the opening of the Gas Hall in Edmund Street, which is part of the Birmingham Museum and Art Gallery. I was the Project Manager for Tarmac-Refurb who were carrying out the refurbishment of the Old Gas Hall and returning it to its former splendour. I was chosen to represent the building contractors.

I felt this to be a great honour for myself as an Irishman, my family and the company I worked for. I never thought as I left Ireland in 1955, the son of an Irish postman, that one day I would meet and talk to the Queen of England in Birmingham.

Left to right are Mick Donnelly, Auntie Etta Donnelly, Karen Garry as a baby, Grandad Lawrence Carroll and the arm of Karen's nan - 'Lil Carroll'.

The Irish Family by Karen Garry

My Mom, Rita Garry, christened Margaret Carroll, was born 20th December 1938 in Dublin. Earlier that year, my grandfather, Lawrence Carroll, had migrated to Birmingham to work at British Timkin in Rocky Lane, Nechells. Mom was born after he'd gone & stayed in Dublin with her elder sister, Elizabeth, known as Etta, the following year when my Nan, Lil, joined my Grandad over here.

Mom & Etta were cared for by my great-grandparents for the next couple of years while Nan & Grandad worked to set up a home. They visited Birmingham a couple of times in that period and then, in 1941, they were coming over for good. Nan came to Dublin to fetch them over on the mailboat. Aunt Etta, who was five, remembers that the boat was attacked by aircraft and Nan was clutching both her and my Mom, who was two, to her as she struggled down the gangplank to disembark. She remembers that the Red Cross were waiting to help them off and gave them a cup of tea in a hut on the dockside.

Then they strapped up my Nan's ankle as she'd twisted it coming off the boat and the heel had come off her shoe.

Nan and Grandad had set up home in a house on Victoria Road, Aston next door to Greasley Norton's Bakery but Mom and Etta hadn't been there long when they were bombed out of it in a raid. The house was too badly damaged to move back in to. So then they moved to Park Lane, Aston where my Mom, Etta and their younger brother and sister grew up. It wasn't a particularly Irish neighbourhood, in fact they were called 'the Irish family' in Park Lane at that time.

They had to walk to and from Park Lane to St Joseph's School on Thimblemill Lane, Nechells, four times every day - as they came home at dinner time and Aunt Etta, being the oldest, had to ferry the younger ones across the main road at Aston Cross. Really, although born in Dublin, my Mom grew up here and identified herself very much as a Brummie - she would never have lived anywhere else.

Very Fond Memories of Aston by Jim Doyle

Jim was born in 1937 in a four-storey tenement house in the Coombe in the heart of Dublin. At the age of seventeen he left Dublin for Leeds, but found it dismal and came to Birmingham.

I lived, at first, with my cousin on Whitehead Road, Aston. She even had a T.V. set which knocked me over. It was about 6" square at front and about 3 foot in depth. I worked at the goods station in Hockley but the money was not so good, so I ended up in Fisher and Ludlow driving an overhead crane. I had left my cousin's house and lived in digs in Dolman Road.

I have very fond memories of Aston in the 1950s. The picture houses I used to frequent were 'The Orient' at Six Ways, Newtown Palace, The Villa Cross, The Odeon Perry Barr and The Birchfield.

The dance halls I used were The Albert Hall, where I was thrown out more than once for jiving!, and The Burlington Hall which was beside the Aston Hippodrome. I went to the Hipp more than once and remember seeing 'Jane' and her sausage dog Fritz!

Beer was cheap but scrumpy was cheaper and when we were short mid-week, I bought a pint at 7d. For food, 'The Blue Star' Café gave you sausage and mash for 2/6d. I also got meals in Victoria Road. There you could buy chips, beans two slices of bread and a cup of tea for 11d. For ${}^{1/2}$d you got an egg as well!

Both a Real Credit to the Irish by Ann Shakespeare

Mom and Dad arrived over here in Birmingham, from Southern Ireland, separately in the April of 1950. Dad had come over to his sister's wedding in Birmingham and mom was "recruited" in Ireland to work on the trams. Mom's name is Bridget Kelly from Galway (McMahon then) and dad is Gerard Kelly from Roscommon. Mom came from a family of three and dad from a family of eleven (he's the baby).

Mom saw an advert in the local paper in Galway that there were jobs going in Birmingham, England. These jobs were on the trams with cost of ferry and "digs" arranged thrown in. She had to travel up to Dublin to attend an interview and medical and then her travel over was arranged. She arrived in Liverpool with about six other Irish folk, none she knew, and they were met and put on a train to Birmingham. Here another lady met them, bought a meal for them all and took them to their "digs". Of course the "digs" left a lot to be desired as there was 16 of them in all and a lively bunch to say the least, with no privacy as you can imagine with such a large crowd. The meals too were sometimes eventful and once they had the left overs from the night before dished up for breakfast!

Bridget Kelly, née McMahon, clippie, 1951.

Mom started her training to be a "clippy" /conductor on the trams. No other badges or pins were allowed on the uniform only the depot/clippy number worn on the lapel. They were trained for 'about a week or two' and then sent to the nearest depot, given uniforms and so the story began of life on the trams. Mom and dad said many a romance/ marriage started on the trams and indeed my mom and dad met here too as dad was a conductor on the trams too.

My mom talks of cycling to work at 4 o' clock in the morning, often almost falling off her bike because it would get stuck in the tram lines in the dark. She said the only people around then were the odd policeman and she was stopped once for having no light on her bike, but he let her go as she was late for work.

She also talks about a sweet shop, on the corner near the Miller Street Depot, where the lady would supply sweets to most of the tram workers and always 'throw in a few extra' even though they were on ration. Mom also said many a time she would 'swap' her sugar, or such ration, with another worker if they needed something that day and had run out.

Mom and dad lived in rooms in Aston when they worked on the trams and their tram was the No 2 from Erdington to Steelhouse Lane. They had many a hard time and were living in what was called 'rooms' with a landlady who could be fierce. When we were small we would often spend happy hours in Aston Park as the enclosed photos show.

Mom left the trams in 1953 as she was pregnant with my sister and dad stopped when the buses came on and he then went to work in Alcan Booth in Kitts Green. It was hard work in the 'foundry' in Alcan's, with shifts and he worked hard, but here again he met and worked with a great group of men, many of them Irish lads, who acted like an extended family to him. Many sadly who are now no longer alive today and very sadly missed but remembered well.

Mom and Dad are both a real credit to the Irish and would 'give you the shirt off their back' if needed and we love them both dearly, and their five grandchildren too! They are living in Castle Bromwich now and in their 70s.

Edward Joseph O'Shaughnessy. A Popular Man by E. O'Shaughnessy.

Edward Joseph O'Shaughnessy was raised in a poor family in Limerick. One of four children he never knew his father as he died shortly after he was born. His mother remarried but his stepfather also died and Edward often told how he would eat raw swede, dug from their vegetable patch, for his dinner. After a couple of poorly-paid jobs and realising that the future looked pretty grim, he travelled to Belfast to join the RAF in 1944. Edward served for three years in the Middle East. After the war he joined his wife-to-be in Lincoln and worked in a factory.

Bridget and Gerard Kelly with daughters, Elizabeth and Ann, in Aston Park, 1959.

During the early '50s he moved to Birmingham, as my mother's sister had told them that there was plenty of work to be had. They were married at St Patrick's church on Dudley Road and their first home was in rooms on the Stratford Road. Their first child was born, Sylvia and, after lobbying the council, he secured a back to back council house at 10/144, Wheeler Street, Lozells. The rest of their family were born there, Patricia and Edward junior, by this time he was working for the BSA (Birmingham Small Arms) in the paint shop.

He quite regularly worked double shifts back to back to boost his earnings until he collapsed from exhaustion and was 'laid up' for some time. I remember him telling me how he had been the one who had sprayed and put the finishing touches to the motorbike used in the James Bond film 'Thunderball'. After 27 years he was made redundant as the company crumbled under the onslaught of the Japanese motorbike industry and poor customer satisfaction.

He then worked for a while for a spin off company NVTG Engineering. The family had now moved and lived in a new development, built in Ladywood, in a maisonette. He left NVTG Engineering and started work for International Plates Strip in Tyseley until again he was made redundant in his late fifties, eventually joining a company called Field and Grant, based just out of the city centre, where he returned to his craft of paint spraying.

They had again moved house and now lived in another new development in Spring Hill, finally getting a house with a front and back garden. When he was sixty seven he finally retired from Field and Grant, but wouldn't rest and started a part-time job, with Forward Trust in Edgbaston. He was employed for five afternoons a week to deliver post and paperwork between floors and also as an odd job man. He fell ill in January 1995 and he asked me to write his resignation and hand deliver it, ten weeks later he had passed away and the requiem mass was held at St Patrick's, the parish he had returned to and the church where he was married some 46 years previous.

He always called Limerick his home and would return on an infrequent basis, using Slattery's Travel from the Irish Centre in Digbeth, to fish the Shannon river with his nephew, see his sister Eileen, drink Guinness, sing Irish songs and 'shoot the breeze' . . .

During his life he was a popular man who sang and played the mouth organ, in the early years playing for loose change on the streets of Limerick. He entertained his friends at many pubs and clubs over the years, regularly doing a 'turn' at the Oratory Club in Plough and Harrow Road on a Saturday night. He was a humorous man, with simple tastes - always with a smile on his face and a mischievous glint in his eye and undoubtedly he is still singing, entertaining and making folk laugh somewhere.

Living in Lodgings

Margaret McNicholas lived nearby in Braithwaite Road. She came over from Ireland in 1933, aged nine, having lived until then in county Sligo. The reason for this was because her father had joined the Irish Guards on 1st January 1940 and her

Before the Second World War, this house in Grantham Road, Sparkbrook, was the home of the late *Evening Mail* columnist Vivian Bird. A formerly middle-class area, many of the homes were turned into lodging houses after 1945. In 1963, 21 people lived here, including two Irish families and one West Indian family.

mother believed he was with other women. So in the March of 1942 she and the five children arrived in Kilburn.

Thomas McNicholas, Mary's husband-to-be, had lived in county Mayo, but arrived in Gloucester, England, in 1946, where he worked on a farm. He had to come to England because, as the eldest child, he was required to send money back to the family. Thomas eventually worked in the construction industry around England before settling in London, due to his marriage.

The McNicholas couple left London in 1956 due to their family claiming that there was plenty of work in Birmingham. They went on to live in Braithwaite Road in Sparkbrook, Moseley, Park Road in Hockley, Rodway Street in Aston and Perry Common.

Living in the Irish Community by Teresa Keenan

Teresa's Dublin parents came to Birmingham in 1939. She was born two years later in Heathfield Road. All her life, Teresa has lived in the Birmingham Irish community.

I went on to marry a Dublin man, Sean Keenan, who I met at The First Garryowen. An old hut when Brendan Joyce first started in the early 60's. We also used to dance at the Casino in Corporation Street, by then I was living with my parents in Erdington (I went to the Abbey School).

Travellers off Ingleby Street, Ladywood 1967. I am conscious that the voice of Irish travellers is missing from this book. Silent to outsiders about their own lives, travellers only seem to gain attention with negative publicity. There is a need to redress the ballance.

My husband, Sean, was a schoolboy boxer in Dublin, and when he arrived in this country with his best childhood friend, Tommy McEvoy, also a well-known boxer, they boxed for Ladywood Boxing Club. Tommy McEvoy was an Irish and British champion. Also at that club was Paddy Lynch, now a wealthy man who owns Lyndon Scaffolding Company, and who is a boxing manager and Dave Tully who has done endless work for youths in Ladywood, and my husband who also is a professional trainer.

All these lads came here very young and were very wild, we used to drink in the scrumpy

houses in the back streets of the Bullring. Then they would probably end up having a fight or two, maybe getting done for being drunk and disorderly and a fine on Monday morning, but they all did a bit of work on the building sites or where they could get it. If times were tough they slept in the Salvation Army and I would take all the dirty washing for mom to do for them.

The most important thing for them was to send money home to their parents every week . . . My husband and Tommy McEvoy were known as hard men because of all their drinking and fighting, but that's what it was like then for survival. There was a lot of hard men in Summer Lane, mostly Northern Irish men, Paddy Fields, Peser Green. I could go on and on, but for all their fighting ways it was always clean fighting (fist fighting), no weapons or dirty fighting, and they'd always shake hands a week later.

Sean still does door work on Broad Street, Tommy McEvoy has arthritis in his feet and still likes his pint, but he is a very well read, intelligent man with a brilliant brain, had he been educated.

Keeping the Links Between Birmingham and Wexford by Eddie Dunne

Eddie Dunne grew up in the historic parish of Oulart in Worth, co. Wexford in the 1940s. Life was tough, yet simple. Eddie's father was paid a pittance and his mom suffered badly with asthma. Like others, Eddie picked blackberries in season and trapped and snared rabbits. He recalls that while 'we never went hungry, our clothes were shabby, holidays were a myth and Daddy Christmas never came'.

Eddie left school at fourteen to work on a farm for two shillings a day. A year later his parents were distraught when he got a job in Dublin at Bolands Mills. He still sent money home and his biggest delight was watching the faces of younger family members as he handed out little presents on return visits. Dublin was heaven, with its dance halls and cinemas. Because of poor pay and a job shortage, sadly Eddie left Dublin for a job as a kitchen porter in Lancashire. Through hard work and determination he worked his way up to 2nd Chef. Then after a spell in Pilkington's Glass Works, in September 1960 he decided to head for London.

But a last minute change of plan to stop over in Birmingham would change my life forever. On arrival I found that the corporation were looking for Bus Conductors with the opportunity to train as Drivers. It was a chance not to be missed. Within weeks of starting, I would meet my wife Maureen and in August 1962 we were married in her home parish of Annyalla, Co. Monaghan. The music provided at the reception was by Seamus McMahon and Tom McBride, who soon after, became famous as Big Tom and The Mainliners. After much illness, my mother sadly died, 6 months prior to our wedding, age 58.

In 1964 and 1965 we were delighted when our two daughters Caroline and Geraldine were born. Both joined the nursing profession and became RGN's working at hospitals in the Greater London area, where they are now married. Our only son, Colin, born in 1968 received an Irish Post Award in 1998 for his achievements in Irish Dancing. Although he qualified as a chartered accountant, he is probably best known for his role in Riverdance.

A snap decision to leave Lucas in 1974 was not in the best interest of family life, as my new job for a building firm involved much travel and living away from home . . . In 1977 I moved to Land Rover Solihull where I remained for 22 years. The opportunity to retire two years early was gratefully accepted.

In 1998 I was honoured by Wexford Corporation, when I was made a member of the Wexford '98 Senate. Senators are not politicians, but a

fraternal organisation that re-convened in 1998, two hundred years after the rebellion of 1798 when the people of Wexford formed its own Government of four Protestants, four Catholics and five hundred Senators in a fight for democracy. However, this was short lived and one month later overthrown. This honour was given to me for keeping the links between Birmingham and Wexford through the County Association.

A Little Ireland by Maggie Bell

Maggie's grandparents, the McDermotts, lived in Monument Road, Ladywood. They died before she was born. Their daughter, Maggie's mom, was born in Limerick. She and her sister each married Birmingham men.

We used to use a couple of fish and chip shops especially on Fridays, the main one, was again an Irish family friend of my parents, Mr and Mrs Wynne. They had a shop in Clarke Street, where we used to have to queue for at least an hour before they opened. I went to the Oratory School, so it was out of the school house, we lived opposite 'park gates' in Monument Road (Chamberlain Gardens), get changed, get some money and up to Mrs Wynne's, my mouth is watering just to think of it.

We had a 'Little Ireland' around us, there were quite large houses in Monument Road and Noel Road that had a set of steps up to the entrance, were owned by a Mrs Ryan, Mrs Hughes and Mrs Baker. They had all the Irishmen who were mainly builders living in them. If one passed early in the morning – I sometimes met them coming back from parties, or going to early mass!!, all you would be saying was 'hello Seamus, hello Patrick'.

Sundays at the Oratory were a hoot, I went to a late Mass, they would all stand at the back and as soon as Mass was ended it was a rush up to the

Ivy Bush on the corner of Hagley and Monument Road, which is still there, or the Roebuck was not very big, they used to congregate outside with their pints on window-sills. I used to hate passing there, you can imagine what they used to say to me, I was a little younger and quite slim and very up to date with fashion as mom was a dressmaker.

My Life was the Richer by Queenie Monaghan

Hailing from Rosbawn, Tinahely, in county Wicklow, Queenie grew up in a poor family because her father had suffered an accident and was unable to work. When she was sixteen she decided to leave for England with a friend who had already emigrated. With a half a crown for her fare lent from an uncle, a shilling for spending and an old cardy from an aunt in place of a coat, Queenie set off for Dun Laoghaire.

I thought my heart would break when the boat sailed away from Dublin. We were on the Princess Maud. There were some black and white cows on the bottom deck and people were getting sick on them. I had a brother Joe in Birmingham so I went to live with him. I got a job in Hercules at Manor Mills in Aston. Ten shillings a week. With my first money I had to send my uncle back 2s 6d.

I started going to Saint Vincent's Dance Hall in Vauxhall where I met my husband Chris, a Leitrim man. We got married in '51 in Ireland. We had three sons, twins David and Alan and Paul. We had our ups and downs but I would not change a day of it.

We had a bad time when the bombs went off in Birmingham. Our friends did not like us. They thought we were all bad. But who could blame them, that terrible loss of life. But I must say my Brummie neighbours were great people, always there to help with hearts of gold. We stayed friends all our lives with most of them.

Birmingham is my home now. My husband lies in English soil and I will be with him when my time comes.

I do remember seeing in a window 'No Irish need apply'. My brother told me it was because they did not understand the Irish. I believed him but now my sons tell me they are Irish Brummies. They all married second generation Irish girls and I am very proud of them all. My life has been the richer because of the people I have met in Birmingham.

CHAPTER TEN
WONDERFUL TIMES: DANCES AND FUN

The Pride of Erin Social Club 1950s.

The Pride of Erin Social Club by Patrick J Doyle.

After the war, when sources of entertainment were limited, a number of Irish lads had the idea to run Irish dances to provide an alternative night out rather than going to the pub in order to meet and make friends. They discovered that school halls could be hired from Birmingham Education Committee for approximately £3 per week and it was decided to hire Hope Street school for Saturday night dances. The first was held in February 1947 under the style of The Pride of Erin Social Club and was a great success.

On the first night everyone gave their names and addresses. 500 membership cards were purchased and handed out at the next dance. The Pride of Erin SC soon began to run dances on Sunday night as well at Hope Street and then on Tuesday night above Burtons, the tailors at the junction of Stratford Road and St Johns Road Sparkhill (a venue which later became the Head Quarters for John Mitchells GAA Club).

The original organisers were Dubliner Eddie Hegarty, Limerick man Harry Hackett, Mayo man John/Paddy Doyle together with Eddie Canning (Mayo), Andy Driscoll (Cork) followed by West of Ireland men John Gavin and John Reilly. To help advertise and personalise the club a banner was made by a Northern Ireland man named Armstrong who lived in Sparkhill. Unfortunately the banner, which can be seen in the photo, was lost since the Club ceased.

The main band was Matt Egan's. Matt played the saxophone and fiddle and they were all good musicians (including an excellent drummer). The second band was led by Billy Ryan and the Club had guest bands from time to time who often came over from Ireland. The photo shows a ceili band from County Galway called Loughrans Slopes. At that time there were numerous good Irish musicians living in the Midlands and this was reflected in the quality of the bands.

The dances were strictly controlled with a strong emphasis on good doormen. No alcohol was allowed on the premises and no admission after 10 p.m. (without a pass-out) and admission was normally 2s 6p (12 1/2p).

Special events such as St Patrick's Day saw dances held at Saltley Baths which could accommodate more people as the attendances were regularly close to recommended hall capacity.

However during the 50s the concept of large clubs with alcohol licences spread from London and dances in school and church halls lost their appeal. Gradually The Pride of Erin Social Club (and others like it) fell away as an active organisation although the memories of those days lives on.

The Harp and The Shamrock by Fred Mercer

In the 50's there were a number of Irish clubs in Birmingham, but the two that I was associated with were the Harp in Walford Road, Sparkhill and the Shamrock in Hurst Street in the heart of the city. Both places shared the same boss, Matty Burns, who was the Heavyweight All-in Wrestling Champion of Ireland and fought as Mike Burns. Matty did not look like a heavyweight, mainly

An evocative photo of a group of Irish Brummies outside the 'Red Lion' on 'The Lane', the Ladypool Road, Sparkbrook. Taken in 1957, it belongs to Willie Hughes, a member of a large and well-known Dublin family who settled in Durham Road, Sparkhill, just before the Second World War. Inter-married with other Dub families like the McGarrys and the Byrnes, the Hughes family were well-respected in Sparkhill and Sparkbrook.

Featured on this photo is Thomas Hughes, Billy's dad, who is in the front row and second from the left. To his right is his cousin, Christy Gannon, a member of another noted Dublin family locally. The lady is Kay Mullins and her husband, also a Dubliner, is Johnny Mullins who stands on the right and is wearing a blazer. Their daughter, Kathleen, is in front of Harry Gillan. Harry is from East Belfast and settled in Brum soon after the Second World War. A passionate Villa fan, as is his mate Billy Hughes, Harry recalls that this photo was taken after Villa won the FA Cup in 1957.

Harry also palled up with my Uncle Ron, who sadly died in 1958 aged 31. My Grandad Chinn used to drink in the 'Red Lion' and Harry tells me that when he found out that the Belfast man was a Villa fan, Grandad sent over a tray of halves of mild for Harry and his crowd. In those days, older Brummies tended to drink 'cow's calves' rather than pints. Also in this photo is Bobby Duffy, who is the tall bloke on the left. He was another Belfast bloke, as was Hughie Owens - whose head can just be seen at the back on the left.

due to his balanced physique. I got to know Matty quite well and he was greatly admired by me as a 'no bull no nonsense' kind of person.

I understood that I was the first trombonist to play in the Harp. At the Harp we played the normal ballroom dances plus the ceilidh music for the dances such as 'The Siege of Ennis' or 'The Walls of Limerick'. On my first night when it came to the Irish dances, Matty stood over to the side of the ballroom to listen and see how I would handle these. I started to play in unison (together) with the trumpet and clarinet, which made the trumpet player Bill Foley say to me:

'Fred, the punters thought it was marvellous to play this stuff on trumpet. God knows what they'll think with you playing it on trombone'.

This photo was taken in 'The Shamrock' club, Hurst Street on Saint Patrick's Day 1968 when Paddy Martin and his pals went there after the parade for some light refreshment and the signing of autographs. Paddy is kilted on the left and is with Tom and Kathleen Maguire and their three children, Kathleen, Kevin and Brian. Tom was from Ballinyaugh, county Cavan and was a former pipe major of the Birmingham Irish Pipe Band. Sadly Tom passed away. The previous Saturday night the band had performed at the Town Hall with Johnnie McEvoy and other artists. Paddy himself is now living back in Ireland.

However, this did not impress Matty who came over to me and said, 'D'you think ya can play that thing like the drone on a bagpipe?' He was absolutely right of course, so I played long notes on the tonic and dominant of the tune which did not require me to double the other instruments. Matty later bought some manuscript books and asked me if I would write out the ceilidh music for the English musicians in the band – the Irish members knew these tunes and required no music.

At the Harp there were two brothers, Seamus and Mike Dunleavy the bouncers (just in case there was any trouble). They later travelled on the wrestling circuit as a 'tag team' as well as fighting solo. I would give them a lift home and when they got out of the van, they would shake the van nearly to pieces; all in fun of course.

Many a Good Happy Night's Dancing by Joe Thewlis

Joe hails from the little village of Carramore, which is two and a half miles from Roscommon town on the main Athlone Road. His dad was a labourer and Joe had various jobs before coming to Yorkshire in 1957, where he worked as a potato picker and then on the sugar beet crop. After a time on the roads, Joe came to

A dance in the Old Sacred Heart Hall, Grange Road, Aston about 1960. Joe and his wife are in the photo.

Birmingham in 1959, where he married the late Bridie O'Connor from Ardagh, county Limerick in the Sacred Heart church, Witton Road. He has worked steadily since then, most recently as a bus driver with West Midlands Travel based at Perry Barr Garage. He still goes to Ireland regularly but has lost some interest in it since his wife died for 'it doesn't seem the same going without her'.

I will tell you an amusing story of the day I left home to come to England. I had arranged to meet my mate Paddy Kelly at the train station on

The Harp and Shamrock clubs Tug-o-War Team 1961, taken by Joe Murray of Murray's Studios. Back row left to right are J. Keegan (Offaly), P. Convey (Mayo), S. Ruane (Mayo) and M. Byrne (Kerry); and on the front are L. Creighton (coach), D. O'Donnell (Roscommon), Martin Gaffey (Roscommon) and T. Kiernan (Roscommon). The team's colours were green and gold with the harp and shamrock on the crest.

Skating Around in My White Coat by Jimmy Loughran

Jimmy Loughran grew up in north Dublin. He started boxing when he was eight and won the Dublin Schoolboys Championships in 1956. During that period, he met two of Ireland's well-known names, Detective Officer Jim (Lugs) Brannigan and Spike McCormick. Jimmy's Uncle Freddie, who lived in Anderton Park Road, Moseley, came home for a holiday and asked Jimmy to go back with him for a holiday. Jimmy has written about the leaving in a poem.

The Exile

A cold winter's October night
He left old Dublin Town
Sailed on board
The Princess Maude
The meanest ship around

Wet wooden gangways
White sheets flapping
Fine damp salty spray
Clinging to each body

His young ear picks up
A different sound
Above the din of the roaring sea
Fiddlers and the craic
The Irish enjoying their outward track

At last the engines
Went quite dead
He guessed
They had reached Holyhead

He left the ship
With no regrets
With sandwiches
Of ham
To last him
On his final journey
To the City of Birmingham

the day of departure. I never told my parents I was leaving because I didn't want to upset them. So I left for work that morning as usual in my working clothes. I had already hidden some good clothes away, which I picked up on my way to the station. I changed into my good clothes at 7.15 in the morning in the open air in Roscommon Golf Links, caught the train and sent my parents a telegram from Dublin to say where I had gone. I wouldn't do it now as I am a parent myself and realise they must have been heartbroken, but you don't think like that when you are young. . . .

This country has been very good to me and I would not run it down to anyone. I have never been out of work since I came here and have no complains whatever. Both my wife and I spent many a good happy night's dancing in the Shamrock in Hurst Street, also the Masque in Walford Road, Sparkhill, the Garryowen in Wordsworth Road, Small Heath, St Mary's in Whitehouse Street, Aston Cross, St Catherine's School Hall in Bristol Street and St Anne's, Alcester Street. Then off to Glebe Farm on Sundays to watch the Gaelic matches. I remember years ago in Brum, every Easter Monday, I think, two of the top County teams in Ireland would play a big match in Perry Barr. I think it's where the Dog Track is now. It used to be packed for the match. Many happy memories, Carl, too numerous to mention.

He found most people
Very friendly
In shop
And in town
They were not
Really bothered
Which country
He had come from

Over forty years
He looked at many
Irishmen here
Sometimes
Shedding a quite tear
Pretending
To be happy
But
Really missing
Their own country
So dear

Jimmy found a job in the Bantam Motorcycle Assembly section at the B.S.A. in Golden Hillock Road, Small Heath. He had never seen so many people in one place at the same time. Jimmy used to give his wages to his auntie who gave him back pocket money. He supplemented this by working at the Embassy Roller Rink at night-time, doing anything from hanging up coats, playing the records, or just watching for any problems arising. It was at the Embassy that Jimmy met his Brummie wife Lynda: 'She was only 14 years of age and I was just a young lad of 16 years'. In later years, Jimmy became active in the Labour Movement.

The 60s Were Wonderful Times by Mary Hickey

Mary comes from Mallow, County Cork. She was the eldest of seven children. Her dad was a farm labourer and her mother often helped out, making hay, thinning beet and milking cows. The family was very poor but happy and united. After five years in service in Ireland, Mary arrived in Birmingham in 1959.

Jimmy Loughran at the Embassy, late 1950s.

I worked for a family in Bunbury Road, Northfield, then I worked for the Head Matron at Yardley Green Hospital. I later moved to Handsworth, and with my sister, Kathleen, began work as a power press operator, at Cheney's in Factory Road, Handsworth. We lived in lodgings, doing our own cooking, it was a happy time, we made many friends and went dancing to the Shamrock Club, The Harp, St. Francis, and also St. Chad's. I was in the 'Legion of Mary' at St Francis Handsworth. We served the teas at the dances and loved Friday nights dancing to The Rooney Brother's Showband from Sparkhill. They were a brilliant group – the 60s were wonderful times.

Skimming the Floor. Granny Wood

For many years, I have dearly wanted a photo of this dance and back in 2002 I was sent one by John Deehan (Snr). Of course, John's son, also John, is the famous ex-player for Aston Villa and now coach with the club. John senior is from Roscommon and he told me that left to right are Jimmy Carew, Arthur Groom, Matt Egan, Freddie Stevens, Albert Cater and Peter Cater on drums at the back. The dance was run by two brothers, Walter and Dick McEvilly from Co. Mayo. Ballroom and ceilidh music went down well there.

Back in the 1950s, the licensee of the 'Old Crown', Deritend was Joe O'Conner. From Galway Bay, he is pictured here outside the pub with his wife, Rose. Rose herself came from County Leitrim and met Joe over here. They were in Birmingham for 60 odd years and they loved their time at the 'Old Crown'. Joe and Rose are remembered with affection by many Irish and English Brummies and their hospitality was such that they were presented with a momento by officers of the Royal Canadian Mounted Police who used to meet at the pub. (Thanks to James Marnell.)

When I was young, Our Mom often told us about the Irish Dance in Whitehouse Street, Aston where she grew up. Held in the Memorial Hall of Saint Mary's Anglican Church, Our Mom learnt many Irish dances there. Her special memory is of my great-Granny Wood coming over at the end of the night and of the Irish lads on the door letting her in. Big as she was she was light of foot and skimmed around the floor. Our Gran was born in The Curragh, and although she was young when she was brought to England she used many Irish expressions – like calling the crocks by the term delf and naming the cupboards the press. When Our Gran died, lots of Irish lads lined the street as the cortege headed off. They told our family that many the time Our Granny had helped an Irish newcomer to Aston and had given them a meal.

Bull Ring Entertainment by Keith and Maureen Neale

Chris Delaney was married to Nancy and their children were Christie, Jimmy, Desi, Vincent and Dolores. Chris could not find work in Dublin in the early 1950's so he travelled to Birmingham, as he knew Maureen's father, William Morgan, also from Dublin, was working and living here. Bill helped him get a job at Wrights Ropes in Garrison Street. He got digs in Victoria Street, Bordesley Green, making ropes for ships. He later worked in a steel cutting yard in Bordesley Green where he lost four fingers in a machinery accident. He then returned to Ireland.

In this scene from the Bull Ring in the mid 1950s, Tralavia the strongman is watched by Dubliner, Chris Delaney, who is on the left and is smoking a cigarette. On his right and with the muffler is Christie Delaney.

All his sons came over here for work when they left school although some returned to settle in Dublin. The often visited the Bull Ring for the entertainment and cheap shopping as it was a very lonely existence living in digs with his family across the Irish Sea. On Sundays they would attend Mass at St. Anne's in Digbeth before taking Sunday lunch at Bill's home.

CHAPTER ELEVEN
A SPORTING LIFE

A sing-a-long at the 'Benyon Arms', Hockley, in the 1950s with players of the famous Shamrock Rovers and their friends and families. Manager Ned Grogan is sitting on the left of the piano. (Thanks to Ned's daughter, Carol.)

More than a Football Club. Shamrock Rovers by Des Kelly

The Kelly family are amongst the many from Ireland who have made their mark upon Birmingham. Raised in Ballymun, then a rural area outside Dublin city, the eleven brothers and sisters knew hard times and eight of them came to England. The oldest daughter, Molly, was the pioneer, settling in Birmingham in 1940 with her husband Mick Kelly, known as MJ. They rented 45 South Road, Hockley Brook in 1940. This became the 'halfway house' for all the Kelly brothers as they arrived and by the mid-1940s,

the house was alive with the families of Mollie and her brothers, Paddy, Oliver and Bluey. There was always a room for anyone else from Ireland who needed a bed and board for a few weeks until they got themselves settled. Aston Villa star Peter McParland also stayed there for a number of months. Mick, Mollie's husband, had spotted Peter playing in Ireland and brought him over for trials with the Villa. And Dennis Howell, the Labour M.P. for Small Heath and Football League referee, held his first political meeting in the front room of the house to an audience of six people!

The Kellys were a sporting family. Their father, John, had played Gaelic football for Dublin; Bluey played soccer for Shelbourne, picking up a couple of Irish Amateur International Caps; and Oliver played for Drumcondra and semi-professional for a number of top clubs in the Midlands. In Birmingham, the Kelly brothers turned out in force for the football team at Lucas Formans Road.

But it was in 1948, when sporting history was made with the foundation of Shamrock Rovers Football Club, in which, at any one time, there could be as many as five Kelly brothers playing together: Bluey a forceful halfback, Mick, a domineering centre half,

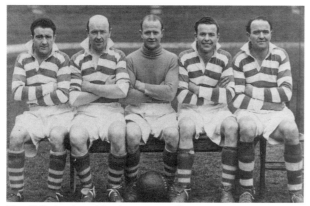

Five Kelly brothers. Thanks to Des Kelly.

Oliver, an agile goalkeeper, Andy, a skilful inside forward and Jimmy, a strong defender, with Kevin a useful fullback, playing in later years. Brother in law Mick Kelly was also club secretary, to keep it in the family!

Shamrock Rovers was formed by eight Irish lads at Mick Kelly's house in South Road, taking their name and distinctive traditional green and white hooped jerseys, from the professional Dublin side. Predominantly, the team was made up from mainly Irish players, but there was some more than useful Brummie lads playing also.

In their first year, playing in front of crowds of hundreds at Lightwoods Park, the Rovers were runners up in their Sunday League also winning

the Wheelers Cup. In the next year 1949/50, they were undefeated champions scoring 87 goals with only 17 conceded. Success continued the following season winning the league championship for the second successive year, losing only one game, with goals for of 94 and 14 against, and again winning the Wheelers Cup.

With their huge numbers of good natured, raucous supporters and their continuing success on the football pitch, The Rovers were soon becoming the leading Sunday team in the Birmingham area.

Shamrock Rovers switched in 1952/3 to Saturday football in the Handsworth League, which was of a higher standard. In their first season they won Division 1B, the Albion Cup, which was played at West Brom's ground, the Hawthorns, and the Divisional Cup. The next year they were champions again and once more won the Divisional Cup and were promoted to Division 1A, where again they were successful.

However, Shamrock Rovers was not just a football club, it was also a social club, involving the wives, girlfriends and children. Every Saturday night all the adults congregated in the club's headquarters, The Benyon Arms in Hockley, where they would gather for a big hoollie. Sixty members paid two bob a week to the club funds, and there was a concert every Monday night in the Benyon.

In August 1951 and again in 1954 the team, their families, girlfriends and supporters toured Ireland, with ninety three people making the second trip . . .

During the 1950's Shamrock Rovers enjoyed continued success, the pinnacle of their achievements was in 1959, reaching the Birmingham Junior Cup final played at Moor Green's ground in Hall Green. This was the premier cup in the whole of the Birmingham area, and was quite an accomplishment for the Rovers to get past the first rounds. Their opponents on that warm May day were the mighty Paget Rangers, one of the top sides in the West Midlands.

Some of the wives enjoying themselves at the 'Benyon'. Thanks to Ned's daughter, Carol Dickinson.

Such was the interest and excitement amongst the Irish community in Birmingham for the match, it resulted in the largest crowd ever seen at the Junior Cup, the vast majority waving green and white flags, banners and scarves. It was a great game, with Shamrock giving their all, but unfortunately losing six goals to three, to the more experienced and fitter Paget side.

Andy, Jimmy and Kevin played that day with Andy announcing his retirement immediately after the game. Shamrock Rovers continued to play with varying degrees of success, eventually disbanding in the late 1960's.

I belong to two cities, Dublin and Birmingham. Apple Brown by Kathleen M. Doyle

Christopher 'Apple' Brown was reared, one of ten children, amidst the dealers of Moor Street Market in Dublin.

He left Dublin at the age of sixteen in 1933 against his mother and father's wishes, but as he said, he wanted to broaden his mind. The B & I cattle boat was to take him to Birmingham and only cost a few shillings, but when he arrived at Liverpool in Lime Street he had no money, so he

went around the corner, got underneath the carriage and boarded the train. On arriving in Birmingham, he slept like a good many Irish men, in the Rowton House or the Sally Anne, as he knew no one in Birmingham.

He worked for Robbie Pryke in the market on a few occasions, and said he was a Gentleman. He also worked at the Grand Hotel Colmore Row; this was around the time he met mom.

He saw her at the Maypole Picture House in Summer Hill, he was wearing his dress suit and dicky bow (his waiter attire), I think that was what won mom's heart along with the blarney. Mom also came from a large family born in Holliday Street 6/205 to Jack and Mary Anne Vennell (nee Curley). They went on to marry at St Peter's Church on Broad Street, and settled down in 31 Latimer Street, Birmingham. Dad took mom, then aged twenty one, to Dublin for the first time. She fell in love with the place, and adored it all her life as we all did.

Apple Brown, Frank O'Sullivan and Robert McCracken. Quiet and always in the background, Frank O'Sullivan is one of those people who make a difference. Through his hard work, commitment and perseverance, he has helped many young men to avoid drugs, drink and crime and he has given them a purpose in life. Reared in county Cork, Frank runs Birmingham City Boxing Club. A boxer himself, he started Ladywood Amateur Boxing Club back in 1956 and is now based at Saint Agatha's Church in Sparkbrook. The best-known of Frank's boxers is Robert McCracken, who became a British champion and fought for world titles.

His trade was as a painter and decorator, and he served five years apprenticeship, I must add, he was first class. When I was a child I loved to watch him rag roll the doors, and to this day I love the smell of paint, it takes me back in time.

Around 1982, he met up with old friends Tommy and Paddy Lynch, boxing promoters, and he helped them in the gym in John Bright Street. He trained many boxers over the years, our own Robert McCracken who was the light middleweight British Commonwealth Champion. Robert was just 15 years old when he met dad, so their friendship goes back a long way, and they all had great times in the gym.

We all have such admiration for the Lynch Brothers, Tommy and Paddy, as when dad was taken ill with heart problems, they did not hesitate to get dad the best treatment, and this most certainly extended dad's life by a number of years. And for that we will be eternally grateful.

Sad to say, mom passed away in July 1998. Dad followed in September 2001, he never really got over losing mom, had she lived a little longer they would have been married for sixty years!

Dad once said, 'I am a very lucky man' I belong to two cities, Dublin and Birmingham. I would like this story to be in memory of two of the most wonderful parents who gave us everything. They will never ever be forgotten.

Dedicated to Doing His Best. Pat Benson

Like Frank O'Sullivan, Pat Benson (front row right) is a man dedicated to doing all that he can for the well-being of young men who come from tough backgrounds. The trainer, secretary and guiding force of the Small Heath Amateur Boxer's Club, a fine boxer himself in his younger days, Pat hails from Ballyhaunis county Mayo. In 1987, Pat's club made sporting history when seven of its boxers reached the quarter finals of the National Amateur Boxing Club Midlands Finals. He gives his time freely, ensuring that young men of all backgrounds are filled with self respect, self confidence and a respect for others. Pat trained Matt Macklin, who is tipped to become one of the big names in British boxing. Matt's father is from Roscommon and his mother from Tipperary. He played minor football for Tipp before turning professional as a boxer after the Athens Olympics.

Gaelic Games - The GAA by Helena Duignan. With thanks to Denis Neenan and Billy Collins.

As far back as the 1930s we know there was non-competitive hurling and Gaelic football being played all over Birmingham, and, with the formation of the Warwickshire GAA County Board in 1939, the competition began!

Ever since, Gaelic football and hurling have been an integral part of the lives of the Irish community in Birmingham. Thanks to the dedication of countless stalwarts who have given their time voluntarily over the years, several generations have grown up playing Gaelic games in Birmingham, while successive waves of emigrants have been able to enjoy playing their sports away from home. It's not only the players themselves who take part in a game – their families, friends, parents, children will all have great pride in their team, and take part in fund-raising for the clubs, driving players to games, holding social functions, etc, so that the whole community is involved.

John Mitchells is the oldest GAA Club in the area and still one of the strongest, drawing on the large Irish community around the Hall Green area. Mitchells tend to place a strong emphasis on training up the young members of the community, and have under-age hurling and football teams.

Erin go Bragh of Erdington competes at all levels in all competitions and has trained many generations of young children of Irish immigrants in the games, which is to be seen in their recent success at under-16 provincial level at both hurling and football.

Fooballers at Páirc na hÉireann.

Sean McDermotts of Small Heath have just completed a six-in-a-row triumph in the Senior Football Championship and tend to draw on strong Irish-born players as well as their own home-grown talents.

St Brendan's of Kings Heath are another strong club with a central role in the life of the local community. Recently James Connolly's of Handsworth has begun competing in juvenile competitions, as has Setanta of Northfield.

The importance of the GAA clubs to the local communities cannot be overestimated, as anyone who watched a game at Glebe Farm in Stechford, could testify. Here thousands of people would turn out to pitches with no facilities to watch their team compete. Competition was always fierce and the craic was always mighty.

Facilities have improved vastly with the move to the Warwickshire GAA's own purpose-built grounds at Páirc na hÉireann in 1990. This facility has proved to be one of the best in the country, and hosts many important tournaments throughout the year, as well as inter-county matches and local games. The ground has been run by dedicated volunteers over the years.

The strength and high standards of the games played in Birmingham can be seen in the impressive achievements of the Warwickshire County teams. It should not be forgotten that between 1968 and 1973 Warwickshire won no fewer than three All-Ireland junior Hurling Finals!

Father Murphy's (All Wexford) Hurling Team, 1961. They took their name from the patriotic priest, Father John Murphy, who was executed for his part in the 1798 rebellion in Ireland.. This photo was taken by Joe Murray who operated Murray's Press and Commercial Photographers on the Stratford Road, Sparkhill. The next year Father Murphy's made hurling history when, as an all-Wexford team, they won the Warwickshire Senior Hurling title at Glebe Farm. To the best of knowledge this was the only occasion outside Ireland that this feat has been achieved. The remarkable team was captained by Paddy Rochford and included: Eddie O'Brien, Hughie McEvoy, Edno Cummins, Mark Colfer, Jim Mullins, J.J. O'Connor, Aiden O'Neill, John O'Connor, Patsy Morris, Gerry Leary, Matt Doyle, 'Blonde' Goggin, Paddy Eames, Nicky Jackman, John Roche, Pat Cullen, Liam O'Brien and John Fitzgerald. Liam O'Brien owns the 'Emerald Club', in Small Heath, which is an important venue for the Birmingham Irish.

In 1968 they defeated Kerry at Glebe Farm, and a whole new team repeated the feat in Tralee the following year. In 1970 they were defeated by Antrim in the Intermediate All-Ireland Final at Croke Park, and in 1973 were defeated by Kerry at the Glebe. In 1973 Warwickshire got back in winning ways by defeating Co. Louth in Ardeagh for another All-Ireland junior title. At its peak there were 12 senior hurling clubs in the county, a huge number which shows how committed the community was to its sport.

The Warwickshire team which won the All-Ireland title in 1969 lined up as follows: Jimmy Gilligan, Don O'Brien, Paddy Grimes, Pat Heffernan, Larry Moore, Liam Dalton, Ricky

Hanley, Tom Crowley, Louie Moloney, Billy Collins, Micky Brennan, Vince Coffey, Johnny McLoughlin, Johnny Brown, Pat Hannon.

Not to be outdone, the Warwickshire footballers reached the All-Ireland junior football final in 1967, losing to Mayo by just 2 points at Glebe Farm.

This strong tradition has continued through the generations, and in 1997 the Warwickshire under-18 football team became the first Warwickshire side to visit New York.

The nineties resurgence of the Irish economy saw a large number of younger Irish emigrants return home, and several GAA clubs have felt the effects of this. However, with so many Birmingham-born players, the games are still thriving. One area of continued migration from Ireland is among students, and the second city becomes home every year to a new influx of young Irish sports people, many of whom become involved with their local club, playing and coaching.

The Erin Go Bragh camogie team.

The recent development of the excellent GAA in Schools Initiative is introducing a new generation of children from all over the city to the skills and excitement of what many regard as the fastest field game in the world. There's a great saying in GAA, well, hurling circles, that goes: 'Those who can, play hurling; those who can't, play football; and those who can't do that, play soccer.

Camogie

Camogie is the women's version of Ireland's national sport, hurling. As such it involves high levels of skill in one of the fastest field games in the world, as teams of 15 compete to drive the ball in for a goal or 'over the bar' for a point. In 1987 at the annual GAA for Africa Festival, the first camogie game in Birmingham took place between members of two Irish dancing schools. The game was a first attempt to introduce the sport in the Midlands, from which was born the Erin go Bragh camogie team, today one of the strongest camogie clubs in the country.

Ever since, Erin go Bragh has been the standard bearer for camogie in Birmingham, competing first in the Gloucestershire County Board competitions before joining the London County Board in 1990 and winning the Junior and Intermediate Championships at the first attempts. The club currently competes in both the Junior and Senior competitions in London, showing great commitment in travelling the long distance to fixtures.

Ever since it began, the EGB camogie team has been run by its dedicated manager Denis Neenan, from Kildare, who has excelled in teaching the sport to youngsters, and who received an Irish Post award in the mid-1990s for his trouble. Other dedicated support has come from Mick O'Hare, and the sadly departed Ted Leavy of Galway, whose driving of the minibus down the motorway to London whilst regaling them with "Delaney's JCB" will never be forgotten by the girls.

Over the years the club has produced a great number of skilful players, born in Birmingham, who compete against Irish-born and taught players admirably, and many of whom have competed against Irish county teams whilst representing London at county level. Indeed, goalkeeper Julie Watchorn became the first Irish

Brummie to play in an All-Ireland competition when she turned out for London against Tipperary aged just 18.

A welcome recent development for camogie in the second city came when John Mitchells GAA club put together a team which competed in the late 1990s in London Junior competitions for a year. Newman College has also put together a team, which now competes in London.

Camogie at Páirc na hÉireann.

Women's Football

Women's Gaelic football is strongly represented in Birmingham under the Warwickshire GAA County Board, with John Mitchell's of Hall Green, St Brendan's of King's Heath, Erin go Bragh of Erdington all competing along with teams from Coventry, Bristol and Cardiff in League and Championship competitions. Competition between the clubs is intense and anyone could foreseeably come out victorious in any game. With a combination of Birmingham-born and Irish-born players, all are welcome, and with many youngsters now learning the game at school in Brum, the prospects are good for keeping competition flourishing in the region. The Warwickshire County Team competes in national inter-county competitions.

CHAPTER TWELVE
IRISH CULTURE AND SELF-HELP

A parade of Irish folk to Saint Chad's Catholic cathedral some time in the 1950s and as can be seen, Irish nurses are in the forefront. Behind them, a man and women are holding a banner of the Sacred Heart. The parade is passing Morgan and Ball, the gent's outfitter's at 124 New Street and on the corner of Burlington Passage, and it is on its way down towards the junction with Corporation Street. Was this a Saint Patrick's Day Parade or was it a parade to celebrate a religious occasion?

Stealing a March on London

The Birmingham Saint Patrick's Parade, 1952. Thanks to Hannah Bergin. Hannah remembers that the people assembled in the West End car park in Suffolk Street and that the parade went along New Street, Corporation Street and Colmore Row and finished back up at the 'West End'. Eileen Combellack recalled that 'The Birmingham Irish brought colour to the City' with the parade and that 'they stole a march on

London by parading forty-five minutes before them and became the first English City to hold an Irish Parade'. Father Sean Connellan, from Limerick, was at Saint Anne's from 1943-53 and it was he who organised this the first Saint Patrick's Day Parade in Brum. (Eileen Combellack, 'Proud Stands My City', unpublished manuscript, 1990, *Birmingham Lives Archive*).

This photo of the Saint Patrick's Day Parade of 1961 appeared in *Trocadó* (meaning 32), a publication that was brought out by the All-Ireland Counties Association, Birmingham. It came about after the Carlow County Association published *The Midland Irish News* in May 1961. The parade itself started in the car park of the 'West End' in Suffolk Street and went via Easy Row, Edmund Street, Congreve Street, Victoria Square, New Street, Bull Street, Colmore Row and Paradise Circus and back to the 'West End'. Walkers were urged to obey county marshals and to keep in formation and not to smoke on parade nor wave to people on the side.

Organising The Birmingham Irish

During the late 1950s and 1960s, the Irish in Birmingham began to organise themselves successfully. Amongst them they boasted many active citizens. Two of them were John O'Connor of the County Kerry Association and Finbar Dynan who belonged to the All-Ireland Counties Development Association Ltd (founded in 1958), which aimed to build an Irish Club as a social, cultural and spiritual centre for the Birmingham Irish. That dream was achieved on the site of the old Saint John's Restaurant on High Street, Deritend. Now called the Irish Club, it continues to be a focal point for the Birmingham Irish. The All-Ireland Counties Development Association Ltd also founded the Trocadó Cost Rent Society to help Irish people get their own homes.

Father Richard Murphy was another man committed to the well-being of the Birmingham Irish. Belonging to the Missionary Oblates of Mary Immaculate, he took charge of the Irish Centre in Moat Row in 1957. This became the headquarters of a number of Irish societies, but

most importantly it was the base for work aimed at the social welfare of newly-arrived Irish immigrants. The centre also founded a Savings Scheme and House Purchase Scheme. Later called the Irish Welfare and Information Centre and based in Plunkett House, by Saint Chad's and now in the Irish Club, this body continues to do good, especially with those ageing Irish people who have not prospered in Birmingham.

These young Irish dancers are in the 1968 Saint Patrick's Day Parade which is going past the Council House and is heading downhill from Victoria Square and into New Street. Gerard Morris is holding the banner. The third boy behind Gerard is J. J. Green and he is followed by Michael Green.

Parades of the 1960s

As a child in the early 1960s, I can recall that each year Our Mom and Our Dad would take me and Our Darryl up town to watch the County Associations and other Irish folk gathering for the Saint Patrick's Day Parade. I have a recollection that then, as now, the parade was on a Sunday and I seem to remember that the bands and everyone associated with the march assembled on a bomb peck - a large bomb site. I could have only been seven or eight at the time, so I'm going back 40 years, and in my memory I can see us standing on the roadside above the gathering and looking down at what was a fascinating scene. I can bring to mind the sound of Irish music, crowds of folk and men and women holding poles on which were attached boards proclaiming the different County Associations.

This photo, from November 1970, emphasises the fact that from its beginnings the Irish Centre, now the Irish Club, in Deritend was a meeting place for Brummies of all origins and beliefs. The Irish Centre was opened in 1967 and fifteen years later a large extension was added.

Irish representation at every level: Larry Dineen 1901 – 1989 by Sean Dineen

Dad came to the UK in May 1942, he was directed to do factory work in Lye Cross, Stourbridge. After about 18 months he moved to Birmingham, to work at Slater's Dairies in South Yardley. He worked there until 1950 rising to Assistant Manager, due to ill health he moved to

out-door work as a door to door salesman for the Kleeneze Brush Co. of Bristol. His sales district being Bearwood and Smethwick. He always said that these were the warmest hearted people he had met in the UK.

The family joined him in 1956 living at Henry Road, South Yardley. He had spells working at BSA Small Heath, working in production control and then at Perry Chains in Tyseley. In 1959 he joined the Civil Service as a Tax Officer and subsequently as a senior grade Tax Official, until his retirement in 1973/74. He then worked as a self-employed tax accountant for many years.

He directed and oversaw funding for our local church, Holy Family, Small Heath, i.e. bingo and raffles. He was also the founding chair of Planned Giving, when it was introduced. He was for many years Financial Director and Trustee Chairman of John Mitchell's Social Club in Stratford Road, Sparkhill, which was one of his main interests.

The Irish Week in 1969 was one of his favourite projects and he spent a lot of time and effort trying to get Irish people interested in local affairs in the city of Birmingham. He always tried to foster good relations with our Birmingham neighbours, and had no time for racism in any form.

His dearest wish was to see Irish representation at every level in Birmingham. Although a very loyal Irishman, he was always proud to have worked and lived in Birmingham. He died in 1989, 5 years after my mother, and both are buried in Ireland.

The first Irish Festival week was held between March 17 – 24 1968 and it aimed to promote Irish cultural and social functions and to sponsor Irish games and trade displays. It involved Feis, Fleadh Ceol, GAA Games, and a small trade display. The minister for health Sean Flanagan and Mr

Bishop Challoner's Irish dancers, late 1950s.

John Danwell were guests of the committee, attending various functions during the week. This promotion was a pioneering and exploratory effort and its committee believed that it was successful in projecting 'to the host community on behalf of Irish Nationals here, the cultural, social and economic face of Ireland' and in promoting 'greater, closer relations in community and so help in the integration of our own nationals'. The 1969 Irish Week was held in the Bull Ring Shopping Centre. Larry Dineen was the chairman of the committee that organised it.

Part of a Wider Irish Community by Carmel Elmes

Carmel Elmes grew up in prefabs in Druids Heath, where there was no real Irish community. She attended Bells Lane School until Bishop Challoner opened in 1953. Her teacher was Mr Cassidy who ran the Innisfail Dancing School which 'I joined and from this came the band,

dancing and playing at the different Irish Association venues. We were now part of a wider Irish community.' As Carmel points out 'how simple our dresses were'. Her maternal grandfather, Monty Riordan, was a Munster Champion step dancer and 'none of his children followed in his footsteps until I started here in Birmingham. He was in his 80s then and used to sit in a chair to demonstrate.'

Fine Irish Dancing

In February 1968 Pat Comerford of the Holy Family School of Dancing in Small Heath won the Bobby Armstrong Memorial Cup when it was presented for the first time at the Colmcille Feis at Handsworth. With Pat is Canon A. W. Emery, the parish priest of St Francis, Handsworth, who made the presentation, and he is holding five-year-old Bernadette Armstrong. The cup was given in memory of little Bernadette's dad, Bobby, who was the husband of Mauretta until his untimely death in 1967. Other local winners included Susan Connors and E. Kelly of the Holy Family School. The photo was taken by M. J. Niels McGuinness.

Birmingham is fortunate to have many fine Irish dancing schools. One of the leading figures in the emergence of the Irish dancing locally is Mauretta Armstrong, née Hallinan. From Ashford, county Limerick she came to Birmingham in 1944 to work for Lucas. Living in digs in Yardley Wood, she was homesick until she met a former schoolpal whose uncle took them to a dance at Saint Catherine's in the Horsefair. Mauretta joined the Gaelic League, which had been revived by Miss C. Brady, and started the Colmcille School of Irish Dancing based at Saint Francis's, Handsworth. Her vital work led to her receiving a Papal Blessing for her contribution to Irish dancing in Birmingham. (Maureen Messent, 'Queen of the Dance', *Evening Mail*, 15 March 2001).

Another special woman in Irish dancing in Birmingham was Catherine Kenny. The daughter of Michael and Kathy from Donegal and Limerick, she battled against cystic fibrosis to become a talented dancer and gifted teacher. Catherine's bravery and charisma led to her receiving an Irish Post award. For her friend, Brendan Farrell, of all the stories he had covered for 30 odd years 'the story of Catherine's bravery

The O'Connor/McCaughey Pipe. Charlie Clark, Carmel's brother, is the piper on the front right. Carmel's husband Mick is in the centre of the second row.

stood out. In particular the trauma of seeing this frail and beautiful young girl connected to drips and monitors in her own small ward in Selly Oak Hospital yet always managing that captivating smile which endeared her to hundreds of people'. Her spirit remains strong in the Kenny School of Irish Dancing run by her brother Michael. ('Memories of a special person', *Irish Post* 7 April 2001).

The 'Jug of Punch' by Tommy Dempsey

Tommy Demspey at the Fiddle and Bone, Birmingham. (Thanks to M. London.)

Tommy Dempsey is a well-known and well-respected Irish singer. He grew up in Dublin when music was an integral part of Irish households.

I began to visit England from about fifteen years of age and in my early twenties I settled in Birmingham. I was singing at work when a mate heard me. He asked me if I'd ever sung in a folk club. I didn't even know what he was talking about! I was singing songs that I had learned as a boy, but this man described them as folk songs. Anyway, he invited me to a gathering at a pub called the 'Big Bull's Head'. I remember it was one side of the Birmingham Civic Hall. On the other side, believe it or not, was the 'Little Bull's Head'.

The organiser was Ian Campbell, along with two men named Dave Swarbrick and Dave Phillips, and together with a few others we formed a group called the Clarion Choir . . . The club in only a few weeks grew to such enormity that we were forced to move premises to the 'Crown' in Station Street. One of our finest nights was a Céilí organised by Luke Kelly and the McPeake family.

Stoically True to Irish Culture by Mick Hipkiss

Mick Hipkiss is from Cork, and although he was brought to England at a young age he remains stoically true to Irish culture in music, Gaelic language and dance. Indeed in his teenage days he was also an Irish dancer, having won many medals in Britain and Ireland.

It all started when I was 17. I saw a poster outside the Abbey Church in Erdington advertising an Irish Concert at Birmingham Town Hall. I joined the Gaelic League, then became founder member of 'Scoil Rinnce Colmcille', Colmcille School of Irish Dancing at St Catherine's School at the back of the church where every Sunday night it was all Ceilidh Dancing.

In 1951 I was also a founder member of Feis Birmingham. 2001 was the 50th year of its foundation and I'm happy to say it's still going though not with all the competitions as in those early days, (language, singing, storytelling in Irish and English, knitting, arts and crafts).

In 1957 I had a bad motor bike accident, I nearly lost my leg and had head injuries, so that put paid to my Irish dancing. I was also a member of the Anti-Partition League. Meetings were held in John Bright Street under the Chairmanship of one Frank Short, Claire Short M.P.'s father. I remember him as a nice man and a good speaker.

So now I couldn't dance anymore, a grand friend of mine, Eilish Mangan of Wexford (RIP) who was a very popular traditional type singer heard me 'trying' to sing along with her in the 'Castle

of Dromore' one night, and told me that I had a good voice and should use it more and learn more Irish songs. I was desperate to be doing something 'Irish' and as well as learning Irish once a week, that I did learn more songs.

A lot of these were in waltz-time, and it was then that I got my first booking. We didn't know the word 'gig' in those days ha! ha! It was at a Ceilidh and Old Tyme, which was held in the Drill Hall in Coventry.

Cumann Céilí na nGael 1961, taken by Joe Murphy of Murphy's Studios. Front Row left to right J. McGowan (Leitrim), J. Lynch (Limerick), Miss K. Larwie (Roscommon), J. McShane (Antrim). Back row left to right F. Flanagan (Roscommon), M. Flanagan (Mayo) and F. Boyle (Fermanagh). Founded in 1960, the aim of Cumann Céilí na nGael was to halt the decline in Irish dancing in Birmingham and to provide an alternative to rock and roll for young people.

There was a very well known pub 'The Red Cow' on the 'Horse Fair' right next door (literally) to St. Catherine's Church. A lot of the Irish lads used it mostly at weekends. I used to go there on Saturday nights for a singing session. The Irish took it over for that night. The lounge in the back was small so you had to get in early for a seat. It was always a lovely night there. Everybody looked forward to the session. No instruments, just unaccompanied singing, and never any trouble, not that I can remember.

The first time I ever saw an instrument there, was one night when a red-headed Dublin fellow came in the last half hour, the pubs closed at 10.30 in those times. Anyway this fellow with the banjo sounded awful. He played awful too; I think he was just starting out, this was about 1959. Anyway this fellow with the 5 stringed banjo turned out to be the great Luke Kelly RIP and as we all know he turned out to be one of the finest folk-singers and one of The Dubliners and famous in his own life time.

In 1966 I started my own club in The Prince of Wales, Cambridge Street, and a year later I moved just down the road to The Cambridge Inn. My club was on a Sunday and was called 'The Skillet Pot', after a song I got from the late Sean O'Tuama – a great Cork Gael. So we had this 'Holy Ground' on Saturday and 'The Skillet Pot' on Sunday. The pub was a mecca for all folk fans and the landlord John Chapman (a Wicklow man) was a very happy man.

Irish singing with Father Sean McTernan and Mick Hipkiss on the right in the mid-1960s. Father Sean began his ministry in Birmingham at The Rosary, Alum Rock, where he was an assistant to Monsignor John Power. Father Sean was then appointed parish priest of Saint Teresa's, Perry Barr, where he and Mrs E. Lawrie started the Birmingham Branch of Comhaltas Ceoltóirí Éireann in 1961. Rehearsals took place in Mrs Lawrie's house and the musicians and singers have helped raise thousands of pounds for charity. Father Sean is still the parish priest, continuing the work of the Church. Monsignor Fallon is another priest who has had a major effect both upon the Birmingham Irish and the people of the city as a whole. Ministering from Saint Francis in Handsworth, Monsignor Fallon is always available to support any good cause

Eventually I moved down to Livery Street, by Snow Hill Station, to the 'Old Contemptibles'. I opened up in that venue with two unknowns, Finbar and Eddie Furey. It was a magical night.

In those days Finbar didn't sing at all, but he did play the pipes for most of Eddie's songs and of course his own beautiful slow airs and his very very fast jigs and reels. The crowd went wild. Shortly after I had two other unknowns, Mike Harding and Christy Moore, now both famous. It was 2/-, two shillings, (10p) to get in and their fee at that time was £12 plus a floor in my house for the night. I was lucky to get artists like these. They were others like The Wolfe Tones, The Yetties, Lyn and Graham McCarthy, TV stars in those days. We really did have fantastic nights at 'The Skillet Pot'

Some time after I decided to form my third group. We met in The Little Bull in Digbeth. I decided to call the band 'Drowsy Maggie', my favourite reel at the time. I met with some opposition, from the others but I won through in the end. The first members of the band were Clive Powers, Keith Kerans, Pete Bispham, Brian Patton, Dave Phillips and myself and I'm delighted to say that though there have been many changes and a few heartbreaks, we had some great talent in 'Drowsy Maggie'. Paul O'Brien was a member for a few years, as was Joe Murphy. I'd like to mention others as well, like Bill Bigg (a Scott), Ronan O'Connor, Patsy Breslin, Mike Stanley, Tommy Dempsey. I feel very indebted to all those who took part in 'Drowsy Maggie' for they all helped to make it a great band, and not forgetting Andy Jones, a great fiddle player.

I am still looking for a permanent singer/guitarist to take the place of Aiden Forde who died in 2001; a great loss to us, and a greater loss to the Folk world in general. He is greatly missed by many and we in the band will always cherish his memory (RIP).

There is one other period I would like to mention. The original Irish Centre. This was opened in the mid 50's. Fr. Richard Murphy (a Belfast man) was in charge. It had been an old shop. Anyway it was very sparse. After a while it took shape. I remember we used to have a Cois Tine (Kush Tannah) (Around the Fireside) on a Tuesday night and anyone who could sing, play a fiddle, melodion, tin whistle etc. would be welcome.

We had some lovely nights there. The Centre was set up primarily to help newly arrived immigrants. It was at this time that Fr. Murphy got a band of men who were members of the Irish Centre to assist by meeting the arrival of the 6.10 am train from Holyhead. We took turns in doing this. Some of us, usually in pairs would get up at 5.00 am, catch the bus into town, put our Irish Centre armbands on and when the train would arrive, we would ask or shout 'are there any Irish here who need help?' Some were a bit suspicious, but we won through in the end.

We would take them back to the Centre where Fr. Murphy would welcome them. We would have someone there to give them a proper breakfast; bacon egg and sausage, plenty of bread and butter and tea. Then he would take their details and try to find 'digs' and a job if they had no one to go to. He did tremendous work for the immigrants. He was a member of the Oblate Fathers based at St Anne's. I shall always cherish his kindness and by the way, after we took these people from the train to the Centre, we would have to go off to work, but we really enjoyed doing what we did. It was to help fellow Irishmen who were less fortunate than ourselves.

A Recognisable Contribution to the Multi-Cultural Makeup by John McMillen

John left Belfast for Birmingham in 1938 when he was fifteen. He lived with his eldest sister, Nell, who was married to Frank Downes and had a house in Clement Street in Ladywood. John met Rose Tullett, his Brummie wife, locally. He recalls the not-easily-forgotten devastation of the Blitz: 'the crash of anti-aircraft guns, the thump of

exploding bombs, the fiercely burning incendiary bombs, and the hours spent huddled in coal cellars and basements is probably an experience that is hard to imagine by those too young to remember it and who, thankfully, have not had to be subjected to such a horrific experience since then. I personally, have thanked God for surviving the explosion to St Paul's Church (St. Paul's Square) where I was 'firewatching' in Brook Street.'

On the morning of the Queen's Coronation in 1953, a member of the Birmingham Irish Pipe Band asked the band committee if it would consider, as a favour to him, entertaining the people of Nechells with some pipe tunes. With some historical irony, these Irish Brummies are marching down Oliver Street and crossing Cromwell Street.

John's first job was making nuts and bolts on capstan lathes and frilling machines for fifteen bob a week. In those days 'they used to advertise their vacancies on boards outside the factories, i.e. "Capstan lathe operators wanted", "Polishers required", etc. Occasionally the boards carried an additional message: "No Irish need apply".'

The Birmingham Irish Pipe Band was formed in 1948. Instruments were bought, donations were made by Irish cultural associations and the members and their wives held dances and raffles to make it a success.

Soon the band had a complete uniform on order which was made by the wife of one of our tenor drummers – John Sweetman – who was also an experienced Irish dancer. She was a first rate tailoress and made individual uniforms that were second to none. The uniforms were so well made that they served the band for many years into the future. The decorations for the uniforms were made by the band members themselves (shawl brooches, cap badges, shoe buckles, etc.) many of whom were employed in the engineering industry. (Thin gauge sheet brass was shaped, engraved, had safety pins fitted and then chromium plated; they looked very smart and really set off our new uniforms.)

In 1958, the Birmingham Irish Pipe Band entered the All-Ireland Fleadh Ceoil under Pipe Major McGuire and won the trophy. Another victory was gained in the 1960 Fleadh Ceoil in Boyle.

The uniform consisted of a navy blue tunic with all the trimmings, a light green kilt, an orange shawl, green stockings with criss-crossed orange tapes from foot to knee and these were topped by a navy blue tam-o-shanter with a green headband and pom-pom. The cap badge consisted of a chromed disc on which was mounted the harp of a 'Free State penny' (also chromed) and mounted behind the badge, a green feather hackle. The body belts were also made by band members, adjustable, heavy duty and with a hook and clasp fitting.

A special word of thanks must also go to Mr Matt Byrne, proprietor of the Harp and Shamrock dance halls in Birmingham for the help he gave to the band in its formative years, and at a time when it was most needed. Engagements at his dances were both plentiful and bountiful and

went a long way towards placing the BIPB on the road to self sufficiency.

The BIPB was, most decidedly, an all-Ireland band, with pipers and drummers from the whole four provinces of Ireland – Ulster, Munster, Leinster and Connaught, and with a fair proportion of Birmingham-born second generation Irish.

Among the long standing members of the BIPB were Tom Finn, the Stanley brothers, Mick, Paddy and Billy, John Kelly, Tom McGuire, Tommy Callaghan, Bill O'Connor, Jimmy Healey, Tony and Joe Hosey, Tommy Harwood, Tony Cuskeran. Tommy and John Farrell, Willenhall Girls Pipe Band pipe tutor, J. Donaghy, F. Short, T. Richards, John Ramsey, John and Pat Sweetman, P. Barr, B. McMullen, J. O'Grady, Bernard McCarthy (Secretary), H. McGuire, G. O'Keefe, P. Bradley, Vincent Hickey, the Stanley and McMillen and Finn (junior bandsmen), etc. Band practice took place at Icknield Street School).

The band played at a wide variety of functions, garden fetes, carnivals, dances, Gaelic football matches (local), concerts at the Town Hall, Nazareth House, St Patrick's Day Parades, etc., and we like to think that we have made a recognisable contribution to the multi-cultural makeup of our adoptive city – Birmingham.

John feels that most of his 60-plus years in Brum have been good and he has been blessed with a good wife: 'Home, however, is where your heart is, and my heart has always nestled in the green hills and glens of Antrim and my native Belfast where my paternal/maternal family lived'.

A Great Stalwart of Traditional Irish Music

'When we were younger we spent many hours playing at Fleadhs, Feis's and music sessions in and around Birmingham. As we got older we

Christopher Jordan was delighted when he saw this photo in *The Harp* in 2002 - for the accordion players are himself and his brother Vincent Jordan, whilst the drummer is their younger brother Michael. 'The boy playing the fiddle is our parallel cousin Paul Jordan and he is being watched by his sister, Helen. The other two fiddle players are Catherine Hennessey and Jo Quinn, the tin whistle players are Paul Kirkpatrick and Keiron Hickey.'

taught various instruments to youngsters at The English Martyrs School on Tuesday evenings and many of our pupils are now playing Irish music around the area. Several of us still play together on a regular basis at Irish music sessions at my pub, The Horse & Jockey Freeford, Lichfield every other Monday evening.

Kathleen Boyle was also pleased to see the photo. She recalls that 'it was taken in The Irish Centre one Sunday afternoon at a Children's Céilí – run by my mother Mrs E. Lawrie, the then Secretary of the Birmingham Branch of Comhaltas Ceoltóirí Éireann. I was the teacher of this junior band and in my early twenties, so it was taken by Brendan Farrell of The Irish Post in the late 1970s.

'This little band started in the mid 60s and was probably the second children's ceili band formed in this country – the first being one that I was in over 40 years ago. Both bands played at many concerts throughout the Midland region and beyond.

My mother was a great stalwart of traditional Irish music in Birmingham. She founded the first

branch of CCE in Birmingham back in 1961 and the Birmingham Céilí Band, which played in venues up and down the country for over 30 years. She had a great gift of organising people to put on functions etc and was responsible for £1,000's being collected for different charities.

She was presented with an award from Comhaltas Ceoltóirí Éireann in Dublin at their 50th Anniversary Banquet in the Mansion House, on 29th September, 2001.'

CHAPTER THIRTEEN
THAT SAVAGE MADNESS: THE PUB BOMBINGS

CONCERT FOR I.R.A. VICTIM

Some weeks ago Charles Long (centre), an L.M.S. locomotive fireman, was injured in a Birmingham I.R.A. bomb explosion in Corporation-street. Last night colleague at Monument-lane locomotive depot organised a concert on his behalf. Left is the organiser, Mr. J. H. Bennett.

D. O'Grogan was one of three boys and two girls, and 'we slept together in a back to back house in Ladywood, in houses with appalling conditions, damp, bugs and no electricity.' In this photo he is on the back row on the left: 'The press took the photograph in a public house at the corner of Station Street and Hill Street, and you note the cause was the IRA. During the War time, as a member of the Home Guard, we guarded Railway Installations, and given instructions to arrest anyone seen shining a torch during bombing raids on Birmingham. The IRA were noted to do that.'

The Pub Bombings

In 1974, the trauma of the IRA pub bombings overwhelmed the people of Birmingham. This was not the first time that the IRA had set off explosions in the city as part of their campaign for a united Ireland. On 22 March 1939, bombs blasts shook Princess Road and Balsall Heath Road, where two Irishmen had set up a bomb factory. The next month sticks of gelignite were found in Martineau Street and there were explosions at Snow Hill Station and elsewhere in the city centre. There were other blasts in May. Fortunately, no-one was killed in Birmingham. However, sadly there were deaths and injuries from bombings in Coventry. Two men were arrested and hanged at Winson Green Prison. In 1969, the real bomber admitted his crime to the *Sunday Times*.

Five years later, The Troubles in Northern Ireland brought death and horror to Birmingham. In 1973 and 1974 a number of bombs were set off locally by the IRA. Fortunately, no-one was harmed and these actions were condemned by Birmingham Irish community leaders. Then on 21 November 1974, the IRA exploded a bomb in the 'Mulberry Bush' pub in the Rotunda and another at the 'Tavern in the Town' in New Street. Twenty-one people were murdered and 160 were injured. Amongst the dead were two Birmingham Irish brothers; whilst Tony Dicksen, an Irishman in the 'Tavern in the Town', was injured. Escaping from the horror, he went back into the ruins to lead others to safety.

There were strong condemnations of the terrible deed from Irish community leaders like Pat McGrath at the Irish Centre and Irish councillors such as John O'Keefe. The Sparkbrook representative made it plain that 'We in the Irish community are doing everything in our power to show we do not support violence of this kind. I would now appeal to English people, despite the

A Civil Rights March in Birmingham in 1969. Formed to achieve full rights for Catholics in Northern Ireland, the Civil Rights Movement was attacked by the police and Protestant mobs in the Six Counties. In Birmingham, a branch of the Campaign for Social Justice was formed and on 16 August 2,000 people from all backgrounds marched for social justice in Northern Ireland.

extreme provocation they are under, not to take it out on the Irish in this city, many of whom feel as they do'. Despite this, there was a backlash and some Catholic churches, schools and businesses were damaged by petrol bombs and the like. Six men were arrested, charged, found guilty and imprisoned for the terrible crime. Becoming known as the Birmingham Six, they protested their innocence. After a long campaign they were released in 1991 after it was revealed that the confessions of the men had been forged by the police and that forensic evidence crucial in convictions could not be relied upon.

In the aftermath of the Pub Bombings, £1,000 was given to the Lord Mayor's Appeal Fund for the bomb victims and their families by the Irish Development Association, which ran the Irish Centre. In the longer term, the Pub Bombings had a drastic and adverse effect on the self-confidence and self-expression of the Birmingham Irish. The Saint Patrick's Day Parade was abandoned and expressions of Irishness were muted. Thankfully, since the 1980s there has been a resurgence of Irish culture and a coming together of Irish and English in Birmingham.

A Tale of Two Second Cities by Frank Murphy

Frank was born in Cork in 1933. After school, he worked in a flourmill until it became part of a multinational company. Concerned at his job prospects, he left with his wife and baby daughter and joined the rest of his family in Birmingham. Luckier than most, the family stayed with Frank's sister until 1960 when he bought his own house.

Working for a transport company Frank settled down slowly, for 'most of my nights were haunted by memories of my beloved Cork, but you soon learn that emigration is not just a change of address and you have to focus on your new life. Nevertheless, emigration for whatever reason is a painful experience. Some of the things that helped us overcome homesickness were new

fangled TV, access to Irish books (for me all the works of Frank O'Connor, Sean O'Faolain's stories of Cork City) also Joyce, O'Casey, McNamara, O'Flaherty.'

Frank is proud of the Irish contribution to the redevelopment of Birmingham, and 'it seemed that every Irish man was involved in construction and every weekend the rafters of the many pubs such as the 'Ship', Camp Hill, and the 'Mermaid'

Birmingham Bus Crews supporting the Civil Rights Movement in 1969. Between 16 December 1967 and 18 May 1973, the *Birmingham Evening Mail* ran a weekly column by John McCarthy. Called 'Irish Mail' it played a major role in publicising events such as this and social gatherings. More than that, the column gave a sense of communal identity to the Birmingham Irish as citizens of Birmingham and Ireland, and it alerted all people to the contribution made to the city by the Birmingham Irish.

would ring to the navvies own anthem, McAlpines Fusiliers. The Irish women made a huge contribution to the economy as nurses, bus clippies, and filled the many vacancies in light assembly work in car component factories.'

In Frank's opinion the Birmingham Irish integrated as workmates and neighbours but 'it has to be said that we lived in an Irish cultural bubble. The church gate remained the meeting place, we socialised at the Irish-managed pubs and church clubs. Our music was 1960s Irish ballads and country & western. Sundays were spent either listening to Gaelic games on radio or playing hurling (and) football in local parks.' Frank has strong thoughts about how the Birmingham Irish were affected by the pub bombings.

The 70s dawned with a growing awareness that some politicians saw emigration from the Republic of Ireland as a threat to national security. When going on holidays we were asked to fill in a detailed security card by the airport security staff. Many of the Irish pub landlords discouraged the singing of Irish rebel songs. There were a number of explosions especially in London but generally the social atmosphere was comfortable except that the usual St Patrick's Day Banquet celebration was somehow overshadowed by the gloomy situation in Northern Ireland.

But it was not all gloom. A lot of positive things were happening. On the work side, Spaghetti Junction brought a lot of Irish workers to Birmingham. The Irish Centre opened and was, and still is, the hub of Irish social events. Irish County Associations were formed and their benefit dances and other fundraising functions generated a lot of money for worthy local causes like St Mary's Hospice, The Children's Hospital and of course the Irish Welfare Centre. There was also a shift in the location of Irish emigrants from the inner city areas like Small Heath, Kings Heath, Moseley, Sparkbrook and Sparkhill to the more affluent leafy suburbs

The full horror of what was happened in Northern Ireland visited Birmingham with the Birmingham pub bombings. I remember switching on in the middle of the news, the screen was filled with chaotic scenes of blue lights flashing, smoking debris, police and other emergency services trying to bring some calm to what was obviously a terrible disaster. It was only when the cameras focused on the Rotunda that I realised the full impact of the situation. My teenage daughter often met her friends in the Talk of the Town before moving to the Irish Centre. She rang me shortly afterwards. I was so relieved.

The result of that savage madness for the Birmingham Irish community

A cloud of shame and guilt hung over the Birmingham Irish. There was almost a total withdrawal of the Irish community in a social and political sense. There were also draconian measures imposed like Stop and Search if you were going into a public house. There was also a rash of institutional discrimination against the Irish. Thousands arrested without charge under emergency laws. The St Patrick's Day Parade stopped. The GAA had planning permission withheld for 6 years before they could develop their stadium in Elmdon. And of course the usual Irish jokes stereotyping the Irish as stupid, illiterate and ignorant were fair game for the TV and radio, so-called comedians, also the social clubs and local press. However it has to be said that the vast majority of people were very tolerant and understanding under the circumstances. There were some dreadful, if isolated incidents. It was often forgotten that one of the victims of the pub bombings was an Irish mother who lost two members of her family. The treatment of the Birmingham Six and their families was appalling.

Summary of that terrible period

The Irish became a silent and invisible community until the mid-80s. I suppose the most significant event since the dark 1970-80 period was the appointment of Fr Joe Taaffe OMI as Director of the Irish Welfare Centre. His appointment was timely. Recession gripped the UK and brought more than a fair share of problems to the emigrant Irish with the collapse of the construction industry. Some of the once powerful McAlpine Fusiliers were elderly and jobless, isolated in multi-occupied lodging houses and fully dependent on benefits.

The courage and vision of Fr Taaffe was the inspiration behind the formation of the Birmingham Irish Forum as a much-needed political lobby. The revival of the St Patrick's Day Parade was also due to his interest and encouragement. The exploits of Jack Charlton's army in Italy also helped the revival of the community. Today we are reaping the results of the seeds planted by Fr Taaffe.

The Whole Situation Was Reversed by Mike O'Brien

Fierce fighting broke out in Northern Ireland in 1969 as the police and Protestant gangs attacked Catholic areas. A number of Catholic refugees fled to Birmingham, where they found support at the Irish Centre. Here in August 1969 a Catholic and Protestant mother from Northern Ireland reach out to each other across the religious divide now that they are in Aston. On the left is Mary Robinson from the Protestant Shankhill Road and she is talking with Betty Hargreaves from the Catholic Falls Road of Belfast. Now living in Sycamore Road, Aston, Betty emphasised how in Northern Ireland the families would not have spoken with each other, but here in Birmingham 'we live together in peace and our children play together. Religion doesn't come into it.' In particular, eight-year-old Alfred Hargreaves and Jean Robinson were good mates. Mary added that both she and Betty loved Belfast and would like to return to the 'best and cleanest city in the world', but that they could not do so because of the fighting there.

Mike's father came to Birmingham from county Clare during the Second World War. After a spell at Windsor Street Gas Works, he worked for a company of steel erectors where it became obvious that whilst he respected heights he did fear them. Amongst the jobs he worked on were the Nechells Power Station, Hams Hall Power Station, the Nechells tower blocks, the Pleck tower blocks in Walsall, and some tall flats in Wolverhampton, and many others. In his later years he went to Twickenham College to train as an inspector of hoists and cranes. It was his job to go around the sites and give the cranes and hoists their monthly inspection.

In the early days, there was a little animosity towards the Irish from the city folk. You have probably heard the stories about the notices advertising `Rooms to let, no blacks, no Irish, no dogs.' This persisted until into the sixties and I remember seeing these notices on a board near Showell Green Lane when I was about seventeen,(1963). However it is also well known that this occurred in other cities in the world at different times, (e.g. Boston when the Irish first started to settle there).

In Birmingham those days had just about passed when the bombs went off. The whole situation was reversed by about ten years then. In fact for a time things were worse for the ordinary Irish population than they had ever been. Apart from the fact that a lot of Irish homes were raided by Special Branch, the Irish in Birmingham, for a time, had to undergo threats and taunts and in some cases beatings by a population understandably in terrible shock. However, I think it went a little too far.

A young fellow I worked with who had an Irish name came to me literally in tears about two or three days after the bombings. He told me that his house had been raided by the police twice, once while his young wife was on her own with the children, and that most of his workmates had stopped talking to him. He asked if I had experienced the same as my name was Irish also. But we hadn't had any trouble from anyone that I can recall. Maybe I was too busy to notice at the time but I don't remember much trouble being caused to me or my family, although as I have mentioned I saw a lot of other people suffering including children at school.

Good Times and the Saddest Thing by Owen Dolan

Married to Mary from Claremorris, co. Mayo, Owen was raised close to Drumshanbo in co. Leitrim. He came to Birmingham when he was twenty to better himself and join his two younger brothers. They lodged in Ivor Road, Sparkhill,

Mike O'Brien's father on a Birmingham construction site.

sharing a room with five strangers. It was hard to get digs anywhere and approximately sixteen people were in the house. Owen paid £1 5s per week in advance, 'and then keep and support yourself after that. All of us had to share a small kitchen between us.' Lodgers were not allowed visitors, had to come in by the back door, were not given door keys and had to be in at 11.00 pm.

Owen started a training course to be a bus conductor. One night he came home after a late shift and to his disbelief, he couldn't get in: 'I couldn't waken anyone to let me in and I had to sleep in the alleyway until the first people started to go to work at 7.30 am so I could get in. In the morning I went to see the landlady, about being left outside for the night. She told me in no uncertain manner, that I would have to change my job, and be in for 11.00 pm. So I found another place in Durham Road to share a room with four others and was given a key.'

One day soon after he started work, Owen went to the garage canteen and found he had no money. He asked the old driver he worked with for 6d to get a cup of tea and two slices of toast, until he got home in his break when he would give the money back. Opposite everyone there he turned and said "No. All the Irish are the same, begging and borrowing, not spending, only sending it back to Ireland." I felt so embarrassed. I left the canteen, and fasted until I got my break. I never spoke to him that day. I later found out that he never mixed or got on with his mates.'

Owen enjoyed a good social life. He was a member of the Catholic Transport Guild which had monthly meetings and the Pioneers – and even though he did not dance he went to many different dances: St. Paul's Hall, Balsall Heath; the Moseley Institute, Moseley Road; St Catherine's; St Chad's Hall beside the cathedral; and Mrs Regan's Hall in Small Heath, now known as the 'New Garryowen'. The only beverages served were tea, coffee, orange juice or lemonade which was enjoyed. Then there was the Harp Dance Hall in Walford Road, Sparkbrook and the Double Dance Hall in Hurst Street over the Hippodrome, which was on the first floor. The second floor was for old time and modern dancing, the third floor was for Céilí dancing.

When the Hippodrome took over the top two floors, an Irish pub was opened on Smallbrook Queensway, known as The Mayfair, then The Four Provinces Club opened in Alcester Road South, Kings Heath. There were many other places to dance, including St Ann's in Alcester Street, St Francis' in Wrentham Road, Handsworth, St Teresa's in Wellington Road and The Irish Centre, now the Irish Club. Most dance halls charged 2s/6d to get in

Those who were not pub-goers would head for parks in Sparkhill, Cannon Hill, Small Heath or Handsworth, 'where large numbers of Irish girls and boys would gather, and hope that someone would have a transistor radio so we could hear football or hurling matches broadcast by the well-known late Michael O'Hehir with his famous voice'. With no Saturday evening mass to fulfil Sunday obligation or no mass on Sunday after midday, many Catholic shift workers had to leave the house at 4.30 a.m. 'to get to the Oratory church, Hagley Road for 06.15 Mass which was the earliest mass said in Birmingham on Sunday'. Owen continues:

In all this time here, I had a good time, mostly enjoyable, people treated me well, I can count on one hand the amount of resentment I ever had about being Irish, this I am grateful for.

I can remember coming home from work, and turning on the news on television, it was covered with the sad news of President John F Kennedy's assassination on that dreadful day in November 1963. For a week or so it was sorrow in any general conversation.

In 1963, the Birmingham Irish spontaneously raised £5,000 for a memorial to the assinated Kennedy. Made of 160,000 pieces of mosaic it is sited close to Saint Chad's; however, with the redevelopment of this area it is hoped that it will be moved to the proposed new Irish Quarter in Digbeth and Deritend.

The saddest thing that sticks in my mind was the bombing of the pubs by the Rotunda and in New Street which caused so many innocent lives to be lost and injuries, which many still have to live with. I was driving a No.5 bus towards the city, on entering Rea Street, I heard an explosion, go

up to the Bull Ring, clouds of dust, Police, fire engines, ambulances started to converge towards the city, at St Martin's, the road was closed and everything was turned back for the rest of the night. It was about two hours later that I became aware that such a tragic event had happened.

The majority of Irish people felt so ashamed that it felt hard to go to work or meet an English person, glad to say that I did not have any resentment from the English people whatsoever. Some people faced abuse and rejection, but I think it was a minority that this happened to. What I did mostly see in some shop windows was notices such as 'Irish Not Welcome', or 'Irish Will Not Be Served', or 'Irish Stay Out'. Thankfully this only lasted a week or two to the best of my knowledge.

A Fantastic Husband and Father. Patrick Augustine Noel Drummgoole by Brenda Drummgoole

Patrick grew up in what was then the small fishing village of Howth, just north of Dublin. After his national service, he found it hard to find work and he moved to Birmingham in 1954.

At first he lived with his mother's cousin, Annie Flannagan, in Sparkhill. He began to work at Lucas making car batteries and was able to send 10 shillings home to his mother every week, no letter, just the money. This left him enough to get by on the bare essentials. At Christmastime he would return to Ireland and he would send his money ahead due to the pickpockets on the journey. Patrick settled down to life in Birmingham with great ease feeling very much at home.

In September 1963, Patrick met his wife Brenda on a blind date arranged by 'Auntie' Annie's daughter Annette. He was 28 and Brenda was 22. After a trip to Howth in February 1964, where they became engaged, they started saving for

their wedding. They married on 12 February
1966 at Our Lady of Lourdes, Trittiford Road and
the mass was celebrated by Father Denis Murphy.

After working for Lucas for 18 years, Patrick was
made redundant. He then went to work at
Clifford Coverings with Brenda's Dad, Cornelius.
After two years, in 1974 he began working at
Cadbury's in Bournville. During the time of the
Birmingham bombings, Patrick suffered a lot of
torment and hassle, name calling and slating of
his race, of which he was very proud. Eventually
things died down and some sort of normality
returned.

Patrick retired from Cadbury's in 1991 after 17
years due to ill health. He kept active by
attending several clubs and did voluntary work
with the Irish Welfare in Moseley Road. Even
after two minor strokes in 1999, he returned to
be an active and hardworking member of the
'drop in'. He was there on 24 December 2001,
his 67th Birthday. Patrick passed away peacefully
in his sleep on Thursday 27 December 2001. He
was a fantastic husband and father and is sadly
missed by us all.

CHAPTER FOURTEEN
REBUILDING CONFIDENCE: FATHER JOE TAAFFE

Father Joe at work helping someone in need.

He is a Great Loss to Us by Dolores Simmonds

Father Taaffe bestrode the Birmingham Irish community. President of the Irish Welfare and Development Centre, director of the Catholic Housing Aid Society and the Family Housing Association, he was the man responsible for setting up a drop-in centre and the Irish Forum. More than that, he championed the innocence of the Birmingham Six, and instigated the revival of the Birmingham Saint Patrick's Day Parade. Father Taaffe came to Birmingham in 1969, replacing Father Paul Byrne. His name lives on,

not only in the hearts and minds of many, but also in Father Taaffe House. This is a sheltered housing scheme for elderly Irish close to Saint Anne's, Deritend, that has been developed by the innovative and progressive Cara Irish Housing Association that is based nearby in Birchall Street, Deritend.

Dolores Simmonds is the daughter of Father Joe Taaffe's youngest brother. Reared in a thatched cottage in Knock, Mayo, one of her earliest memories is of the excitement felt in the house in Knock when Uncle Joe would be coming home on holiday. Her beloved uncle would take her on visits to relatives in Castlerea, Roscommon: 'I loved these days out with Uncle Joe'. In 1957, Dolores came with her mother and father to live near Warwick. Fr Joe was then ministering to construction workers building nuclear power stations in North Wales. He lived with the labourers in just one room of one of the many huts constructed to accommodate the workforce. Tragically, Dolores's father died suddenly. Immediately he received the news, Father Joe drove straight to Warwick.

Father Joe and his brother, the father of Dolores.

Although he was devastated at the loss of his younger brother, 'he was a tower of strength to all the family especially to my mother and myself. He bore his own sorrow with great dignity. Fr Joe always put others before himself.' Dolores brings to life a man who was a family figure as well as a public figure.

After the unexpected death of my father, Uncle Joe became a father figure to me. To help us over the Christmas season, he came, most years, to be with us on Christmas afternoon and stayed until the next day. He always went back to Birmingham on St. Stephen's Day evening (Boxing Day) when he and other people got dressed up in fancy dress and toured the pubs and clubs collecting money for charity. This group was known as the Wren Boys,(an Irish custom).

We had great fun trying to advise him on what to wear. At first, he went out without his glasses so as not to be recognised and he usually wore a long dress and a blue curly wig which our girls used to play dressing-up games with. Not wearing glasses had its difficulties as he couldn't see where he was going so he had to hold on to the person in front. This worked well and he was always very pleased with the kindness and generosity of people. However, on one occasion, he decided to wear his glasses and the response was even greater. So, from then on, he got dressed up but always wore the glasses and lots of money was raised for very deserving charities.

Amongst his prized possessions were some socks that had been knitted for him; they were green, white and orange and he always wore them on St Patrick's Day. Whilst mentioning St Patrick's Day, he was so thrilled that the St Patrick's Day Parade started up again in Birmingham after a lapse of about 20 years. I thank God that he saw that first Parade as he proudly stood on the open-top bus.

1994 was his Golden Jubilee year. In June of that year, the Birmingham Irish community laid on a fantastic party for him at the Irish Centre in Digbeth. It started with concelebrated Mass and continued with a marvellous buffet. This was followed by many presentations of gifts and cards. He was very appreciative of peoples generosity of the gifts they gave him and the time people had given up to prepare the room and the food etc.

During the celebrations at the Irish Centre,

Brendan Farrell gave him a copy of the *Irish Post*. Pieces of type had been cut out and stuck across the front page saying "Missing" and "Fr Joe is Missing". Brendan said it was the only copy of the *Post* he could find which did not have a photograph of Fr Joe in it. This was indeed quite true because himself and Brendan seemed to follow each other to functions so he was always getting a mention.

His prayer books and rosary beads were his most precious possessions and, as to be expected, there were rosary beads under his pillow and prayer books on his bedside table. These were in addition to those he had with him when he died.

I was really touched on the day of his funeral when an elderly gentleman spoke to me whilst I was sitting in the funeral car. He raised his hat and said 'he was the only man in Birmingham who could get me a hot dinner for 50p'.

During his time in Myton Hospice he spoke to his two sisters and myself about his place of burial. He wished to be buried in Birmingham and be amongst the community he worked with and loved so much. His wish was granted and his friends, family and Irish community erected a lovely gravestone (Brandwood End Cemetery) in his memory. He is still loved and greatly missed by all his family. May he rest in peace.

Happy Times in Birmingham by Josie and Brendan Mulvey

My first visit to Birmingham was back in 1966, I was one of the coach drivers involved in the World Cup, I was driving members of the press. I was living and working in the London area where even back then people were busy going about their business and hardly had time to bid each other the time of day.

What a breath of fresh air to arrive in Birmingham it was just like my native Leitrim

people were friendly and relaxed, the police officers who were in charge of movements of vehicles were so helpful, as a stranger to the city I was worried about getting lost, not so the police escorted us everywhere. It was a memorable time especially having a seat at Wembley to watch the final.

Over the years I made countless trips to the city, it was 1980 before Josie and myself actually moved to live in the great city. Josie took up nursing and enjoyed taking care of the Midland people, she made many good friends over the years both in nursing and outside.

I enjoyed the life on the open road as a coach driver, I had the honour to work on many major events in the city, I was part of the driving team on The G7 and G8 summits, I also drove some of the team back in 1988 who were looking at Birmingham regarding their bid to host the 1992 Olympics, another memorable day was setting off from The Sky Blues ground with Coventry City to the great F A Cup Final when they defeated Tottenham Hotspur and lifted the cup.

In the early nineties I took a change in career and began working with the National Blood Service as a driver, such a rewarding worthwhile job rushing urgent blood to save someone's life, my last three years with the service until I retired in 2001 I held the position of marketing co-ordinator for the service.

Away from work Josie and myself were involved in the running of our much loved Lady of Fatima Parish in Quinton, also we were part of the wonderful Saint Patrick's Day Parade and the Birmingham Irish Pipes and Drums, we were honoured to be members of the committee who helped to get an Irish pipe band back on the street, however just like the parade the band is part of the community at large in the city and are pleased to help out at any event they are invited to take part in.

The Birmingham Irish Pipes and Drums in Annyalla, Monaghan, 2002. This was the home of their pipe major, Frank Brennan, who is second from the left on the back row. Sadly, a short while after this trip Frank died suddenly. His influence will live on through the band he loved so well.

We are both now living in the Hills of Sligo but still a big part of the community of a wonderful friendly city whose people can get on together and share the happy and sad times and give support to one another. With God's help we will be delighted to help with the parade and our lovely band.

Renewed Confidence

The Birmingham Irish Pipes and Drums arose from the Saint Patrick's Day Parade in Birmingham. Revived in 1996 the Parade has become a symbol not only of the renewed confidence of the Birmingham Irish but also of the way in which the Irish community has reached out movingly to others. Its first committee included Father Taaffe, Pauline Roche and her Welsh husband Ted Ryan; Noel Mulvey, now a key figure in the Irish Welfare and Information Centre; Willie Finnegan, a motivating force in the Monaghan Association; Jim Barron; Ewan Lenoch, who was studying in Birmingham at the time; and Sylvia Murphy-Brennan who runs a well-respected school of Irish Dancing and whose husband Pat is a fine

musician teaching Irish music in schools. Second generation Irish Brummies were represented by Anthony Duffy, Paul McElroy, Paul Smith, Celine Finn and Laura Grigg. Now one of the biggest Saint Patrick's Day parades in the world, in 2002 it drew over 100,000 people to the streets of Digbeth and Deritend. Many of them had no connection with Ireland but were drawn in by the vitality and inclusiveness of the Birmingham parade. Similarly, the Birmingham Irish Pipes and Drums attends a wide-range of functions, supports a variety of good causes and leads parades on Remembrance Sunday.

Other organisations have also been crucial in reinforcing the self-confidence of the Birmingham Irish and in raising a positive profile of the community in general. They include the Irish Heritage Group, which meets regularly and is aiming for a permanent centre of Irish history in the city, and the Birmingham branch of Conradh na Gaeilge, the Gaelic League. Called Craobh Phádraig Mac Phearais, after Patrick Pearse, it was founded in 1976 and its primary aim is to promote the use of An Teanga Ghaelige, the Irish language. This is achieved through Irish language evening classes at Birmingham's Irish Club. The branch has also been active in staging plays, providing speakers for talks and lectures and in driving forward three national conferences on the Irish dimension in British education. Held annually from 1985, these 'became the precursor of present Irish sporting and music activities currently available in a number of Birmingham schools. Six years before, the branch had celebrated the centenary of the birth of Phádraig Mac Phearais with a large concert and seminar at Saint Anne's, Alcester Street. His Excellency, Mr Kennedy, the Irish ambassador to the United Kingdom, was in attendance. It is believed that the branch was the first Irish organisation outside London to have an Irish ambassador as guest of honour. (Gearóid Mac an Mhaoir, 'A Brief History of the Current Branch of Conradh na Gaeilge in Birmingham', February 2003).

CHAPTER FIFTEEN
THE LEGACY

His Legacy Lives on. George Patrick by Rod Presley

George hailed from Enniskillen, county Fermanagh. His mother died while giving birth to him and, with his father going to Belfast for work, George was granny-reared. At fifteen he joined the British Army and fought at the battle of El Alamein. After the war he was stationed in Wigan and met his wife, whose mother came from Belfast. Because George was a Catholic and his wife was Protestant they faced prejudices and were told the marriage would not last. It did for 50 years. His son Rod carries on:

Mom's sister had also married a 'squaddy', a fine jolly man, Bill Lee, a Brum through and through. Mom and dad had moved to Brum some months earlier and had found work and above all somewhere to live. The accommodation was an ex-Army camp - mom and dad were officially squatters.

Work was plentiful and dad tried many jobs. For most of his working life he was employed by Hardy Spicers in the heat treatment department. Prejudices were shown as there were signs outside the factory gates: 'No Blacks - No Irish'!

Although we moved from one camp to another, life was good. My first recollection of life was growing up on an ex-Army camp in Oaklands recreation grounds in Yardley. I have many happy memories spending good times with my aunt, uncles, cousins and my 2 sisters.

I am now fifty one and have many happy memories of my childhood, even though I was very aware of our Irish background. I am extremely proud of my parents and their impoverished beginnings, all this makes me very

Anne and Mary Mooney of the Colmcille School of Irish Dancing. In 1976 the school entered the All-Ireland Championships in Dublin for the first time and Anne won the intermediate All-Ireland Solo Championship. She produced 'the performance of a lifetime'. It was believed that Anne was the first Irish dancer from Birmingham to gain such an accolade. Her sister Mary danced in the figure championship in which the Colmcille team was runners-up, the highest placing until that time for a Birmingham school. The Mooneys lived in Acocks Green with their Leitrim-born mother and Dubliner father.

proud of my roots. The West Midlands and in particular Birmingham have given me a good living from humble beginnings. I have been in business for 25 years and have built up a very successful company, so I do like to think that my background has benefited me because in my parents' younger days, tolerance and understanding were in short supply.

As I said, dad is no longer with us, but his legacy lives on - his softness of voice and manner, his acute awareness of other people's feelings and above all fairness to all.

Growing up in Sparkhill in the 1960s by Steve McCabe

Being young in Sparkhill was nothing special. Or so it seemed at the time. In retrospect, though, it had qualities that made it wonderful. It was a place where, similar to the present day Asian community, the Irish could feel as much 'at home' as was possible in a foreign country. It offered reasonably priced accommodation which, for many, was a room in one of the many large houses. For many, like my parents, the dream was to own your own house.

So it was for my mother and father. We lived in Castleford Road and all my early memories revolve around that house and the surrounding area. The back garden was, of course, sufficient most of the time. However, the place that every kid wanted to be was Sparkhill Park. It was where I learned to ride my bike. It was a place to meet others. I can remember being there in summer and seeing lots of other families who would meet there to talk about the recent events and what was happening 'at home' in Ireland.

For children, Sparkhill Park was a place where you could feel free (surrounding roads were a lot less busy then). There was the playing equipment, which is still located at the top end behind the baths; that required money and was a 'special treat'. The bandstand could be imagined as a spaceship or base, which some would attack and others defend. I don't remember a band playing there. It's probably a good thing because we kids wouldn't have welcomed intruders with musical instruments!

Those younger than forty probably won't remember that there used to be a paddling pool that occupied much of the bottom end of the park closest to Springfield. In summer you'd get

in and splash about with whoever else happened to be there. I don't know why it was filled in but I think that this happened in either 1967 or 1968. I recall the sadness that accompanied the earth machines that were brought to the park to do this.

Christmas is always a special time for children. In Sparkhill this meant that there was the nativity scene to marvel at. It was always set up in the park and faced out onto the Stratford Road. The figures were life-size and when it was lit up at night it provided a marvellous attraction. It also provided a constant reminder of the religious significance of Christmas and what we might receive on December 25th. We would go and see Father Christmas at Lewis's department store. However, as was tradition then, he would travel in his sleigh along the Stratford Road and I vividly remember going out on cold winter's evenings to watch him go past the end of Castleford Road with other children and parents. To help in our choice of presents, regular trips were required to Woolworth's which was situated between Durham Road and Newton Road. I also remember excited trips to a toyshop just around the corner from Castleford Road. It was more or less opposite to what was the Cascade Club. This club existed until the 1980s when, very appropriately, given its name, the building suddenly collapsed late one Saturday night with, thankfully, no injuries.

My parents, like the majority of the Irish who arrived in Sparkhill, maintained their religion. This meant regular attendance at church and school. In the case of the former, the huge numbers meant packed masses and the use of the hall behind English Martyrs on Evelyn Road. In the case of the latter, the local school couldn't cope and until the opening of St. Bernard's on Wake Green Road. This meant I attended Springfield for a year followed by St. John's for two years. At the time this seemed normal. Now I can understand the annoyance of parents like my mother who had to walk past the door to either walk or get the bus to a school much further away.

Such irritations were, I believe, cancelled out by being part of a wider community that looked after themselves. For example, many women needed to work and those that didn't were prepared to provide child minding for them. Because mom worked at the MEM factory on Foremans Road, I was looked after by Lily Lynch who would go on to run the Corner Shop on Court Road with her late husband Ben. I know that she had a particularly difficult time with me because of my ability to get into scrapes (including trying to climb out of a bedroom window on the first floor!) The other thing I recall was that shopping always seemed to take ages. In the days before refrigeration, fresh food had to be bought daily. Given that every family did this, the shops along Stratford Road became a 'community centre' for meeting and exchange of gossip.

Married men, of course, didn't shop. Instead, they met in locals such as The Antelope, The Bear, and The Mermaid. I am informed that The Harp Club, which until it closed, was a place where it was possible to meet someone who might be prepared to 'step out' with you. Such were the origins of some of the families that exist today in Birmingham.

Sparkhill is very different today. The culture that predominates is one that is created by newer immigrants; Asians. In the 1970s and 80s Irish families moved out to areas like Hall Green. As they did, the 'Irishness' that was very much a feature of Sparkhill lessened. Undoubtedly, my parents may have felt great sadness at being away from home. For the young like me, however, home was Sparkhill.

Proud to Sport the Blue and Gold of Tipperary by Paul King

Stephen King's granddad, John Anthony King, was born in Nenagh, co. Tipperary in 1930. The oldest of five children, from the age of nine he saw himself as the 'provider' after his father went to serve for the British Army in India. His father died when he was still young and John was just fourteen when he first came to work in England. After returning home, he came to Wolverhampton in 1954. Two years later he moved to Birmingham. He told his grandson that 'his first memories were seeing a sign in a shop window saying "No Dogs. No Irish". However horrifying this might have been, he would always speak very highly of Birmingham and the tolerance of its people. His father had told him that it was a privilege to work, and my grandad greatly respected the opportunity the city gave him to find employment. He would say that in those days you could leave one job in the morning, and get another in the afternoon along the 36 bus route.'

John married Barbara Wilson, a proud Brummie, and the two of them got married at English Martyrs, six weeks after they first met. The Wilsons were not overjoyed that their daughter had married an Irishman, particularly a Roman Catholic one, 'but my Nan and Granddad would remain happily married for 42 years'.

John and Barbara prospered but an unfortunate business deal led to John losing his money and having to send his son and daughter to live in Ireland, while he and his wife lived with relatives in Birmingham. They fought back, cleared their debts and bought another house.

Stephen takes up the story.

Shortly afterwards he worked at the Bakelite Factory, (where he was employed for 16 years) and was also employed by Commando's

Industrial Cleaning at the weekends, cleaning paint at Rover. My Dad was also taken along and recalls a definite feeling of hostility between certain Irishmen (who did most of the cleaning) and certain Brummies who were known to urinate in the areas where the Irish would have to clean. It was a case of the Irish 'doing jobs that the Brummies wouldn't do'.

Wedding reception of John and Barabara King held at 429 Somerville Rd, Small Heath (August 4th 1956).

My grandad was always very conscious of trying to integrate, and whilst he mixed with many Irish, he would always have an abundance of Brummies whom he could call friends. He would never drink at home, preferring to join in the craic with virtually anyone who might be in the pub, where he was well known for singing in his terrific baritone voice, and for his deep, smoke filled laugh. (In Ireland and England he was affectionately known as Old Man River by friends, his favourite party piece).

This may have been one of the reasons why my family got so much support during the pub bombings, because my grandad was so well liked. He was overwhelmed by the support he got from many neighbours in the wake of the bombings, where they vowed to support him if anyone accused him of being involved. This was particularly valued after the next door neighbours were taken in by the police for questioning.

Despite his love of Birmingham and the family that had grown around him, it is fair to say that my grandad's heart never really left Ireland. We would all cram into his Ford Escort to make the long journey to Ireland every year, and would often visit my great-grandmother who had outlived virtually everyone in the town; hence we are still unsure of her age when she died. (What an advert for 40 fags a day and a glass of stout!).

Yet he gradually found it harder to leave Nenagh after holidays, and would often talk about returning home, even though he spent far more time in Birmingham than he ever had in Ireland. In 1995 my Dad bought a piece of land in Puckane, just outside Nenagh, and built a house overlooking the Shannon. My grandad was overjoyed when he was invited to live there, and in June 1998 he and nan left their home in Castle Bromwich, and were finally able to retire from work; he sadly died in November of the same year.

I suppose my grandad's legacy is the example he set, and the history he has given us. He had a tremendously positive attitude on life, was happy as long as he had enough money for a packet of fags and a pint, and was always laughing and joking. He was also tremendously generous, and greatly disrespected those whom he described as having short arms and deep pockets!

He was also determined that his family would have the opportunities that he didn't, and valued education above almost anything, which is why he would have been so proud to see me at Birmingham University. On passing my exams, my uncle Sonny (grandad's brother) sent me a card with the words 'verbum – satis – sapienti', which is on the lines of 'through words we are wise'. This epitomises my grandad's attitude, in public he would simply smile at people who called the Irish stupid, in private he was determined to prove them wrong.

In simplistic terms I represent his life by wearing a Blues shirt during the football season, and being one of the proud few to sport the blue and gold of Tipperary at the St. Patrick's Day Parade. In coming to Birmingham he has raised a family in one of the greatest cities in the world, where we have been given the luxury of good jobs, homes and education. Yet he has also given us a proud Irish heritage, a wealth of family and friends in Tipperary, and a sense of being among friends wherever we go in the world. I can never repay him for that.

'The Englishman' by T P McManus

I went to London first on 28 August 1935 at the age of 17 – 18 years. I held many jobs – a male nurse, bus conductor, worked for the express dairy delivering milk with a horse and trap to a wide area around Norwood. These jobs took up 18 months of my time. Next I started in the licensed and catering business at Waterloo Station, I became a relief barman after 12 months. I would be sent out to any of their branches all over London, often working in 3 – 4 different pubs every week. I worked in Norfolk and Suffolk from 1942 to the end of 1944 (aerodromes) two beautiful counties. I came home at Christmas 1944.

I went back again, to Birmingham on 9 January 1955 to work as a blacksmith for 12 years. I must say this and pay a little compliment to dear old England, I still have pleasant memories of past times and my relationship with English people. When I went back to Ireland, the local community gave me a new title: 'The Englishman'. I told them it was the greatest compliment ever.

Always a True Dubliner. Thomas Joseph Pullen by Joyce Pullen.

Tom came over to England from Dublin as a 14-year-old boy looking for work, along with a friend called Littler Butler. They worked cash in hand for various firms of builders being put up in Salvation Army hostels or bed and breakfasts.

Katie Jordan playing the bodhrán at Carl Chinn's BBC WM show on 16 March 2002 at the Irish Club. Her dad, Vince, is playing the accordion, and Daniel O'Connor is on the guitar.

Tom was a good, diligent worker and in time got taken on to work permanent with Babcock & Wilkins who already employed his older brother Jack. They worked on building the Hams Hall cooling towers (now gone!).

Then with being in lodgings in Stechford Tom found work with Monitor Engineering firm next to Parkinson's Stoves. That is where we met!! Love at first sight and for ever since. The Second World War was still raging. Air raids and bombs and everywhere posters urging people to JOIN UP AND DO YOUR BIT FOR BRITAIN. So we did. I joined the Land Army and Tom went in the Merchant Navy. Those were anxious years never knowing if we would meet again on leave. Lots of letter writing and on one leave we became engaged. Then in July 1946 we married at Corpus Christi, Stechford.

Tom was at sea for a further 6 months but decided to sign off as we were expecting our first child. He worked for a few months at Dunlop, but did not like the factory so he went to Nuffield Metals Products in Ward End. He did well although work conditions were not so good. Not much safety procedures. Long hours. Always trouble with the Unions. Tom rose to be a Convenor and fought for several changes for the men on his section.

Tom was always a true Dubliner. Thinking about and talking about "HOME" as much as possible. A deeply loyal family man. We went across to Dublin every year in the summer and sometimes Christmas too. Tom was a strict man but loving and loyal too and at times very generous, such as birthdays and Christmas, but only wanted the simple straightforward things in life . . . When he died on 17th July 1990 we took his remains over to be buried with his parents in Glasnevin Cemetery. He had talked about this previously.

Memories Old and New from 'Going to England' by Rose Ward

'Mom' he said

'I've met a girl.'

'Oh that's nice love', I said

I was bending down emptying the washing machine, Chris, my youngest was home from Dublin for a few days, he's been working over there recently. It's 1996.

The previous year he'd said to me casually one day, 'I might go to work in Ireland for a while Mom, a mate of mine says he's been there and he can get me about 6 months work on a building site if I want it.'

'He says he's living in a pretty nice place near to the job and he can get me in there too. Whadeya think Mom?'

Well, my mind reeled back to the early 1950s. It was like history repeating itself. I well remember a day in 1951 when my Dad told my Mom that he had a friend who'd told him, that he could get him a job if he wanted one and board and lodgings too, if he was interested.

'It's all there for the taking if you're prepared to chance it. Cross the Irish Sea and try your luck,

why don't you?' his friend said.

Well it was the same story, and to me now, it was just like déjà vu. The difference was that we would be crossing the Irish Sea in the opposite direction, because in those days we lived in a small village in a small farming community in the West of Ireland. Dad's friend, home for the holidays, was talking about finding a job and digs in Birmingham.

I remember Dad saying to Mom, 'Well, what do you think, I may as well go mayn't I?'

'What have I to lose?'

'I might do all right, but I'll never know if I don't try, will I?'

With these words he persuaded my Mom, and she agreed that he should go by himself for the time being. Then, if after a few months, things worked out, and he ended up with a steady job, and could afford the rent on a place for us to live we would go over and join him.

So, in his best suit and with collar and tie on, his raincoat over his arm and carrying just the one big suitcase, he crossed from Dun Laoghaire to Holyhead. Then he caught the train to Snow Hill, a railway station in the centre of Birmingham. When he came home for Christmas he was able to tell Mom that yes, he had a steady job in a factory and he was making enough money to rent a flat for us.

'Well that's settled then', she said, 'when it's time for you to go back in the New Year, we'll all go.'

That New Year was 1952 and I was 10, and an avid reader of adventure stories. I was jumping up and down with excitement when I heard Mom confirm that we would be going. I remember thinking what a great adventure it would be, to go to another country and live in a big city. I recall being able to tell my friends, that when they went back to school after Christmas I wouldn't be there. Mom, or Mammy as I called her then, would be writing a letter to my teacher, explaining, that we were going to England.

January 1952 then, brought worrying times for my Mother and Father but exciting ones for me. Now, here I am in the 21st Century making the by now familiar crossing again. This time we are on our way from Holyhead to Dun Laoghaire to see Chris who has since settled down in Ireland and got married to a beautiful Irish girl, our lovely daughter-in-law Louise, and we're going to see our equally lovely Irish grandson Charlie.

I feel as if the wheel has truly turned full circle, and my son who was born in Birmingham and supports Aston Villa has returned to our roots. I often wonder, when my Grandson grows up, which team will he support? And what will his outlook on life will be? Which seas, if any, will he take a notion to cross.

Expressing My Irish Roots by Katie Jordan

Vince Jordan is a leading light with the South Birmingham Branch of Comhaltas Ceoltóirí Éireann. Formed in 1972 it includes many young musicians like Vince's daughter, Katie. She stresses that 'Traditional Irish music has been a major part of my life for as long as I can remember. It has given me the opportunity to go places and meet people I wouldn't have otherwise. As a third generation person living in Birmingham, traditional Irish music has given me the chance to express my Irish roots and to be proud of who I am and where I have come from. I have found that Irish music has the ability to bring people together no matter what their age, ethnic origin and ability. Irish musicians are brought together in their love and understanding of the music and its origins. By playing and teaching Irish music we are keeping the traditions of our ancestors, which is very close to my heart.

Members of the Birmingham Tyrone Association gather by their county banner for a Saint Patrick's Day Parade in the city in the 1960s. Second from the left and holding the flag is P. J. McKenna.

Traditional Irish music is important to me because it enables me to express myself. It's a major part of my past, present and future.'

The Pilgrimage by Mary M. Donoghue

Mary M. Donoghue is the author of an evocative and insightful book about growing up in Small Heath and called Smells of Childhood (1997). Mary's mother, Jane, was from Dublin and her father, William Joseph Kiernan, from a small village in county Wexford. After serving in the Royal Air Force he fetched Jane to war-torn Birmingham. Their children grew up hearing tales of Ireland, joining in Irish songs and fetching *Ireland's Own* for their mom. Mary was enthralled and held fast to the expectation that one day her dad would take her to Ireland. From when she started work she prayed for the day 'when we would go on our travels together'. But money was scarce and Bill died before he could ever fulfill his daughter's wish. In 1994 Mary made that trip and stood with her dad's brother, Pat, and looked at her family's cottage.

My Pilgrimage

I'm here, in the cottage where my Father was born,

Unable to speak
On this lovely May morn.

For years I have longed to visit his land
Where a stranger is welcomed
With the touch of a hand.

I learned of the little folk, the cute Leprechaun,
And the wailing Banshee –
Disappearing at dawn.

He told me of the mountains, rivers and streams,
Filling my young mind
With beautiful dreams.

Breath-taking sunsets, the vivid sunrise,
And the millions of stars
That filled the night skies
With reverence he told of the fields of green,
And I longed for the vistas
Yet to be seen

His soft, lilting voice filled me with awe
When he spoke of the history
And his country's folklore

He promised that some day he'd take me there
To see all the wonders
That, together, we'd share.
My dreams, at last, are all coming true,
And as I traveled
I saw wonders anew.

Marring the pleasure in fulfilling my dream
Is walking alone
Where he has been

Now I am here, holding things he has touched,
Feeling his presence,
Missing him so much.

Afterword

Since the hard days that followed the Pub Bombings in 1974, there has been a strong coming together of Irish, English and other communities in Birmingham. Irish people have played a leading part in the building of a successful multi-cultural city in which people can be proud of their distinct communities but also can be proud of that which we share in common: our humanity and our belonging to Birmingham. With no natural, geographical or physical features to contribute to its growth and strength, Birmingham is a city made by its people. In that making and remaking the Birmingham Irish have taken a leading role and have contributed vibrantly to the well being of all Brummies. The Birmingham Irish have made, and are continuing to make, their mark upon this, our city.